SO-AKS-723

The Master Plan

God's Hope to Heal Humanity

Kevin McCarthy

New Family and Church Foundation
a project of The National Heritage Foundation

Copyright © 2003, Kevin McCarthy

Published by **New Family and Church Foundation, a project of The National Heritage Foundation,** 4124 Hoffman Drive, Dale City, VA 22193.

All rights reserved.

ISBN: 0-9727864-0-5

This book, or parts thereof, must not be used or reproduced in any manner without written permission. For information address the publisher, New Family and Church Foundation, 1610 Columbia Rd. NW, Washington, DC 20009

Scripture taken from the HOLY BIBLE, NEW INTERNATIONAL VERSION®. Copyright © 1973, 1978, 1984 by International Bible Society. Used by permission of Zondervan. All right reserved.

Acknowledgement of brief excerpts from Divine Principle, Copyright © 1973, by The Holy Spirit Association for the Unification of World Christianity.

For information address the publisher, New Family and Church Foundation, 4124 Hoffman Drive, Dale City, VA 22193.

Printed in the United States of America

Dedication

To Rev. Sun Myung Moon—
For his vision and teaching
that stand as the foundation of this book.

Acknowledgments

To Anne Ulvestad, for her artistry, design and unlimited patience.
To Vicki Phelps and Debbie Scott for their extensive editing skills.
To Christoph Wilkening, for his assistance and support.

Special gratitude goes to Reverend In Hoi Lee and Andy Weiss for their advice and support which was crucial for this project.

Cover and Book Design and Layout: Anne E. Ulvestad/*Dancing Design*
Copy Editors: Vicki Phelps, Debbie Scott

The
Master Plan

God's Hope to Heal Humanity

Kevin McCarthy

New Family and Church Foundation
a project of The National Heritage Foundation

Table of Contents

Foreword

As we endeavor to gain greater enlightenment into the depth of God's Word, I find that this book is deep enough for scholars to dive in and never reach the bottom, yet shallow enough for babies to swim in and not drown.

In addressing the issue of universal oneness, and the phenomenon of sin, the author discusses aspects such as the causes of sin, as well as the necessary procedures and measures it takes to set man free from the bondage of sin. The Apostle Paul wrote to the church at Colossae and told of his great burden and desire for the believers in Colossae to be filled with the knowledge of the will of God and with spiritual understanding.

Colossians 1:9-10
For this cause we also, since the day we heard it, do not cease to pray for you, and to desire that ye might be filled with the knowledge of His will in all wisdom and spiritual understanding; that ye might walk worthy of the Lord unto all pleasing, being fruitful in every good work and increasing in the knowledge of God.

There was a reason behind Paul's desire. We find that reason in verse ten of Colossians, chapter one. He wanted the believers at Colossae to know how they could "walk worthy of the Lord," to live the Christian life that would bring glory and honor to the Lord. This is the life that is pleasing to him. According to Paul, increasing in spiritual understanding leads one to live the life that is fruitful in every good work and increases in the knowledge of God (**Colossians 1:10**). That ought to be the goal of every saved person - to live a life on this earth that reflects the life of Christ in such measure that others see the effects of salvation and have a desire to know the one who can change lives in such a wonderful way.

This book is designed to help you increase in "the knowledge of God and spiritual understanding." As you do, you will experience a wonderful transformation in your Christian life. For as the Bible says, you will be "strengthened with all might, according to his glorious power unto all patience, longsuffering and joyfulness." **(Colossians 1:11)**

If you are studying this course in a classroom atmosphere, be faithful in your attendance. Remember, it was a Sunday night when Jesus came to visit His disciples after the resurrection and Thomas was not among them (John 20:19-25). Thomas missed out on the blessings of seeing the Lord because, for some reason, he skipped the meeting! It is often true that the lesson you miss will be the one that you would have enjoyed and gained the most.

Be faithful and don't miss out on the blessings within *The Master Plan*.

Bishop C. Phillip Johnson, Th.D., D.Min.
New Prospect Family Praise and Worship Center, Inc.
Washington, D.C.

Introduction

This book is for Christian leaders who resonant with Jesus' prayer in **John 17:23**. We are to be one "as God and Christ are one.

Paul says that we are to be "perfectly joined together in the same mind and in the same judgment." This means God's people should be the foundation of common sense in society. The body of Christ should establish the sense of national morality. It is what, in the past, stimulated "firm reliance on the protection of Divine Providence." Is this being done today?

Aren't we observing the opposite in society? Aren't Christian values losing their effect on a growing number of people? Aren't a growing number of Americans, especially youth, of the mind that no one can know what is true?

Despite its *Christian heritage*, the United States leads every other nation in the industrialized world in a array of social illnesses that find their root in the decline of the family.

This confusion in values finds its root in the Church. Christians are unclear on what the Bible expresses with regard to marriage and family:

- 67% of Americans believe that sex is permissible outside of marriage.
- 56% of single fundamentalists engage in sex outside of marriage.
- It is a growing problem for the clergy as well.

A 1988 survey of nearly 1,000 Protestant clergy by *Leadership Magazine* found that 12% admitted to sexual intercourse outside of marriage.

Jesus is the visionary of Christian unity. Jesus not only prayed fervently for Christian unity but indicated that there would be an important effect of that unity, as well.

John 17:23

*May they be brought to complete unity **to let the world know that you** **sent me and have loved them even as you have loved me.***

Our inability to provide our nation with sound judgment is directly attributable to our resistance to Jesus' prayer. Also, that the world is still unaware of the quality of Christ's love is directly attributable to Christians having yet to fulfill the vision of Jesus' prayer. Many would dispute the conclusion that Christians are not sufficiently united. Some would say the diversity of Christian belief is not a problem. But it is important to note that Jesus himself articulates a clear definition of the level of unity he expects. **John 17:21** "As God and Christ are one" is the standard he lays down for believers.

What are some of the elements that have prevented this "oneness" from being achieved? Probably the most obvious reason are issues of doctrine. Certainly over the course of Christian history there have been many cultural, political and racial reasons for the division of Christianity, but eventually all contributing circumstances trickle down to the all-pervasive common issue of doctrine. It is doctrine that dictates, for example, whether baptism will be by full immersion or by sprinkling. It is doctrine that prepares us for an imminent return of Christ or a return that will be preceded by a series of events. Ultimately, it is doctrine that can and does divide us.

Many Christians approach the objective of Christian unity by suggesting that we should avoid doctrinal issues altogether. "Doctrines divide-Mission unites," is a cry now heard frequently. "Let's agree to disagree," is another. While these are good, positive ideas, doctrine cannot be avoided because it *is* important.

Doctrine is the vehicle that transports the truth to the believer. It forms the justification for his actions and, more important, it is the ultimate source for the believer's sense of well-being and peace. Suggesting an alteration in doctrinal position is not easily implemented.

Typical of doctrinal belief and equally problematic is the "all or nothing" attitude. If I find out that some portion of my doctrine is wrong, it opens the door to the possibility that other areas may be wrong. Most believers will try to avoid that position at all costs.

The objective of doctrine is to elicit conviction, "to win souls" and to generate loyalty among the adherents. Thus, any suggestion that doctrine needs to be altered or adjusted is perceived as something that could have negative impact upon the loyalty of its adherents. Naturally, Christians approach with trepidation the idea of reconciling doctrines.

What is the objective in attempting to reconcile doctrinal differences? It is not to redefine the root of Christian faith, but rather to define and accomplish the *fruit* of Christian faith. That is, our mission is to fulfill the final hope for which Christians are waiting.

How shall Christian unity be achieved without the careful process of transcending the differences of doctrinal beliefs? Remember, the standard articulated clearly by Jesus is "as God and Christ are one." Certainly there are no doctrinal contentions between God and Christ.

Clearly, we must begin by trying to envision what God and Christ's perspective must be as they survey the present circumstances of world Christianity, especially in this age when it appears that the moral influence of Christians in the world is on the wane.

There could only be three scenarios to describe the nature of divided Christianity. One possibility is that there is one denomination that has the "correct" perspective and everyone else is wrong.

Most ministers would agree that this would be the case; however, hopes for achieving a consensus on this important issue would be dashed when we realized that each minister, no doubt, would feel that it was his own church that was the only correct one.

A second possibility is that every doctrine is completely wrong. Not surprisingly, no minister would ever consider that, but it could be an explanation for the extreme diversity in doctrinal belief.

A third scenario and the most likely possibility is that most doctrines have truth but also, in varying degrees, elements that are not true. Thus, we could expect, at a certain key moment in history, God would begin a process to help resolve the differences by magnifying our shared truths while lovingly shedding light on new areas so as to help facilitate a new basis for discovery and agreement. In this way we will be able to accomplish the vision for which Jesus prayed. Hopefully this book can help to facilitate that process.

In fact, even if only one doctrine and church had the truth, wouldn't it be incumbent upon that church to also report to the world the deep sorrow of God caused by such a sorry state of affairs, especially if we consider the sentiments of a God who "so loved the world, that he gave his only son." In other words, it is not sufficient that only one church is correct. God's goal embraces the entire world. God wants you to be saved, yes, but your salvation is not His only or ultimate goal. This higher, ultimate interest of God must be articulated and serve as the moral impetus for Christians to defer their individual church interests toward that higher fellowship. This interest is articulated through God's Word.

The Master Plan is the story of God's effort to recover humanity as his very own. God created in order to realize the ideal of love. As a loving Parent, God sought His own uncontested lineage of loving sons and daughters. He instilled in them a vision of becoming true husband, true wife, and True Parents. Henceforth, God's lineage would be a co-project of God and humanity. It would expand in perpetuity to the family, society, nation and world. Not only would we see God in each person, when we saw the family, we would see God, the society, we would see God, the nation, we would see God and the world, we would see God. This was the basis of the Kingdom of Heaven.

This dream of love was dashed, however, by the fall of the first human ancestors. God became a God whose heart was filled with sorrow and tears. God began the long arduous path to recover humanity.

The Master Plan seeks to answer questions that have long been asked by serious Bible students:

Why did God create mankind?

Did God know man would fall? If so, why does He grieve so in **Genesis 6:6**?

Why does God allow good people to suffer?

Why didn't God just stop the fall?

Why does it appear that God favors the younger brother, such as Abel and Jacob, over the elder?

How did Satan become god over man?

Why is the story of Tamar preserved? Why did God so summarily dispose of Er and Onan?

Why are there so many parallels between Jacob, Moses and Jesus? (For example, Jacob had 12 sons and 70 family members, Moses had 12 tribes and 70 elders, Jesus had 12 apostles and 70 disciples.)

Why was striking the rock twice such a mistake for Moses?

How does God fulfill His Will and what is our role?

Why did Jesus tell his apostles, "Don't go to the Gentiles or any house of the Samaritans, go rather to the lost sheep of the house of Israel?"

Why did John the Baptist say, "Are you the one who is to come or shall we look for another?" Why was this so offensive to Jesus?

Why was Jesus grieving the night before his cross?

How will Christ come again and what will be our mission?

I hope *The Master Plan* will be a blessing for you. This book is telling a story. It is not a textbook or Bible handbook. Although it is based upon the teachings of Rev. Sun Myung Moon, it is by no means meant to be a full exposition of those teachings.

Chapter One

The Principle of Creation

At the center of everything is God's love. God needs love, man needs love, and the angelic world also needs love. If the world had been centered upon God's love from the beginning, it would have been not only an ideal beginning, but the direction and the final results would have also been ideal. God, man and the angelic world would have formed one perfect world, freely communicating with each other centering upon God's love.

Sun Myung Moon

In this chapter we are pursuing the original purpose for which God created. When man fell into sin, he fell away from the ideal of creation. The literal translation of the Hebrew word *chata* for "sin" is "missing the goal." We will explore the nature of "the mark" that was missed.

This is relevant, not in order to alter the root of Christian faith, but rather to be best able to define the ultimate fruit and fulfillment of the Christian age. That fruit is, in fact, the very "mark" that was missed in the beginning of time.

Central to this will be the institution of marriage and family. We will find that these are not merely inventions of man, nor are they just based on biblical imperatives, but they are, rather, institutions that find their origins deep within the very nature of God and are central to the accomplishment of His purpose for creating.

There are several important resources for our discovery of God's original purpose for creating. The first and foremost is expressed in:

Hebrews 1:1–3
*In the past, God spoke to our forefathers through the prophets at many times and in various ways, but in these last days he has spoken to us by his Son, whom he appointed heir of all things, and through whom he made the universe. The Son is the radiance of God's glory and **the exact representation of his being**, sustaining all things by his powerful word.*

All principles and truths related to the nature of God and His purpose for creating are expressed in the manifest relationship between the Father and the Son. Our second resource will be the authorized assertions manifested through God's Holy Word and expressed in the Bible. Our third resource will be the manifestation of God via the "things that He has made" as indicated in **Romans 1:20** and **Psalms 19:1–2**.

Romans 1:20
For since the creation of the world God's invisible qualities—his eternal power and divine nature—have been clearly seen, being understood from what has been made, so that men are without excuse.

Psalms 19:1–2
The heavens declare the glory of God; the skies proclaim the work of his hands. Day after day they pour forth speech; night after night they display knowledge.

The Nature of God

In order to understand our relationship with God, of course, we need to be clear about the nature of the God with whom we seek to relate.

Genesis 1:27
So God created man in his own image, in the image of God he created him, male and female he created them.

Scripture states that God's image is male and female. In this sense, it appears that God is a being of two, male and female. However, in Mark 12:29, Jesus asserts, "God is one." How could God at the same time be "one" and yet display the pair of male and female? What about the Trinity of the Father, Son and Holy Ghost? Is God one, two or three?

We can understand that, in a sense, it is all of those. Think of it in this way: red and blue when engaged in a circular motion reveal the color magenta. God is magenta. Magenta is "one" color, so God is one. However, magenta appears on the foundation of the engagement of red and blue. So God is also two, red and blue, as in "his image, male and female." Thus, God is also three: red, blue and magenta, as in the Trinity. All biblical reference to the idea of becoming "one" involves a type of relationship between two. Jesus prayed, for example, in **John 17:21** that all believers should be "one" as God and Christ are "one."

This is why we see the system of pairs as such a fundamental dynamic of the creation. It is because the pair system is the very groundwork of God's own existence, His "image." This is why Paul could explain, although God Himself is invisible, the things that God has made are a visible manifestation of His invisible nature. The pair system of the universe, then, is the visible manifestation of God. In the creation of man and woman, it is His very image.

We find another type of pair dynamic in God that is manifested in the character and form pair structure of the individual human as described by Paul in:

1 Corinthians 15:44
*It is sown a natural body, it is raised a spiritual body. If there is a **natural body**, there is also **a spiritual body**.*

God is described as "spirit" in **John 4:24**. This is God's external manifestation. In **Exodus 33:20–23,** we find another very interesting record:

"But," he said, "you cannot see my face, for no one may see me and live." Then the LORD said, "There is a place near me where you may stand on a rock. When my glory passes by, I will put you in a cleft in the rock and cover you with my hand until I have passed by. Then I will remove my hand and you will see my back; but my face must not be seen."

However, just as we would have to delve into the internal nature of a human to understand his true being, likewise in order to know the fullest nature of God one must transcend a surface understanding of His existence. Instead, scripture leads us into the innermost regions of God's internal and personal nature. It is here that the foundation of our relationship with Him is discovered. It is here, then, that our position in the universe, our fundamental unique value and identity, is realized. Who am I? I am the one who is loved by God.

1 John 4:16

God is love.

John 3:16

God so loved the world . . .

Exodus 34:6–7

The Lord, the Lord, the compassionate and gracious God, slow to anger, abounding in love and faithfulness, maintaining love to thousands, and forgiving wickedness, rebellion and sin.

Of course, a concordance search focused on the word "love" will certainly generate a wide array of scripture that will provide overwhelming testimony to the loving nature of a mighty God.

This fundamental nature of love is what dictates the process, function and purpose of creation. Reverend Moon explains:

What is the purpose of the pair system? Why did God create in this way? The Creator divided all things in male and female so that they might unite through their give and take of love. Through the action of love, each species multiplies and extends its lineage.
—The 11th World Media Conference, April 10, 1990

Creation is structured to facilitate the operation of love, for "God is love." (**1John 4:16**) The pair system is the central principle of the universe, love is the center of all pairs, and therefore, God is the center of the universe.

Jesus declared most simply, yet profoundly, the nature of God:

Matthew 6:9

Our Father, which art in Heaven, . . .

Jesus called God "Father." This means that God's nature of love is of the parental, sacrificial, and unconditional type. God's purpose for creation, His will, His plan, our purpose and destiny are all extensions of a Supreme Parent of love. This is the key to all theology. When we ponder the mysteries of God, we must first know that His thoughts, plans and actions are all motivated from the heart of a True Parent.

The Origin in the Foundation of Power

As we have mentioned, the pair system or principle is the groundwork of the universe, encompassing all existence. Again, consider Rev. Moon's insight:

> When we observe our universe, we recognize that every being exists through the union of paired elements. This is true on all levels, beginning even with the mineral realm. Molecules are made from the union of a positive ion and a negative ion. On the level of plants, existence and reproduction require the union of stamen and pistil, representing the male and female aspects.
>
> **The pair system** is even more obvious on the level of animals. Fish, birds, mammals and all animals exist as male and female. Finally, the supreme creations of God, human beings, are either men or women. The first man, Adam, and the first woman, Eve, were the original ancestors of mankind.

Remember, God did not "invent" the pair system. It is the groundwork of God's own existence. "I am that I am" God told Moses. Jesus said in **John 5:26,** "The Father has life within himself."

John 1:1–2
In the beginning was the Word, and the Word was with God, and the Word was God. He was with God in the beginning.

The Word, or "Logos," is that principle of God's own existence as a being of "oneness". The Word "became flesh" is also the expression of "the Son," because "God and Christ are one." The statement that "through Him all things were made" is the affirmation that the fundamental principle of God's existence is likewise the principle by which God created all things.

Thus, God and His creation exist and act via the same principle, the "Logos." This is why we can look at the creation, as Paul states in **Romans 1:20**, and perceive the visible expression of God. More important, this is why humans, man and woman, stand as "the image" of God. God created us via the "Logos," the principle by which He, Himself, exists.

Division in the Foundation of Power

God, the creator who is "one," creates via the pair system. However, both members of any pair begin their process as separate and distinct entities. That is, entities that must orientate toward each other around a common protocol, interact, trade elements, and then merge into oneness.

Science can observe the give-and-take action between plus and minus particles in the forming of an atom. However, the stage prior to their engaging is still rather mysterious. What cosmic force causes plus and minus to attract and then establish a reciprocal relationship? It is as if all things in creation are driven by a predetermined sense of destiny and purpose. All things other than humans, that is. We are the ones that have fallen off the path, having "missed the mark," as it were.

Before two can engage in a reciprocal relationship, first a common protocol must be established. Simply, a common base must be shared for give-and-take to ensue.

One way to visualize this it to imagine a conversation with another, someone you have never met. You are sitting on the train. A person sits in the seat next to you. What do you do? The feeling of unconnectedness is awkward and uncomfortable. Most people quell that discomfort by intensifying disengagement. We do not acknowledge the alien presence in our space. The other course of action is to engage and familiarize. I express pleasantries and openness. I probe for common experience and likes. If my seatmate, for example, is from Boston then I say "How about those Red Sox!" We search for a commonality because give-and-take action operates around an established common base. It is one reason we talk about the weather in order to "break the ice."

All pairs within the pair system of creation are attracted toward each other and into reciprocal relationship because each member of each pair holds something in common with its pair partner. A plus particle and a minus particle have a common base that brings them toward engagement. The common needs of hydrogen and oxygen bring them into engagement in the creation of water molecules. Red and blue have a common base that brings them toward engagement. Certainly, man and woman have something in common that brings them toward engagement. What is the common base of all created pairs and from where does it originate?

The destiny of all pairs is to achieve the status of "oneness." That standard of oneness is the Logos, the Word through whom all things were made. God is the archetype of that design. In other words, red and blue are created around the design of magenta, patterned after God. Man and woman are created around the design and purpose of their union, likewise patterned after God This design preexists the creation and was with God and is God. It is the structure of love. This design, that two should become one, is the common base between the members of all pairs. That is why Jesus' relationship with God, the relationship of Father and Son, is the core of "Logos." "As God and Christ are one" is the prime design through which all pairs are made.

There is a new movement within the field of science called "Intelligent Design." Intelligent Design theorists are now finding a multitude of ways for science to demonstrate that natural things have been intelligently designed. This was precisely the goal of St. Thomas in his work, *Summa Theologiae*, on the five proofs of God's existence, especially the fifth proof, which concludes: "Therefore, there is something intelligent by which all natural things are ordered to their end, and this we call God." God is not only the first cause, but He is also the pattern and archetype, or design, of all creation.

When God creates in pairs, He endows each member with the nature to place priority on the design, the Logos. This common nature, for example, in plus and minus particles causes them to attract and move toward a reciprocal base. The pinnacle of all pairs is man and woman, God's image. This is what attracts men and women into relationship. It is because the union of man and woman is an idea and design deep within the very nature of God. Jesus refers to this:

Matthew 19:4–6
*"Haven't you read," he replied, "that at the beginning the Creator 'made them male and female,' and said, 'For this reason a man will leave his father and mother and be **united** to his wife, and **the two will become one flesh.'"***

The most essential "common base" between man and woman, however, is not just that they are reflective of God's design but that both have been endowed with God's own nature, the nature of sacrificial love. This is what sets humans apart from all other creations.

Genesis 2:7

*The Lord God formed the man from the dust of the ground and **breathed** into his nostrils the **breath of life**, and the man became a living being.*

John 5:26

For as the Father has life in himself, so he has granted the Son to have life in himself.

1 John 4:12–13

. . . God lives in us and his love is made complete in us. We know that we live in him and he in us, because he has given us of his Spirit.

Giving and Receiving Action

Around this common base, giving-and-receiving action ensues. Through this action of give-and-take all the forces necessary for existence, action and multiplication are generated.

The idea of "image" therefore implies a type of relationship between man and woman. In other words, a man and woman standing next to each other are not necessarily manifesting the image of God. They must become one as the Lord is one. What is the process for man and woman to "become one"?

What brings two into one? In creation we see a core virtue defining and shaping all relationships toward oneness. Consider Jesus' words:

Matthew 6:26–29, 33

Behold the fowls of the air: for they sow not, neither do they reap, nor gather into barns; yet your heavenly Father feedeth them. Are ye not much better than they? Which of you by taking thought can add one cubit unto his stature? And why take ye thought for raiment? Consider the lilies of the field, how they grow; they toil not, neither do they spin: And yet I say unto you, That even Solomon in all his glory was not arrayed like one of these.

But seek ye first the kingdom of God, and his righteousness; and all these things shall be added unto you.

Matthew 10:39

He that findeth his life shall lose it: and he that loseth his life for my sake shall find it.

Jesus is describing the virtue of sacrificial love. First, give, then after that, receive. Paul describes Christ's sacrificial love for the church as the model for the relationship of husband and wife.

Ephesians 5:32–33
This is a profound mystery—but I am talking about Christ and the church. However, each one of you also must love his wife as he loves himself, and the wife must respect her husband.

When husband and wife implement the virtue that brings two into one then they are united *"so they are no longer two, **but one**."* On this foundation they become "one with the Lord."

1 Corinthians 6:17
He who unites himself with the Lord is one with him in spirit.

Therefore, God is drawn toward and within the relationship of sacrificial love between husband and wife.

1 John 4:24
God is love, he who lives in love, lives in God and God in him.

This is the "gyroscope" of love. In other words, when the wheel turns (live in love) a vertical axis appears (lives in God and God in him). To try to balance a gyroscope without turning the wheel is very difficult. However, if the wheel spins, it will balance on its own.

This is also why whenever two become one, a higher value appears that is greater than even the sum of the two parts. Magenta, for instance, is not merely red and blue. Salt is not merely sodium and chloride. This mysterious higher value stumps scientific materialism to this very day. How does one plus one equal three? It is because a deeper, more reflective connection is made between God and the unified pair *no longer two but one.*

Rev. Moon explains:

Another way of interpreting this formula of origin, division and union is the Origin which is God's position and can be interpreted as plus. The union can be interpreted as man's position, which is minus. Once this union takes place, bringing absolute unity between husband and wife, do you think that God is pulling this union toward Himself, or is this union pulling God toward them, or are they repelling one another? Which

one? Does no one have the answer? When God sees this perfect union tak-
ing place, don't you think that He would want to draw that toward Himself?
Don't you think the couple would also want to pull God down toward
them? It functions in such a way that God will pull this united couple
up as strongly as He can and the couple will pull God down as strongly
as they can. Therefore this circular motion takes place.
—True God's Day, January 1, 1996

Based on all of this, we can conclude that God's objective is to become one with parents who are one with the Lord. What is His purpose?

The Purpose of Creation

We can conclude that God created an "image" so as to duplicate His love-giving nature in a created being. For God, as for anyone, perfect love is not only in giving love but also in responding to love given. Without man and woman, how could God have that experience? With whom else was God to engage in the actual experience of love? This was the mission of Adam and Eve. God gave "His blessing" to them. What is that blessing?

Genesis 1:28
God blessed them and said to them, 'Be fruitful and multiply, fill the earth and have dominion over it.'

The Three Blessings

1. The First Blessing: "Be Fruitful"
The First Blessing calls us to the full realization of each individual as a true child and person in the image of God.

Matthew 22:37
Love the Lord your God *with all your heart and with all your soul and with all your mind.*

Matthew 5:48
You must be perfect as your Heavenly Father is perfect.

Therefore, before Adam and Eve could multiply they were to perfect God's love within themselves.

1 John 4:12

. . . if we love one another, God lives in us and his love is made complete in us.

The pair system operates on the individual level. Individual Adam and Eve, likewise, are structured via the pair system.

1 Corinthians 15:44

*It is sown a natural body, it is raised a spiritual body. If there is a **natural body**, there is also **a spiritual body**.*

Also, **Ecclesiastes 12:7**

And the dust returns to the ground it came from and the spirit returns to God who gave it.

Therefore, to achieve perfection, Adam and Eve must unite "with the Lord" their personal "husband and wife," that is, their own spirit and natural body.

Ephesians 5:28–30

In this same way, husbands ought to love their wives as their own bodies. He who loves his wife loves himself. After all, no one ever hated his own body, but he feeds and cares for it, just as Christ does the church— for we are members of his body.

The unity of Christ and the church, the unity of husband and wife, the unity of spirit and body are all based on the same design, the "Logos." Thus, the path to becoming "fruitful" is the path to establish the submission of the flesh to the will of the spirit. This was Adam and Eve's premarital responsibility. Without accomplishing this responsibility, they would not be able to "multiply" in accordance with God's expressed will in **Malachi 2:15**

Has not the Lord made them one? In flesh and spirit they are his. And why one? Because he was seeking godly offspring.

In their premarital state, before they are to multiply, their bodies are to be in submission to the Lord:

1 Corinthians 6:13

The body is not meant for sexual immorality, but for the Lord, and the Lord for the body.

1 Corinthians 6:18

Flee from sexual immorality. All other sins a man commits are outside his body, but he who sins sexually sins against his own body.

God's commandment to Adam and Eve to not "eat the fruit" places them in the position to exert the authority of faith in God's word toward the submission of their flesh. This is the path of maturity, spiritual perfection, and character development. Even Jesus walked this course:

Hebrews 4:15

For we have not an high priest which cannot be touched with the feeling of our infirmities; but was in all points tempted like as we are, yet without sin.

Hebrews 5:8–9

Though he were a Son, yet learned he obedience by the things which he suffered; And being made perfect, he became the author of eternal salvation unto all them that obey him.

During this time of maturing, Adam and Eve were to achieve "oneness with the spirit of the Lord" **1 Corinthians 6:17**. God's spirit is to indwell in them for they are "temples" of the Lord **1 Corinthians 3:16**. As "temples" they are to become "sacred" **1 Corinthians 3:17**.

Having lost the three Blessings, humankind does not understand how important it is to perfect one's individuality. As a true individual we can experience sacred and eternal conjugal love. Most of today's youth are not educated in a thoroughgoing way about the importance of keeping purity before marriage and reaching individual maturity through true love. Thus they do not understand the value of true love, which is the fundamental root of joy, happiness and all ideals.

Rev. Sun Myung Moon

On this foundation, they would be ready to begin their married life.

2. The Second Blessing: "Multiply"

Malachi 2:15

Has not the Lord made them one? In flesh and spirit they are his. And why one? Because he was seeking godly offspring.

God was seeking godly offspring. Jesus referred to God as "Father" over 50 times in the Gospels. In the first blessing, God bequeaths His life to Adam and Eve. In the second blessing to "multiply," God bequeaths His role, His love and lineage, to Adam and Eve.

God created Adam from dust and Eve from Adam's rib. However, after that God will not create His offspring on His own. Henceforth, God wanted His offspring to emanate from Adam and Eve. The creation of God's eternal, uncontested lineage will be a co-creatorship between God and true parents. That is, had Adam and Eve not fallen.

In order to become sons and daughters of God, we must come into God's own lineage. Our bloodline must become connected to God. What if there had been no fall of man? In the first place, we would automatically be born as children of God. The fall of man was the severing of man from God. Illicit love brought about the fallen lineage. Instead of Adam and Eve uniting under God, the serpent and Eve united. The serpent took God's position and subjugated all mankind, and all mankind came under Satan instead of God.

Rev. Sun Myung Moon

In marriage, the Lord's authority over the body is transferred to husband and wife:

1 Corinthians 7:4

The wife's body does not belong to her alone but also to her husband. In the same way, the husband's body does not belong to him alone but also to his wife.

If Adam and Eve's children could have been born as "godly offspring" then we would have seen the social expansion of the image of God. Not only would we be able to say "as you see me you see the Father," but we would be able to proclaim, as you see the family you see God, as you see the society, you see God, as you see the nation and world, you see God. The entire world of humanity would be God's "exact representation."

That would have been the Kingdom of God on Earth and in Heaven.

This is how the process of creation originally took place: God created all things first and then Adam and Eve. Finally they were supposed to become the True Parents of all mankind. The ultimate goal was the complete unity of Adam and Eve's family with God's love.

The family is the building block of the Kingdom of Heaven. The family is the boundary line that separates the heavenly world from the satanic world. God's plan is to hold Adam and Eve in His arms, within His domain. If God rules the husband-wife relationship, He has all other relationships and all things of creation as well.

Rev. Sun Myung Moon
"True Parents and Our Responsibility", 1981

3. The Third Blessing: "Have Dominion"

Originally, God created Adam with the goal of making him the perfect substantial representation of God. Adam was to be God's substantial vessel. No one but God the Creator can have complete dominion over all things. That is because in order to have complete dominion it is necessary to have complete knowledge. Only God knows all things completely; therefore, complete dominion is possible only by God. Adam himself is a created being, and it is impossible for a created being to have complete dominion over the creation. Therefore, God made Adam in His image so that He might live directly in him. In other words, God intended to make Adam stand in the position of God's resonator and wanted to control the universe directly through him.

Psalms 8:4–6

*What is man that you are mindful of him, the son of man that you care for him? You made him a little lower than the heavenly beings and crowned him with glory and honor. When **you made him ruler** over the works of your hands; **you put everything under his feet.***

The first Adam was to inherit the authority of God. Thus, God would receive joy and stimulation from the creation through His children. God would have direct dominion over creation through

Adam. Therefore, when Adam fell, all of creation lost that vital connection to God the Creator.

Romans 8:18–21

I consider that our present sufferings are not worth comparing with the glory that will be revealed in us. **The creation waits in eager expectation for the sons of God to be revealed.** *For the creation was subjected to frustration not by its own choice, but by the will of the one who subjected it, in hope that* **the creation itself will be liberated** *from its bondage to decay and be brought into the glorious freedom of the* **children of God.**

After the first Adam's fall, the "last Adam" fulfilled that role.

1 Corinthians 15:27–28

For he "has put everything under his feet." Now when it says that "everything" has been put under him, it is clear that this does not include God himself, who put everything under Christ. When he has done this, then the Son himself will be made subject to Him **who put everything under Him, so that God may be all in all.**

"So that God may be all in all." Again this indicates that God rules through the position of the Son. From the standpoint of God's dominion, Adam and Eve, as True Parents, would pass on and expand the dominion of God through His "Godly offspring."

The Three Blessings given to Adam and Eve were the cornerstone of God's plan to establish and expand His kingdom in perpetuity.

The Position of the Son in the Universe

The Creation of Adam

How could God work through the form of Adam? God created all things with forms, but the invisible God does not have any form.

In terms of largeness, God is infinitely large, and in terms of smallness, God is infinitely small. Material things, no matter what kind of form they may have, cannot receive direct dominion from God. Therefore, in the created world of material things, God created man, who has His spirit, to be the master.

God must have dominion not only over all earthly things, but also over the infinite spiritual world. Archangels and all other spiritual beings are invisible substantial beings. A certain central form is also necessary in order to have dominion over the invisible substantial world.

Then where was that form available? It was only through the position of the Son that God could have such a form. Accordingly, through Adam's form, God planned to have dominion over both the spiritual world and the physical world, with Adam as the center. That was the purpose of creation.

1. The Son Is a Microcosm

Therefore, the form of creation was patterned after the Spirit body–Natural body form of the Son. Jesus, then, stands as a "microcosm" of a universe that is composed of a time/space physical world and an eternal world of spirit. This corresponds with the flesh and spirit of Christ.

John 1:10

The universe was made through him . . .

In **Hebrews 1:1–3**, Jesus is described as "the exact representation" of God. Because God is perceived in "the things that he has made," then all things are patterned after the Son.

2. The Son Is a Medium of Harmony

We can see that Jesus was in contact with both worlds. Whether in heaven or on earth, Jesus engaged in direct communication. Jesus moved freely between the two worlds.

Matthew 17:1–5

After six days Jesus took with him Peter, James and John the brother of James, and led them up a high mountain by themselves. There he was transfigured before them. His face shone like the sun, and his clothes became as white as the light. Just then there appeared before them Moses and Elijah, talking with Jesus. Peter said to Jesus, "Lord, it is good for us to be here. If you wish, I will put up three shelters—one for you, one for Moses and one for Elijah." While he was still speaking, a bright cloud enveloped them, and a voice from the cloud said, "This is my Son, whom I love; with him I am well pleased. Listen to him!"

3. The Son Is Lord and Ruler Over Both Worlds

Psalms 8:4–6

*What is man that you are mindful of him, the son of man that you care for him? You made him a little lower than the heavenly beings and crowned him with glory and honor. When **you made him ruler** over the works of your hands; **you put everything under his feet.***

1 Corinthians 15:27–28

*For he "has put everything under his feet." Now when it says that "everything" has been put under him, it is clear that this does not include God himself, who put everything under Christ. When he has done this, then the Son himself will be made subject to him **who put everything under him, so that God may be all in all.***

Once we are saved, with that salvation comes a hope for future glorification, i.e., the redemption of our bodies. At his second coming, Jesus restores to the believer the original position and status that was to be established by Adam. It is because we are of the same family as Jesus:

Hebrews 2:11

Both the one who makes men holy and those who are made holy are of the same family. So Jesus is not ashamed to call them (the saved) *brothers.*

Our dominion is not only on earth, but also over the angels.

Hebrews 1:13–14

To which of the angels did God ever say, "Sit at my right hand until I make your enemies a footstool for your feet"? Are not all angels ministering spirits sent to serve those who will inherit salvation?

The Relationship of the Two Worlds Centering on the Son

1 Corinthians 15:44

*It is sown a natural body, it is raised a spiritual body. If there is a **natural body**, there is also **a spiritual body**.*

The universe, created through the design of the Son (the Word, Logos), therefore reflects the spiritual body and natural body configuration of Jesus. Thus, the universe is structured via the pair system.

The universe, then, is composed of a visible substantial world, or physical world, and an invisible substantial world, or spiritual world. The physical world corresponds to the flesh body of Christ and is patterned after Jesus. The spiritual world corresponds with the spirit body of Christ and is likewise patterned after the Son.

The Physical World

The physical world is a temporal world. Our physical bodies are temporal, as stated in **Ecclesiastes 12:7**. What is the purpose of this temporal existence with an average lifespan of 75 years?

We can compare it to another temporal life that each of us experienced. It was our life in the womb of our mother. This time Dr. Hak Ja Han Moon gives us a perfect analogy:

> To the fetus, the aquatic world of its mother's womb is a world of total freedom. Interestingly, although it is constrained within the confines of the womb, the fetus feels completely free. In the womb, it can't stretch its legs as much as it would like, and the fetus relies on an umbilical cord to breathe and receive nutrients for survival since its nose and mouth are both useless in this world. Nevertheless, to the fetus, the world in the womb is one of complete freedom.
>
> As soon as the baby is born, it begins to cry. At the same time, it starts to breathe through its nose and becomes linked to the second world, the world of air.
>
> As the baby leaves the womb to enter the world of air, the umbilical cord is destroyed along with the water sac and everything it needed in the world of the womb. With the death of these things, the baby is born into the bosom of its new mother, the planet earth. Once born, the baby begins to eat with its mouth and breathe with its nose. The food we eat on Earth nourishes our physical bodies, but it does not contain the essential element of life. This life element is nothing other than love. Thus, while we are in this world, we also need to breathe the air of love. We need to inhale this air of love from our mother and father.
>
> **"The Path of Life for All Humankind", March 19, 1999**

In other words, the purpose of life in the womb is to grow and develop the capacity for the new life in "the next world." Likewise, the purpose of life in the physical world is akin to life in a "second womb." In this second world, we must develop the spiritual capacity to live in the next dimension of life in the world of spirit.

Just as when a baby completes its growth inside the womb of its mother, it is born to its new life in the physical world. The placenta, once so vital for its survival, is purged from the womb and is useless. In the same way, when one completes one's growth and spiritual development in the physical realm, the time arrives for "death." This death is, in fact, meant to be a "second birth." Just like the placenta at the first birth, the physical body, having completed its usefulness, returns to the soil. Rev. Moon speaks on this:

There is an intrinsic difference between God and men of flesh. There must be some way that man, who is spiritual and physical, can fulfill the things as does the totally spiritual God. We must have some kind of body that is similar to the body of God.

The day we receive new birth, becoming persons with God-like bodies capable of following God anywhere, is the day that we call "death" here on earth. Does it seem that we should welcome death, then? What is the purpose of dying? We die in order to fulfill our craving to experience all the love of God, which is limited here on earth. In a way, physical death is the discarding of our clumsy physical bodies, these "vehicles" we have used on earth. God enjoys total freedom in the universe; so when He sees His children suffering from so many things here on the earth, He can hardly be happy about it. In God's scheme of creation, "death" is another birth for man. We can achieve liberation from the shackles of our physical bodies and enjoy the kind of freedom God enjoys; so death is really a second birth.

"Victory of Home Church", January 1, 1982

The physical world and the physical body is the soil in which the spirit is to grow. Once the "fruit" is ripe, it falls from the tree. Once our spirit is fully matured in God's love, it is ready to separate and begin life in spirit only, as God is spirit only.

The Spiritual World

As we can see from his experience at the Mount of Transfiguration, Jesus was in contact with the vast realm of spirit. This interaction between the two worlds centering on Jesus did not seem unusual or frightening to him at all. How different would our reaction be if we received a similar visitation from the departed?

In the following parable, Jesus gives us a glimpse into the nature of the unseen world.

Luke 16:19–31

There was a rich man who was dressed in purple and fine linen and lived in luxury every day. At his gate was laid a beggar named Lazarus [a different Lazarus from the one Jesus raised from the dead] *covered with sores and longing to eat what fell from the rich man's table. Even the dogs came and licked his sores.*

The time came when the beggar died and the angels carried him to Abraham's side. The rich man also died and was buried. In hell, where he was in torment, he looked up and saw Abraham far away, with Lazarus by his side. So he called to him, "Father Abraham, have pity on me and send Lazarus to dip the tip of his finger in water and cool my tongue, because I am in agony in this fire."

But Abraham replied, "Son, remember that in your lifetime your received your good things, while Lazarus received bad things, but now he is comforted here and you are in agony. And besides all things, between us and you a great chasm has been fixed, so that those who want to go from here to you cannot, nor can anyone cross over from there to us."

He answered, "Then, I beg you, father, send Lazarus to my father's house, for I have five brothers. Let him warn them, so that they will not also come to this place of torment."

Abraham replied, "They have Moses and the Prophets; let them listen to them."

"No, father Abraham," he said, "but if someone from the dead goes to them, they will repent."

He said to him, "If they do not listen to Moses and the Prophets, they will not be convinced even if someone rises from the dead."

Jesus describes two basic realms in the world of spirit at that time. One side he refers to as "Abraham's side." On this side of the spirit world are Abraham and Lazarus. The other side below is called "hell" and is the dwelling place of the rich man "in agony." Between these two realms "a chasm" has been fixed, "so that those who want to go from here to you cannot, nor can anyone cross over from there to us."

This parable is noteworthy for several reasons. One is that we see Abraham and Lazarus, though not saved Christians, are not in hell. They appear to be in some intermediate realm corresponding to the dimension of righteousness they were able to achieve during their life on earth. God has a plan for these righteous saints who passed before the coming of Jesus Christ:

Hebrews 11:39–40

These were all commended for their faith, yet none of them received what had been promised. God had planned something better for us so that only together with us would they be made perfect.

The second noteworthy element from the parable is displayed in Jesus' description of the forms of Abraham, Lazarus, and the rich man. The rich man's natural body had died and "was buried" as per **Ecclesiastes 12:7**. However, his spiritual body ended up in hell. For all intents and purposes, though in their spiritualized form, they all appear very similar as they did on earth. It is likewise true for Moses and Elijah, on the Mount of Transfiguration.

They seem to display all the same senses of sight, taste, touch, smell and hearing in their spiritualized form as they had in their physical forms.

A third noteworthy element to the parable is expressed when the rich man in hell pleads with father Abraham. He asks him to send Lazarus from the world of spirit back to the earth in order to warn his five brothers "so that they will not come to this place of torment." Abraham tells the rich man that if his brothers will not listen to Moses and the prophets, they will not listen "even if someone raises from the dead." This seems to indicate a potential for those in the realm of spirit to make a return appearance on the earth plane as did, apparently, Moses and Elijah. This "appearance" is referred to as "raising from the dead."

Most Christians are rightfully wary of spiritual communication. However, scripture never declares an unconditional moratorium against any and all spiritual interaction. Rather than shutting ourselves off from the spiritual world completely, scripture indicates that communication can and does take place. However, we must discern by "testing the spirit."

1 John 4:1–3

Dear friends, do not believe every spirit, but test the spirits to see whether they are from God, because many false prophets have gone out into the world. This is how you can recognize the Spirit of God: Every spirit that acknowledges that Jesus Christ has come in the flesh is from God, but every spirit that does not acknowledge Jesus is not from God. This is the spirit of the antichrist, which you have heard is coming and even now is already in the world.

If the physical body is the soil unto which the spirit grows, what is the nature of the exchange? What are the specifics of spiritual growth on earth?

The Structure and Function of a Human

As per the pair system, God has created the Son with a spiritual body and a natural body. The perfect Son stands as a microcosm of the universe. Thus, the universe is created via the pair system as spirit world and physical world. The two worlds, then, harmonize and become "one" centering on the Son who stands as the microcosm of oneness, that is, the unity of his spirit and flesh. Jesus achieved this, as testified to in **Hebrews 5:7**.

Just as the unity of Christ and the church and the unity of husband and wife are of the same design as the unity of spirit and flesh, the two worlds follow the same design toward achieving oneness between the two. The two worlds, however, must have something in common around which exchange and harmony can be achieved.

That common base between the two worlds is the microcosm of the perfect Son. Jesus, perfectly united in spirit and flesh, was the link and conduit between the two worlds. This is why there was such a high degree of spiritual phenomena around the person of Jesus Christ.

However, since Jesus left this world, believers have not been able to duplicate the same high standard of unity between flesh and spirit.

Romans 7:21–24

So I find this law at work: When I want to do good, evil is right there with me. For in my inner being I delight in God's law; but I see another law at work in the members of my body, waging war against the law of my mind and making me a prisoner of the law of sin at work within my members. What a wretched man I am! Who will rescue me from this body of death?

Thus, the two worlds remain separate and detached. The result is that knowledge of life in the spirit world is still vague and obscure. Our understanding of the reality in heaven becomes subject to an ever-increasing proliferation of dogma. Humans, even believers, on various levels still fear death. Therefore, with our salvation comes a hope for future glorification, the "redemption of our bodies" at Christ's return.

Romans 8:23–25

Not only so, but we ourselves, who have the first fruits of the Spirit, groan inwardly as we wait eagerly for our adoption as sons, the redemption of our bodies. For in this hope we were saved. But hope that is seen is no hope at all. Who hopes for what he already has? But if we hope for what we do not yet have, we wait for it patiently.

When the redemption of the body is accomplished, then mind and body can fully unite and all believers can stand as the perfect image of Christ. On that foundation, the two worlds can become as one. This is a fundamental quality to the Kingdom of Heaven on earth and in spirit.

The Relationship of Spirit Self and Physical Self

As we have seen, Paul indicates the original form or model of spirit body and natural body in **1 Corinthians 15:42–44**. The relationship of the spirit body and the natural body is reflective of the ideal relationship of husband to wife and Christ with the church. **Ephesians 5:31–33** The body is the soil for the spirit to grow. What are the necessary components for spiritual growth to take place? The following five steps are the fundamentals in the relationship of spirit and flesh.

1. The spirit self needs life elements: God's love and truth.

What is the foundation for spiritual growth? It is the Word of God. In the beginning, Adam and Eve were given the Commandment of God. Maintaining faith in God's word is the foundation of life.

Matthew 4:4

Jesus answered, "It is written: 'Man does not live on bread alone, but on every word that comes from the mouth of God.'"

1 Peter 2:2

Like newborn babies, crave pure spiritual milk, so that by it you may grow up in your salvation.

2. Once we receive God's word, we are compelled to put that word into practice.

In other words, life elements must manifest as action. This involves a transfer from spirit to flesh.

James 2:17

Faith without action is dead.

Matthew 7:24–25

Therefore everyone who hears these words of mine and puts them into practice is like a wise man who built his house on the rock. The rain came down, the streams rose, and the winds blew and beat against that house; yet it did not fall, because it had its foundation on the rock.

3. We must take care of our body, the "temple" of God's spirit.

Ephesians 5:29

After all, no one ever hated his own body, but he feeds and cares for it, just as Christ does the church.

Our natural body needs sunlight and air just as our spirit body needs God's love and truth. Also, just as our natural body needs food, water and nutrients, our spirit body needs additional nourishment besides love and truth.

4. Through acts of righteousness a nurturing grace or "vitality element" is returned from the natural body to the spiritual body.

Romans 6:13

The body is an instrument of righteousness.

Proverbs 11:25

A generous man will prosper; he who refreshes others will himself ***be*** ***refreshed.***

2 Corinthians 9:7–8

Each man should give what he has decided in his heart to give, not reluc-tantly or under compulsion, for God loves a cheerful giver. And God is able to make ***all grace abound to you****, so that in all things at all times, having all that you need, you will abound in every good work.*

5. A growing healthy spirit manifests in physical well-being. A "spirit element" is returned from the spirit body to the natural body.

Psalms 92:12–14

The righteous will flourish like a palm tree, they will grow like a cedar of Lebanon; planted in the house of the Lord, they will flourish in the courts of our God. ***They will still bear fruit in old age, they will stay fresh and green.***

Through this cooperation between God and man, man would grow spiritually. Once Adam and Eve achieved perfection, becoming one with God, multiplying and exerting dominion over all things, then they would be ready to "pass away" to the eternal world of spirit.

Why did God set up a system that seems to require human effort and cooperation with God?

The Growing Period for Created Beings

As Paul tells us in **Romans 1:20**, God reveals His way in the things that He has made. When we "consider the lilies" as Jesus advises us, we find a deep message in the way of God's creation. We see that God creates in such a way as to involve all things in a pro-cess of growth and completion. In other words, the lily begins as a seed, it grows over time and then in a glorious consummation of its purpose, explodes in a magnificent springtime blossom.

Humans, too, must go a course to completion. Growth, both inter-nal and external, is a vital element in our life. We can examine Jesus' own life as a model for our own.

Luke 2:40, 52

And the child grew and became strong: he was filled with wisdom and the Grace of God was upon him. . . . . And Jesus grew in wisdom and stature, and in favor with God and men.

Luke reveals the two types of growth. "Jesus grew in wisdom and stature." Jesus grew internally, or spiritually, and he grew externally, or physically. Of course, the most important and most challenging aspect of growth is the internal spiritual growth.

Hebrews 4:15

For we have not an high priest which cannot be touched with the feeling of our infirmities; but was in all points tempted like as we are, yet without sin.

Hebrews 5:8–9

Though he were a Son, yet learned he obedience by the things which he suffered; and being made perfect, he became the author of eternal salvation unto all them that obey him.

We can observe that external growth is mostly governed by natural law. Assuredly, given the right amount of food, water and nutrition, everyone will grow externally much in the same way as nature, likewise governed by natural law. However, as we can see with Jesus, internal or spiritual growth involves a much higher degree of participation. It is not the domain of natural law. It is not automatic. It is the domain of love via obedience. Therefore, the core of spiritual growth is the growing of our capacity to love as God loves via the path of obedience to His Word. We mature and stretch our capacity until we can become the recipient of God's own love.

1 John 4:12–13

. . .God lives in us and his love is made complete in us. We know that we live in him and he in us, because he has given us of his Spirit.

In this way, we can observe the distinct nature and potential of humans in relation to the rest of creation. Nature is governed by the laws of nature; thus, we never see nature engaged in sin. Nature cannot disobey natural law and therefore never is in a state of disobedience and sin. Man, in contrast, is not controlled by natural law and, instead, must take responsibility to adhere to a moral code laid down by God.

In fact, we may even ponder why God would not exact the same measure of control over humanity. Why has God opted for His children to play a key role in the process to spiritual perfection? This question resides at the heart of theological query into the meaning of man's broken relationship with God. What conclusions are we to draw from the corruption of humanity and the decline into sin? Why would God establish a process that contained a potential for the entrance of sin into the world? It is not extraordinary that so many theologians conclude that God, in some way, must have intended or permitted sin. Unfortunately, such conclusions lead us away from understanding the nature of God's grief, as expressed in **Genesis 6:6–7**.

We must begin to understand by reminding ourselves of God's core purpose for creating mankind. God is love and God, as love, is seeking to engage in the relationship of love with an object of love. That object of love must be able to not only receive God's love but also have the capacity to give God's love to God as well. This object must, then, be more than a mere creature of God. This object must be able to stand in the same dimension of love as God. This is why we are referred to as God's image and why Jesus cited the Old Testament declaration that states, "ye are gods." **John 10:34**, **Psalms 82:6**. This is why we must go a course to inherit God's love. God is then able to "control" man through love, rather than natural law. In perfection, Adam inherits God's life, love and lineage. On that foundation he is qualified to establish the "godly offspring."

For Adam to inherit God's fundamental nature of love, Adam must stand in a position to inherit. What position is that? Adam must stand in God's position. What is God's position? It is the position of the Creator. God places Adam in the position of the Creator. He does so by sharing His role with Adam. Adam receives from God a portion of God's role as creator. Adam is given the responsibility to partnership with God in the creation of Adam, Eve, Parents, Children, and the universe. This is the role that Jesus accomplished after the first Adam's failure. **1 Corinthians 15:27–28**

By standing in God's position and successfully carrying out God's creator role, then Adam is able to inherit the nature of the Creator. This is similar to a computer downloading its files to another computer. There must be a link and common protocol between computers for the exchange to proceed. God places Adam in a position to share God's protocol. That is, God's destiny to be consummated in perfect love is indelibly intertwined with man's destiny. God and man share a common destiny. The achievement of that common victory requires two victors, God and man, to stand as one.

How, then, does God place Adam in the Creator's role? God places Adam in the position to complete the creation. For example, God creates man's spirit and body; however, Adam must complete the creation by bringing spirit and body into "oneness." This means that Adam must exert authority over his flesh body. Remember the body is the "inner wife" and it is the "inner church." For Adam to have dominion over all things, he must first establish the authority of the creator over his own body of flesh.

God bequeaths His authority to Adam through His Word: the Commandment, "Do not eat the fruit." Adam must generate the power of faith and exert that power over the desire of the flesh body. By maintaining faith in God's word, Adam exerts the authority of the creator over his body of flesh. In this way, the spirit and body move toward oneness and perfection. Thus the creation of perfected Adam involves a partnership between God and His son. Through faith in God's word, Adam plays an active role in his own creation. He, thus, stands with God as co-creator. By Adam successfully fullfilling this responsibility, he inherits the role of son of God, sharing in his Father's destiny of ideal love.

The key for man to inherit God's nature and be able to rise above the dimension of mere creature is to successfully exercise the responsibility that God has given. Man alone must fulfill his portion of responsibility. God will not do it for him. This is why God does not exert the same degree of control over man as He does with the rest of creation. He has given man a portion of responsibility. In **Romans 6:20**, Paul speaks about "the control of righteousness."

Romans 6:20,22
*When you were slaves to sin, you were free from the **control of righteousness**. But thanks be to God that, though you used to be slaves to sin . . . you have been **set free** from sin and have become slaves to righteousness.*

2 Corinthians 3:17 indicates that freedom is a by-product of closeness to the Lord.

Now the Lord is the Spirit, and where the Spirit of the Lord is, there is freedom.

Responsibility, though, has a dark side. For a responsibility to be genuine, there must be a potential for failure. If there is no potential for failure, then the responsibility is not real. It is here that God recognizes the potential for Adam to fail, to betray. However, God has entered into a relationship of love bound by an entrustment. Even for God, there are no guarantees He will never taste the sting of unrequited love.

The potential for failure and betrayal is present not as a manifestation of a proposed Will of God. In no way is God hoping for the failure of His ideal and the subsequent pain and suffering wrought by betrayal and sin. The potential for failure is present so as to give validity to Adam's role of responsibility. It gives definition to his real role, just as a shadow gives depth to an object bathed in light.

In order for man to inherit His nature, God gave man the role to complete the creation of man. God created the parts, but it is man that must bring the parts into "oneness." God created mind and body; man must unite them and become one with the Lord. God created man and woman; they must unite centering on God's highest purpose. God created the universe but will only rule all things through perfect humans.

This is why Adam and Eve must go through the period of maturity. This is why they do not grow automatically. This is why they must take responsibility to apply the tool of faith in the commandment toward that goal.

By doing so, *they* assume the position of children of God and are joined in partnership with God in the creation of ideal man, family and the universe. By taking on a portion of God's role, and having the same mission and purpose as God, Adam and Eve inherit the nature and authority of God. Thus, they were to become "rulers" of the universe. When they become "one" with the Lord, the joy of God and man is the exhilarating joy of a common victory.

It is this conditional nature of relationship with God during the growing period that opens the door for the potential for sin. If Adam and Eve could have fulfilled the course of maturity by keeping faith and accomplishing their portion of responsibility, they would have established an unwavering, direct and unconditional relationship with God that would have stood impervious to sin.

On this foundation, we can begin to understand the conditions that led to the fall of man and the loss of God's ideal. Most important, we can begin to grasp the deep nature of God's disappointment and grief as a result of man's fall. In this realization, we can begin to discover the burning heart of God moving through history in search of His lost beloved children.

A Testimony

A few years ago, I had struck up a friendship with a Methodist minister in North Carolina. He admired the work of Reverend Moon and was deeply inspired by the heart and sincere efforts of our members. Of course, many times I would take the opportunity to share with him Reverend Moon's message.

He was intrigued by much of it, but the part of Reverend Moon's message that mystified him the most was the teaching concerning God's heart and suffering. He just could not, for the life of him, fathom it. Often he would say to me, sometimes even laughing, "God doesn't suffer....God is perfect!" It is a typical attitude about God.

The amazing thing is that though we deeply agree with the Christian affirmation about the perfection of God, we make exactly opposite conclusions. For most Christians, God's perfection precludes suffering. However, in Reverend Moon's experience, because God is perfect, He suffers.

My Methodist minister friend went on to discover the reality of God's suffering heart in a very personal and dramatic way. One day, he was on his way to a family outing. His fiancé and his youngest daughter were traveling in a vehicle following his car.

His youngest daughter was 12 at the time. She was his baby. I have rarely observed a father who so loved his daughter as he loved her. She was a beautiful girl, an Amer-Asian child with deep brown eyes and the most beautiful long brown hair with natural chestnut highlights. He loved watching her walk home from the school bus stop every afternoon. He looked forward to it so much that he had a special window in his home office built just so he could get a better view from his desk as she walked home. He often mentioned how much he loved watching the wind blow her beautiful hair and how the bright sun made her chestnut highlights sparkle. She was his prize of love.

They never made it to their destination that day. As they rounded a curve in the highway, a driver coming from the opposite direction fell asleep at the wheel and swerved into their lane, clipping the rear of my friend's car and plowing head-on into the trailing car. His fiancé was killed instantly and his daughter critically injured.

After they were transported to the hospital, he called me urgently, explained quickly what had happened, and then asked me to meet him at the hospital. When I arrived there, he was inside the ICU with his daughter. She had received severe head trauma and was experiencing swelling in the brain. The doctors ordered emergency surgery on her brain to help alleviate the swelling. In order to perform the surgery they had to shave her head completely. Her long brown hair with chestnut highlights was stuffed into a clear plastic bag and handed to her father as they wheeled her away to surgery.

Devastated, my friend wandered out of the ICU and into the waiting room. I went up to him and we embraced. In his hands, the plastic bag stuffed with her hair, spotted with his tears. This was all that was left him. He collapsed in my arms and set free a cry from deep within his trembling soul. After several minutes, he gradually lifted his head and appeared to be gazing far, far away, as if in a dream or in remembering. It was then that he said the most amazing thing. It was something I will never forget:

"Kevin," he said, "I never understood what Reverend Moon meant when he said that God suffered . . . but now . . . I know, . . . now I know." And with that, he slowly lowered his head and continued to softly cry, lost in a sea of sorrows.

The years passed by until one morning she quietly passed away, and for all that time his beloved never awoke for a final moment to share her tender love with her grieving father.

Chapter Two

The Fall of Man

When will we see the alleviation of the sorrowful feelings planted deep inside the heart of God since the fall, after the creation of the world?

In its most basic form, the story of man's fall is the foundation to understand our need for salvation and the process of that salvation. In other words, before one can hear and understand "the Good News," one must come to grips with "the bad news." The bad news is that we descendants of Adam are "born in sin."

There has not been a more significant and urgent hour to understand beyond mere basics the detailed implications of the fall.

There probably is no greater shocking statistic than the one that demonstrates that despite its Christian heritage, the United States leads the industrialized world in a growing number of social ills that all find their root in the breakdown of the family.

This suggests that a degree of contemplation and self-reflection is in order. As one proceeds in that direction, it should be stressed that the Word of God has the answer. In fact, the Bible's first chapters not only report that God's original family broke down, but reveals the significant process that led to that sad end. Indeed, all subsequent familial impairments can trace their root to the demise of that one central family. Thus, by thoroughly reexamining, through God's Word, the circumstances of the archetypical family breakdown, we gain deep spiritual insight into the ways of the modern family decline. In view of the accelerating rate of family breakdown, it is indeed wise that we begin the process of reexamination.

A growing number of pastors and Christians are becoming sensitized to the issue, as more Christians have direct experiences with this phenomenon of decline. For the first time, many pastors are recognizing that the decline of the surrounding society is now encroaching upon their own church community and is having an adverse effect on the quality of worship.

One frustration felt by many Christian leaders is the increase of social science solutions that beckon believers away from traditional answers. They have been barraged by a growing number of adherents who see Bible solutions as ineffective and shallow. The problem, however, isn't that God's Word is insufficient, but rather God's Word has been mischaracterized in that way by those whose interest it is to do so (the social scientists with their lofty promises, hourly rates, and array of medications). Christian ministers should always stand strong and be heartened by the affirmation that God's Word has the answers for our life.

This chapter on the Fall of man declares that God has an answer. For this reason, we revisit His word in search of a deeper understanding of the root of family breakdown.

The Root of Sin

The Meaning of Eating the Fruit

Genesis reveals that God had placed a mysteriously desirable fruit "in the middle of the garden." This is the fruit that is the object of God's commandment. It is the fruit that creates the context for Adam and Eve to exert the control of righteousness.

Genesis 3:1–4

Now the serpent was more crafty than any of the wild animals the Lord God had made. He said to the woman, "Did God really say, 'You must not eat from any tree in the garden'?"

The woman said to the serpent, "We may eat fruit from the trees in the garden, but God did say, 'You must not eat fruit from the tree that is in the middle of the garden, and you must not touch it, or you will die.'"

"You will not surely die," the serpent said to the woman. "For God knows that when you eat of it your eyes will be opened, and you will be like God, knowing good and evil."

What is the nature of this fruit? What could it be? An apple? An orange? Perhaps, even, a mango? Believers debate and divide between applists, orangists, mangoists, and figists. We could suggest an ecumenist solution: the fruit was a fruit salad. But, sadly, that would probably not suffice to turn the tide toward the ideal of "same mind and judgment."

Some argue that the meaning of the fruit is insignificant and that the only salient point is that Adam and Eve disobeyed God's commandment. This would not be wrong on its face; however, there are degrees of disobedience. For instance, I asked my son to mow the lawn. He did not. This infraction would be far less than others that come to mind (especially in today's world).

Adam and Eve's act of "eating the fruit" had the effect to change their very nature and status with regard to their relationship with God. It transcended their earthly life and passed on death to all their descendants. This was something far more serious than eating the Hostess Twinkee that Dad was hiding in the fridge.

In terms of degrees of sins and their consequences, Paul affirms the idea.

1 Corinthians 6:16, 18

*Do you not know that he who unites himself with a prostitute is one with her in body? For it is written "the two will become one flesh." . . . Flee from sexual immorality. **All other sins** a man commits are outside his body, but he who sins sexually sins against his own body.*

Could this be an indication that the fruit is something more than any ordinary fruit?

Some believe that the placing of the fruit was a test from God. Many point to the example of how God tested Job. But for God to test Adam as he tested Job would be inconsistent with the love relationship in which God was engaged.

There is a very significant difference between Adam, before the fall, and Job. Adam, before the fall, is in the state of sinlessness and is within the parameters of God's love. Job, unlike Adam, is born with sinful nature and in need of salvation. God needs to test sinners. Adam was not yet a sinner, he was a pure child of God.

God giving the commandment, therefore, *was not a test, but a responsibility*. God was giving Adam the opportunity to share in God's role by joining with Him in the responsibility to exert control over self. That is, Adam would play a key role in the government and discipline over self. Fulfilling this role would give Adam the moral base for his freedom and thus open the potential for Adam to inherit God's love.

The key is in understanding the difference between a "test" and a "responsibility." You test someone to evaluate whether he can assume a responsibility. God was not testing Adam; he was fully entrusting him with a portion of responsibility: to assume the role of "co-creator."

Another indication that the fruit was something more than a regular fruit is by the intensity of their desire for it. They were willing to risk their lives to eat it. Remember, God told them that of any other tree they could freely eat, but of the single tree they could not eat.

Do you think that you could be tempted to risk your life to eat something when hunger was not involved at all? Even Satan knew he would have to wait for Jesus to fast for 40 days before his temptation to turn the stones to bread would wield any influence. The list of things that one desires more than life itself is a rather short one. I doubt that desire for a literal fruit makes the list.

Jesus indicates a deeper root to sin.

Matthew 15:11, 15-20
"What goes into a man's mouth does not make him 'unclean,' but what comes out of his mouth, that is what makes him unclean. . . ." Peter said, "Explain the parable to us." "Are you still so dull?" Jesus asked them. "Don't you see that whatever enters the mouth goes into the stomach and then out of the body? But the things that come out of the mouth come from the heart, and these make a man 'unclean,' **FOR OUT OF THE HEART** *come evil thoughts, murder, adultery, sexual immorality, theft, false testimony, slander. These are things that make a man unclean."*

Jesus indicates that the root of sin is "from out of the heart." Thus "eating the fruit" and the corruption of love are one and the same, one a symbolic expression and the other literal.

Let's place the fruit to the side for a moment and move on to other important elements in the story of man's fall. As we clarify each element of the story, the meaning of eating the fruit will become abundantly clear.

The Serpent
The serpent is significant because he is the first one to call attention to the fruit. He contests the moral code laid down by God concerning the fruit. He takes upon himself the ambitious task of redefining the meaning of God's commandment, suggesting to the daughter

of God that his assessment of the issues at hand was much more reliable than God's.

In many circles, debate rages concerning the identity of the serpent, much in the same way there is debate over the meaning of the fruit. According to some, the serpent is a literal talking snake in Eden. In fact, because the serpent was cursed after the fall to "crawl on its belly," some insist that, therefore, before the fall the serpent was upright. Thus the debate addresses the mode of the serpent's mobility: did he have little legs that dropped off when he was cursed or did he bounce around like a pogo stick?

Could Adam and Eve be so gullible as to be tempted by such an aberrant, alien appearance? In fact, if we examine the history of Satan's temptation, don't we find that typically Satan's most influential schemes are delivered via a more subtle agent: the known and trusted entity? Indeed, the serpent is called subtle, but how subtle is an upright, talking serpent bouncing through the garden?

Clearly, the dialogue recorded in **Genesis 3:1–4** between Eve and the serpent is one that displays familiarity. It suggests that this was not the first time they had met.

Genesis 3:1–4 reveals the serpent to be an intelligent being able to communicate comfortably with the daughter of God. Most revealing, however, is the fact that the serpent is conscious of God and His Word. This suggests that the serpent is actually a being with a spiritual nature. Does scripture give us a clear insight into the actual identity of "the serpent"?

Revelation 12:9

The great dragon was hurled down, **THAT ANCIENT SERPENT** *called the devil, or Satan, who leads the whole world astray. He was hurled to the earth, and his angels with him.*

The "serpent" in Eden is none other than Satan himself.

Good and Evil

When we delve into the deep origins of evil, a fundamental question arises: Did God create Satan and evil? Did evil always exist side by side with good? Or did evil come about through an unsanctioned process?

Some point to **Isaiah 45:7**, where God declares that He brings both good and evil. However, "evil" used in this context does not mean moral evil. It is referring to calamity or natural disaster.

Genesis 1:31 states that God proclaimed all things to be "very good" at the conclusion of the creation process. God gave no indication of the existence of any evil entity. Because we affirm the ex nihilo (out of nothing) nature of creation, we could not adhere to the dualist notion that suggests a co-existing god of evil outside God's power to affect.

Therefore, we conclude that Satan's existence finds its origins in the corruption of good. That is, an unsanctioned process transforms a good being, created by God, into the monster of evil we refer to as Satan.

Scripture overwhelmingly supports this conclusion.

Revelation 12:7–9

And there was war in heaven. Michael and his angels fought against the dragon, and the dragon and his angels fought back. But he was not strong enough, and they lost their place in heaven. The great dragon was hurled down—that ancient serpent called the devil or Satan, who leads the whole world astray. He was hurled to the earth, and his angels with him.

2 Peter 2:4

For if God did not spare angels when they sinned, but sent them to hell, putting them into gloomy dungeons to be held for judgment.

Jude 1:6

And the angels who did not keep their positions of authority but abandoned their own home—these he has kept in darkness, bound with everlasting chains for judgment on the great Day.

Job 1:6

One day the angels came to present themselves before the Lord, and Satan also came with them.

What are we able to observe in each of these Bible verses related to our topic? Read them carefully. It is this: angelic beings, originally dwelling in heaven with God, are found to be lacking as a result of some sort of sinful action.

God casts them out of heaven and into "gloomy dungeons" where they are being held for judgment. Also, we see that "the ancient serpent called Satan" seems to have a type of authority or position over this particular group of angels ("his angels"). Thus, the casting out of Satan is of note because he is a figure of high esteem and position in heaven.

This does not mean that "Satan" was "in heaven" with God. We are stating that a being of goodness, related to angels, with a position of authority over a portion of angels, engaged in corrupt activity and was disqualified from heaven. The term "Satan" is used to identify this being post-corruption. However, we need further investigation to discover this being's pre-corruption identity.

The Identity of Satan

Revelation 12:7–9 clearly testifies that the entity cast out of heaven has a position over a portion of angels. The verse also makes a direct comparison of "Michael and *his* angels" with "Satan and *his* angels." It would tend to follow that if Michael is an archangel, the being called Satan likewise was an archangel before he was cast out of heaven.

The identity of the fallen archangel is revealed in **Isaiah 14:12**. Isaiah introduces us to "Lucifer."

Isaiah 14:12-15

"How art thou fallen from heaven, O LUCIFER, son of the morning! How art thou cut down to the ground, which didst weaken the nations!" You have been cast down to the earth, you who once laid low the nations! You said in your heart, 'I will ascend to heaven; I will raise my throne above the stars of God; I will sit enthroned on the mount of assembly, on the utmost heights of the sacred mountain. I will ascend above the tops of the clouds; I will make myself like the Most High.' But you are brought down to the grave, to the depths of the pit.

Here, Isaiah reveals that Lucifer is struggling with his pride. He seems to be dissatisfied with his station in life. When we consider the consistent use of the image "star" to refer to God's children (**Revelation 22:15–17**, "star" = Jesus), Lucifer seeking to raise his throne above the "stars" of God indicates jealousy toward Adam and Eve.

Another oracle is even more explicit in describing aspects of the fall in Eden.

Ezekiel 28:12–19

Son of man, take up a lament concerning the king of Tyre and say to him: "This is what the Sovereign LORD says: You were the model of perfection, **full of wisdom** *and perfect in beauty.* **You were in Eden, the garden of God;** *every precious stone adorned you: ruby, topaz and emerald, chrysolite, onyx and jasper, sapphire, turquoise and beryl. Your settings and mountings were made of gold; on the day you were created they were prepared.* **You were anointed as a guardian cherub,** *for so I ordained you.*

You were on the holy mount of God; you walked among the fiery stones. You were blameless in your ways from the day you were created till wickedness was found in you. Through your widespread trade you were filled with violence, and you sinned. So I drove you in disgrace from the mount of God, and I expelled you, **O guardian cherub,** *from among the fiery stones. Your heart became proud on account of your beauty,* **and you corrupted your wisdom** *because of your splendor. So* **I threw you to the earth;** *I made a spectacle of you before kings.*

By your many sins and dishonest trade you have desecrated your sanctuaries. So I made a fire come out from you, and it consumed you, and I reduced you to ashes on the ground in the sight of all who were watching. All the nations who knew you are appalled at you; you have come to a horrible end and will be no more."

One of the most important additional benefits of this scripture is that it helps to establish the proper timing of the fall. In other words, Ezekiel's oracle helps to establish a clear time-line that indicates Lucifer did not fall until after the creation of Adam and Eve. The "guardian cherub" is in Eden, the garden of God, and has not yet fallen. Later, when we study the course and motive of the fall, we will discover that it was the very appearance of the maturing Adam and Eve and the subsequent change of order that precipitates the fallen reaction of Lucifer.

Many Christians adhere to a theory that has Lucifer falling even before the creation of the world and Adam and Eve. It is referred to in theology as "the gap theory." The gap theory alleges a "gap" of time between **Genesis 1:1** and **Genesis 1:2**.

However, the essence of scriptural teaching on the fall shows that Satan's very existence is predicated on the voluntary cooperation of man. Without a condition established by man, Satan could not become "god and ruler" over man. That is, Satan could not become Satan. The focus of the fall, then, is on the conditions that brought about this "change of lineage" from God-centered to Satan-centered. In other words, there is a huge difference between a "rebellious angel" and an angel who has risen to a position of god and ruler over humanity.

Another important conclusions we can draw from **Ezekiel 28:12–19** is the description of the angel as a "guardian cherub" in Eden. This helps to establish a God-centered original paradigm for the relationship between Adam, Eve and the archangel.

Lucifer is present in Eden as a protector and helper. There are all sorts of analogies one can imagine to help visualize the nature of their intended relationship. For example, in the movie *The Last Emperor*, the English teacher of the boy emperor (played by Peter O'Toole) would be a fitting example. The teacher is older, wiser and more experienced than the young emperor. . .but ultimately the teacher must acquiess to the maturing emperor's position of authority.

Another important element from this oracle is the description of the guardian cherub as "full of wisdom" and the statement that the cause of his downfall involves the very corruption of his wisdom. This is important because it links directly to the "serpent" of **Genesis 3:1** and to the meaning of the symbolism of "serpent." For example, Jesus characterized the Pharisees as "a brood of vipers" not because they had scaly skin, but because, like Lucifer, they were very adept at twisting their wisdom toward achieving their own interests.

Thus, Lucifer, an archangel having a position of authority over other angels, is in Eden with the role and duty to watch over, or protect, Adam and Eve. At some point, he becomes disenchanted with this role and instead is drawn to Eve. Through employing corrupted wisdom, he (one and the same with the serpent of **Genesis 3:1**) seeks to tempt Eve to partake of the fruit in direct insubordination to the expressed word of God.

What circumstances could set in motion such a dire chain of events? What could cause Lucifer's sudden dissatisfaction with his ordained role and purpose? In Lucifer's corrupted view, what was to be gained through enticing the daughter of God?

The Course and Motive of the Fall

The position of Adam and the Angels

To adequately explain the course and motive of the fall, we must clearly explain the intended nature of the relationship of Adam, Eve and the archangel. One challenge in clearly describing their relationship is that the point where we enter the Garden of Eden is a moment when the relationship of man and the angels is undergoing a fundamental, scheduled transition.

Lucifer, the covering cherub, was finishing up his duties as protector and guide. Now Adam was emerging toward lordship, co-creatorship and the vision of **Psalms 8:4–6:**

What is man that you are mindful of him, the son of man that you care for him? You made him a little lower than the heavenly beings and crowned him with glory and honor. When **you made him ruler** *over the works of your hands;* **you put everything under his feet.**

Up until this moment of transition, Lucifer could relate directly to God conditionally with regard to his position as "guardian cherub." We can speculate a time when Lucifer and angels were the highest created beings, prior to the creation of Adam and Eve.

The creation process rendered in Genesis shows clearly that mankind was the last element of the creation. The claim for the pre-Adamic existence of angels can be based upon that clearly stated order of creation.

Again, the point is that Lucifer, since he was created before Adam, had enjoyed a period of exclusive relationship with God as the highest created being to that moment.

The next important point to establish is that Adam was to emerge to a new position of "dominion," including dominion over the angels. An issue that must be resolved concerns the statement of **Psalms 8:5** that man was created a little lower than the angels. In view of this, how can we assert that man was to have dominion over the angels?

If we were to take the 8th Psalm as meaning that man is lower in quality and position than the angels, then we must conclude that Jesus is likewise lower in quality and status than the angels because the writer of Hebrews uses the same **Psalm 8** to describe Jesus (see **Hebrews 2:6–9**). If that was our conclusion, of course, we would be in error. A more proper exegesis of **Psalms 8** and **Hebrews 2:6–9** would be . . . Man was created for a *little while* lower than the angels.

In other words, while Adam was still growing, he was under the protection and care of the guardian cherub, but once Adam had perfected himself, he would then exert the full dominion of the Son of God over all things, including the angels. That's why, though **Hebrews 2:6–9** repeats the 8th Psalm, the first and second chapters of Hebrews are an unabashed declaration of the superiority of the Son and the children of God (over the angels).

Some feel that Hebrews, chapters 1 and 2, are teaching that Jesus, not a man in general, is superior to the angels. Other scripture help to clarify the position of those who stand in the position of God's children.

Hebrews 1:14 declares angels are "ministering spirits" sent to serve the heirs of salvation. This shows that the authority of the Son is bequeathed to us and as a result we stand, likewise, as God's children. As such, we also gain the right to judge the angels (see **1 Corinthians 6:3**). Jesus was crowned with glory (**Hebrews 2:7-8**) and everything was put under Him.

Hebrews 2:10 says that Jesus, in dying, brought us to glory. **Hebrews 2:11** states that both the one who makes men holy and those who are made holy are of the same family, so Jesus is not ashamed to call them (believers, not angels) brothers. **Hebrews 1:5** asks, to which of the angels did God ever say, "You are my Son; today I become your Father." This inheritance is shared with believers, not with angels. **Romans 8:17**

Another bit of evidence indicating Adam's dominion over the angels is manifested in the order by which the Commandment is given. The scripture reveals the order by which the commandment is passed. God gives the commandment to Adam, Adam gives the commandment to Eve and Eve (**Genesis 3:1**) is to give the commandment to the archangel. God gives Adam the commandment prior to the creation of Eve in **Genesis 2:17**. Eve is clearly explaining the meaning of the commandment to Lucifer that, of course, he contests in **Genesis 3:1**.

Having faith in the commandment is Adam's central responsibility to achieve dominion, to become co-creator, as we previously studied. Therefore, giving the commandment to Eve who is to give the commandment to the archangel is the core manifestation of Adam's authority for dominion, as the head of the family and over the angels.

The Process of the Fall

Failure to see Adam from God's viewpoint

The first step of the fall is Lucifer's rejection of Adam's emerging new authority. Lucifer was greatly challenged by the reordering of his relationship with Adam dictated by Adam's emerging new position. Lucifer was an angel, an archangel. Prior to Adam's rise, he had enjoyed a position of direct access to God. God created the angelic world and assigned Lucifer to the position of archangel. Lucifer was the channel of God's love to the angelic world. In this position he virtually monopolized the love of God. However, at no time was the nature of God's relationship with the angels anything more than "Lord and servant."

Hebrews 1:14
Are not all angels ministering spirits sent to serve the heirs of salvation?

and Hebrews 1:5
To which of the angels did God ever say, "You are my Son, today I become your Father."

God's relationship with Adam and Eve was of a higher order: parent-child. Therefore, God's relationship with His children would take precedence over God's relationship with the angels. God loved Adam and Eve many times more than He had ever loved Lucifer. When Lucifer saw that God loved Adam and Eve more than him, he felt as if there had been a decrease in the love he received from God. It is important to stress that God was loving Lucifer the same amount as before the creation of Adam and Eve. God was not reducing his love for Lucifer; He was increasing the caliber of love for His children.

This is similar to the parable of **Matthew 20:1–16**. In it, the laborers in the vineyard who had worked since morning received a fair wage; when they saw that those who came later and worked less received just as much, they suddenly felt underpaid. This is a classic "fallen nature." It started with Lucifer.

Second, because God was transferring His role to Adam, God's destiny was to rule all things through the position of perfected Adam. Thus, **Psalms 8:4–6** explains that Adam was to be a ruler with all things under his feet. Also see **1 Corinthians 15:27–28,** which explains God's plan to rule all things through the position of His son.

This means that Lucifer must learn a new channel of access to God. Lucifer must acquiesce to Adam's position because this will be the new channel by which he will experience the love of God.

At this critical juncture, it is vitally important for Lucifer to not focus narrowly on his own interests, but rather, to focus on the interests of God in having Adam assume this position over Lucifer. Obviously Lucifer faltered and could not rise to the challenge to put aside his own interests and viewpoint to focus on the interest of God. We could speculate how he viewed his interests. He was probably feeling that he was losing the direct access to God that he had enjoyed previously. He also, no doubt, knowing Adam so well, was not impressed with Adam, who was still growing and not yet perfect.

This personal failure on Lucifer's part leads him to the next stage of the fallen process.

Lucifer leaves his proper position

Lucifer's position is to receive God's love through the channel of perfected Adam. However, because he cannot connect to God's interest for Adam, Lucifer feels no motive to harmonize with the position of Adam. Lucifer becomes distant from Adam and thus from God. The sensation of love and validation seeps away.

Lucifer must now make an evaluation. Is this feeling of alienation from God a result of something he has done to God, or is it a result of something God has done to him? He must choose between two opposite views of God:

1. God loves me absolutely; it is I who has shut him out, and it is I who must accept the channel through which love will reach me. God will never change His love for anyone. He is absolute.

Or,

2. God changed His heart toward me because circumstances didn't favor Him continuing to love me. God doesn't need me because He has Adam and Eve. God acts based on His own interest, at my expense and the expense of others.

Lucifer chooses the latter and not the former. Now our angel is growing in his potential for disaster. Cut off from the channel of God's love and feeling a withdrawing of love, he begins to fabricate a relativist mind-set that will permit him to do whatever he must do to fill this growing void in his soul. In his view, God betrayed him; thus, he feels the license to strike back. Like a ticking time bomb, he moves to the next phase in the process of the fall never realizing that he alone was the cause for his diminishing perception of love.

Reversal of dominion

In Lucifer's confused mind, he believes that God is changing His commitment toward him. Thus, Lucifer feels fully justified to pursue his own benefit and, as a result, feels fully excused from commitment to a moral truth from this God. With such a convoluted mind, he ponders Eve. She is beautiful and stimulating, even though he knows she is not meant for him. He cannot stop drinking in her beauty; he feels a stirring in his soul, he waits for her, reaches out to her, until he decides he must have her.

Thus, the original sin, like all sin, finds its root in the desire to seek a replacement for God's True Love. Now we are ready to understand fully the actual meaning of "eating the fruit."

Genesis 3:1
Now the serpent was more crafty than any of the wild animals the LORD God had made. He said to the woman, "Did God really say, 'You must not eat from any tree in the garden'?"

The woman said to the serpent, "We may eat fruit from the trees in the garden, but God did say, 'You must not eat fruit from the tree that is in the middle of the garden, and you must not touch it, or you will die.'"

"You will not surely die," the serpent said to the woman. "For God knows that when you eat of it your eyes will be opened, and you will be like God, knowing good and evil."

The Meaning of the Fruit

The following scriptural references will reveal the true nature of "the fruit." The fruit is a symbol of love.

Proverbs 30:20
This is the way of an adulteress: She eats and wipes her mouth and says, "I've done nothing wrong."

Song of Solomon 4:12–16

(Solomon to his bride): *"You are a garden locked up, my sister, my bride; you are a spring enclosed, a sealed fountain. Your plants are an orchard of pomegranates with* **choice fruits***, with henna and nard, nard and saffron, calamus and cinnamon, with every kind of incense tree, with myrrh and aloes and all the finest spices. You are a garden fountain, a well of flowing water streaming down from Lebanon. Awake, north wind, and come, south wind! Blow on my garden that its fragrance may spread abroad."*

(The bride's response): *"Let my lover come into his garden and taste its* **choice fruits***."*

Therefore, Lucifer tempting Eve to "eat the fruit" means that Lucifer was seeking to consummate a love relationship with her on the sexual level.

From a theological standpoint, the theory of angelic fornication with women on earth is not a new idea. It finds a long tradition in Hebrew mythology and certainly was readily acceptable by the early Church Fathers of Christian history. The view has fallen in and out of vogue several times since. Its acceptance as a credible view is based on the overwhelming use of the Hebrew "bene Elohim" (sons of God) for angels. This is supported by New Testament Greek in **Jude 1:7** which states, "Even as Sodom and Gomorrah and the cities about them in like manner, giving themselves over to fornication."

This does not mean Satan had a physical body and engaged in a physical relationship with Eve. Lucifer was an angel and had a spiritual angelic body only. However, the scriptures show us that there is a point of contact between beings in the world of spirit and beings on earth.

Genesis 32:22–32

Jacob wrestles an angel (confirmed by **Hosea 12:4***)*

Genesis 19:3

Lot prepares a meal for angels and they eat!

Hebrews 13:1

"Keep on loving each other as brothers. Do not forget to entertain strangers, for by so doing some people have entertained angels **without knowing it.** *"* (This means angels can be in our midst and we would not neces-

sarily notice. This indicates angel's ability to interact in time and space and maintain a low-profile, non-distinct manner.)

Sexual union is not just a physical event; it also bears a spiritual manifestation. This is why Paul indicates that sexual sin is unique in magnitude in **1 Corinthians 6:16, 18**. All other sins are outside one's body, however sexual sin causes one to "sin against his own body."

The Sin of the Fallen Angels

The sin of the angels is likewise the sin of fornication. Remember, these angels that sinned are the same angels that were thrown down with Lucifer. They were "his" angels and are reciprocating that which they observed their leader doing.

Jude 1:6–8
And the angels who did not keep their positions of authority but abandoned their own home—these he has kept in darkness, bound with everlasting chains for judgment on the great Day. In a similar way, Sodom and Gomorrah and the surrounding towns gave themselves up to sexual immorality and perversion. They serve as an example of those who suffer the punishment of eternal fire. In the very same way, these dreamers pollute their own bodies, reject authority and slander celestial beings.

"In the **very same way**, these dreamers **pollute their own bodies.**" Not only does the verse indicate that the angels and citizens of Sodom and Gomorrah share the same sin, it describes it explicitly with the phase "pollute their own bodies." Remember Paul's words on sexual sin? It is the only sin that was a sin against our own body.

Again, these fornicating angels and the angels that fell with Lucifer, "his angels," are one and the same.

2 Peter 2:4
*For if God did not spare **angels when they sinned**, but sent them to hell, putting them into gloomy dungeons to be held for judgment.*

Revelation 12:9

*"The great dragon was hurled down, that ancient serpent called the devil, or Satan, who leads the whole world astray. He was hurled to the earth, and **his angels with him**."*

Genesis 6:2
"The sons of God (the angels) saw that the daughters of men were beautiful, and they married any of them they chose."

The sin of Lucifer's angels is, therefore, the same sin as Lucifer. Lucifer engaged in the sin of fornication with Eve, and his angels followed suit with the daughters of men.

Spiritual Fall Leads to Physical Fall

After Eve commits the spiritual fall with Lucifer, she is consumed with guilt and fear. She is filled with "knowledge" of good and evil and becomes "like god," but which god? The true God knows both good and evil. However, God knows both good and evil not through the practical experience of evil, but rather by being the paragon of good. As the paragon of good, anything not in relationship with God is, therefore, evil. God recognizes evil by its inability to relate to Him.

Eve became like "god"; however, it was a mere cheap imitation. She bought the $100 Rolex off the street. She gained the knowledge of good and evil through the practical experience of evil. She became the paragon of evil and as the paragon of evil, anything not in relationship to her must be good. She knew she was cut off from God and from Adam because they were good and she, now, was not. This sudden turn of fortune deeply terrified her. She knew she had been used and that Lucifer's promises were empty and only reflective of his needs and wants. She desperately wanted to return to her former position and status.

Sin multiplies

Rather than walking the path of responsibility by confessing her wrong to Adam and throwing herself before the mercy of the court, she seeks instead to include Adam in her iniquity. Because of the destruction of her self-esteem through sin, Eve seeks comfort and acceptance. She follows the path of her god who imposed his will upon her through trickery and deceit. Adam eats the fruit offered him by Eve.

Genesis 2:25
Before the fall, Adam and Eve were naked and unashamed.

Genesis 3:7
After the fall, "their eyes were opened" to their nakedness.

Job 31:33
If I covered my transgressions as Adam, by hiding mine iniquity in my bosom.

The Results of the Fall

Result of the Fall: Original Sin

Without a doubt, the single most significant result of the fall is that mankind's lineage was changed. We want to understand clearly the nature of "the change of blood lineage." Christians have a very solid understanding of the universal manifestation of sin. Scripture is very explicit in that regard:

Romans 5:12–14
*Therefore, just as **sin entered the world through one man**, and death through sin, and in this way death came to all men, because all sinned; for before the law was given, sin was in the world. But sin is not taken into account when there is no law. Nevertheless, **death reigned from the time of Adam** to the time of Moses, even over those who did not sin by breaking a command, as did Adam, who was a pattern of the one to come.*

1 Corinthians 15:22
*For **as in Adam all die**, so in Christ all will be made alive.*

Results of the Fall: Change of Blood Lineage

Thus, fallen man's essential problem is that he has an ancestoral link to the dead Adam. It is why fallen man's salvation will require a "new Adam," and will necessitate a grafting process into the lineage of the new ancestor of man.

However, the biblical view goes to a much deeper level in understanding the foundation of man's historical problem with sin. Sin is defined as any thought or action in violation of God's Heavenly Law that makes a base for Satan to have give and take with me.

The key point of the fall is not just that man sinned, but that man's sin set up a condition for Satan to exert a claim over the lineage of Adam and Eve. How could an archangel, who was meant to serve man, obtain the position of "god" and "ruler" over man? The scriptures reveal that the archangel could not establish this on his own, by his own volition. He needed to elicit the voluntary cooperation of man.

Genesis 3:1 indicates the process Lucifer used to gain dominion. Lucifer took the position of "god" by tempting Eve, first in refuting the commandment of God and then by replacing God's true word with his own. In effect, Lucifer is challenging the validity of God's Word and offering his own word as a replacement: "Did God say you will die? I say you will surely not die!"

God's role is to give the authorized Word. By giving the Word, God is giving man the opportunity to share His role and His nature. If man had fulfilled, God's coronation as substantial God, Father, and King would have been achieved.

Lucifer hijacks the power of coronation given to man by God. Lucifer gains the position of god over Eve by giving her his word, which was a false word. However, for Lucifer to gain dominion as god, he needs Eve to voluntarily submit to his word. By submitting to his word through the action of the spiritual fall, Eve validates his position as "god." She tragically obliges him. This pattern is repeated with Adam. Thus, through the condition committed by Adam and Eve themselves, Lucifer is able to seize the position of dominion over them as "god," "ruler" and father." This was the "change of blood lineage" at its core. See scripture:

2 Corinthians 4:4

*The **god of this age** has blinded the minds of unbelievers, so that they cannot see the light of the gospel of the glory of Christ, who is the image of God.*

John 12:31

Now is the time for judgment on this world; now the prince of this world will be driven out.

John 8:44

*You belong to **your father**, the devil, and you want to carry out your father's desire. He was a murderer from the beginning, not holding to the truth, for there is no truth in him. When he lies, he speaks his native language, for he is a liar and the father of lies.*

Result of the Fall: Fallen Nature

Fallen nature is the original nature of the fall. It is the process of sin transformed into a nature. Therefore, fallen man has the nature to sin. That nature to sin is the process of the first sin. We are following the ways of our father the devil. We inherited his proclivities toward sin. Thus, our fallen nature has components that reflect the key steps in the process of the fall, that is, the process by which the archangel Lucifer left his position and gained dominion over the position of Adam and Eve.

Romans 7:21–24

So I find this law at work: When I want to do good, evil is right there with me. For in my inner being I delight in God's law; but I see another law at work in the members of my body, waging war against the law of my mind and making me a prisoner of the law of sin at work within my members. What a wretched man I am! Who will rescue me from this body of death?

Reverend Moon spoke on this very clearly:

You know that you are important and that you love yourself. But then, which self do you love, the original self or the fallen one? The original mind wants to go in a certain direction, but the body is like a slave to the fallen nature so such separation exists between the original mind and the body. Imagine the feeling of someone who goes to the spirit world and can see very clearly the existence of God as well as the course human beings should walk, but he is incapable of going that way. Even though he can see it clearly, he won't have a physical body anymore, so he won't be able to do it. There is no greater tragedy than to see the goal clearly but to be unable to move even one inch in that direction. Do you follow?

Do not look for heaven and hell elsewhere. It is all within you. Just from the guidelines I have given you so far this morning, you can determine whether you are heading for heaven or hell. This is the reason the path has always been to deny one's self, take up the cross and follow. Anything the body enjoys, you must learn to deny. Something your phys-

ical eyes like to see will often be disliked by the eye of your original mind. What the body wants to do, the original mind doesn't want to do. When we really look at this situation, we realize the incredible paradox within man. Everything within you is contradictory.

If someone explained clearly how that contradiction came about in human nature, his would be the greatest of all contributions to human-ity. Furthermore, if there were some prescription, some method of elim-inating that contradiction, that would be a truly priceless gift. Each per-son can feel the contradiction within himself and his own behavior. The original mind wants to do one thing but the body doesn't want to do it. However, the original mind is not God's will itself; it is a sensitive agent which can detect the will of God. You can see how far we have deviated from the original course of God's will.

"God's Providential Course And The Course Of Human Life,"
January 11, 1987

Lucifer started the fallen process because he couldn't:
- Love Adam from God's viewpoint
- Keep his position with Adam (receive God's love through Adam)
- Accept Adam's dominion
- Multiply goodness under Adam's authority.

Fallen nature upsets the natural order. Therefore, our flesh body, like Lucifer, does not want to accept the authority of God via our spiritual self. This is also why the pattern of salvation involves rever-sal of the fallen nature and the process of sin. Jesus is in Adam's position, while sinners are in Lucifer's position. In order to be saved we must reverse the process of the fall:
- Love Jesus from God's viewpoint
- Come to the proper position to Jesus: He is Lord!
- Accept Jesus' dominion: Come into my life, take over my life.
- Multiply goodness: Obey His commandments! Put His words into practice.

Result of the Fall: God Suffers
In **Genesis 6:6** we see that God's heart was "filled with pain" as He observed the results of the fall. This is, above all, the most tragic consequence of the fall. A God who was to experience the joy of fulfilled love instead became a God of sorrows who would have to pursue man in an arduous historical process of recovery.

Previously, we explained the significance of the prophet's oracle. The oracle gives us insight into the events of the distant past in the Garden. Ezekiel chapter 16 is another example of such an oracle. The contemporary circumstance is a disobedient and unrepentant Jerusalem. God asks Ezekiel to express God's frustration and pain and to confront Jerusalem with her detestable practices.

From what deep well does God draw upon for the imagery He uses to express, so overwhelmingly, His sense of pain and grief? As you read the 16th chapter of Ezekiel, the longest chapter of any book of the Bible, you will begin to sense that this God is displacing the sorrow of a long-ago, unspoken tragedy. Jerusalem is merely the contemporary echo of that past, opening the floodgates of pent-up grief and inconsolable sorrows. How did Almighty God learn so well the vivid images of betrayal and the eloquent prose of unrequited love?

Reverend Moon explains the consequences of the fall for God:

What is the pinnacle of God's suffering? There is no question that the fall of God's children, Adam and Eve, is the focal point of His difficulty. Their separation from God was a very pitiful and tearful situation. God is the Father of mankind and Adam and Eve are His first children, the ancestors of fallen mankind. When these children fell, the consequences had a direct impact on God and caused Him incredible suffering. Because the fall was a physical act, God lost His connection with the physical world, and in addition, He endured suffering of the mind and suffering of the soul. The seeds of man's suffering throughout history were planted by Adam and Eve being corrupted at the beginning of human history, and from that time on suffering was handed down from generation to generation.

The fall of man brought three consequences: God lost His children and He lost His temple, because man was to be the dwelling place of God. Furthermore, God lost the only home in which His love could be manifested; Adam and Eve were not only to be the children of God but to be the recipients of His love. With the fall of man God lost everything He had hoped for in the love of His own children, the love between husband and wife, and the love between parent and child.

"The Pinnacle of Suffering," June 26, 1977

In our next chapter we will discover the meaning of history. God is engaged on an arduous journey to recover His lost loves

Chapter Three

A Good God—An Evil World

Probably the most often asked question pertains to the entrance of evil into God's world. Humans have pondered since the dawn of humanity this most mysterious of life's questions. We grapple with the great paradox before us. A good God of absolute sovereignty seems to tacitly allow for the entrance of evil into His world. If this almighty God is truly all knowing and all powerful, then how could there be such an end without the approval of the all-encompassing God? Does not God become the author of evil if, indeed, the entrance of evil into the world was intrinsic to God's design? Conversely, if evil's entrance into the world takes place in violation of God's plan and Will, does not that call into question the very sovereignty of God?

Why, then, do bad things happen? Why does it appear that God allows the forces of evil and selfishness to gain the upper hand? It can appear that God was standing by aloof and unconcerned when the serpent was tempting Eve or when Judas' mind was taken over by Satan to betray the Christ. Why doesn't God come down to prevent the overturning of a church bus and the death of four children?

It is why many have relinquished their faith in God. In a moment of gripping tragedy and loss, the extent of one's trust in God is challenged. For those who have walked in the valley, the specter of Christ looms as our only hope to dispel the gripping fear that God could be indifferent to our plight. But if God is in control of everything that takes place, how is the purpose of love served by imposed tragedy?

God is not a "do it all for you" God. God has relinquished a portion of His sovereignty. God doesn't exert an unconditional sovereignty over humanity. Understanding why He has done so will help us to deal with many important issues.

The Force of Love, the Force of the Principle and the Reason for the Commandment

The commandment is a tool that, if applied, gives man the opportunity for self-government. Having this role to govern one's self is the essence of what gives man the potential to rise above the realm of creature and into the realm of descendant and image of God. We need to look at all the forces facing man in his quest for perfection.

We can observe two major forces with which man must contend. One is the force of nature, or natural law, and the other is the force of love. Scripture indicates that the force of love is to be magnified and completed in each person through a cooperative effort between man and God. These two forces are potential partners, but also potential foes. That is because the objective of love and the objective of natural law are not always in sync. The force of natural law pertains to physical functionality and self-preservation. It directs all entities toward the fulfillment of their purpose, i.e., perfection. Creation is controlled by this power.

The force of love, however, is the force that transforms two into one. The reason man is not to be controlled essentially by natural law is that God's purpose for man is to engage in relationships centered in love. Remember **1 John 4:16**, "He who lives in love, lives in God and God in him." Therefore, man is to be controlled ultimately by love. Also, **1 John 4:12,** "If we love one another, God lives in us and his love is made complete in us," indicates that our "perfection" is to be the perfection of love. Thus, love is essence and is a stronger force in man.

The Force of Love Is Stronger than the Force of Principle
This poses a potential problem. Adam and Eve should not become "one" with each other until they become "one" in their mind and body and, therefore, become "one with the Lord." They must be "fruitful" before they "multiply." Natural law will tell them it is time for relations. By physical functionality, they will be "ready"; however, in terms of the purpose of love, they will need more time. What force can be imposed over the demands of the flesh so as to provide the necessary time for the perfection of love? If such a power cannot be implemented, no doubt, the demands of the flesh will entice them to become "one" with each other before becoming "one with the Lord." Such a circumstance will usurp God's purpose in making them "one":

Malachi 2:15

And why one? Because He was seeking godly offspring.

See 1 Corinthians 6:13

The body is not meant for sexual immorality, but for the Lord and the Lord for the body.

See again, **1 Corinthians 6:16, 18.** Paul describes sexual immorality as the most serious sin. Jesus indicates that there are no grounds for divorce "save for adultery." If Adam and Eve become one before perfection they will impede God's most fundamental purpose: to have "Godly offspring." This is why sexual sin is the worst of all sins. Conversely, if sexual relations proceed after they achieve perfection (become fruitful) then their sexual union will be the very accomplishment of God's purpose. It isn't sex that is inherently "ungodly." It is the timing and sequence of sex that will determine godly outcome.

However, a lesser force (natural law), with its objective of self-preservation and functionality, cannot direct a greater force (the force of love) with its objective of Adam and Eve becoming "one flesh." Thus, it stands to reason that a premature or "immoral" consummation was possible unless a third element of control was issued.

Therein resides the reason for the commandment, "Do not eat the fruit." The power of faith emerges within Adam and Eve relative to receiving and adhering to that Word. Is faith an applicable force? Indeed it is.

Matthew 17:20

He (Jesus) replied, "Because you have so little faith. I tell you the truth, if you have faith as small as a mustard seed, you can say to this mountain, 'Move from here to there' and it will move. Nothing will be impossible for you."

Adam and Eve would be able to remain focused on the path of maturing love and becoming "one with the Lord" if they kept faith in the commandment. It would instill within them the moral means to say "no" to the creature urges of natural law. Obedience to God's word would be their pathway to the higher plane of love. Thus, during this growing period, Adam and Eve would stand as brother and sister, forming a partnership of faith in God's word.

With this empowerment of faith, the force of natural law and the force of love achieve a cooperative alliance toward the ultimate fulfillment of the purpose of creation. That is, flesh and spirit become partners to fulfill God's desire to have an expanding "godly offspring."

More on the Purpose for the Commandment

Man Is a Co-Creator with God

Why does God require man to complete a "co-creator" mission? Is God dependent on man? It is not dependency that motivates God but rather His will to share His nature with us. Man gains the potential to inherit God's nature when man stands in the role of God as "co-creator."

How does the act of faith in the commandment position man in the role of God? As was mentioned in the first chapter, God's role is that of the Creator. His mission is to create. God created man and woman; however, God did not "complete" that creation.

It is man's co-creator role to complete the creation. God created the parts, but it is man that must bring the parts into "oneness." God created mind and body; man must unite them and become one with the Lord. God created man and woman, but it is man that must "love his wife" and it is woman who must "respect her husband." God created the universe and seeks to rule all things but will do so only through perfected humans. Thus, the creation is "groaning in travail" until that objective is fulfilled.

God wants us to share His nature. We are created in His image. We are to be the objects through which God would experience love. The process by which God will transfer His nature to us is the process of man fulfilling his portion of God's role and responsibility.

We could say, figuratively, that God has given us a 5 percent portion of His role and responsibility.

The main point is not the amount of the percentage, but rather, the *content* of the responsibility. God is sharing a portion of *His responsibility,* as Creator, with man. Man, by receiving this precious gift and carrying it out successfully, will inherit God's nature (of love). By receiving the commandment and taking responsibility to discipline ourselves centering on that moral law, we gain the nature of the Creator. This is the process of qualitative growth from creature of God to living descendant of God.

This is why Adam and Eve must go through the period of maturity. This is why they do not grow automatically. This is why they must take responsibility to apply the tool of faith in the commandment toward that goal.

By doing so, *they* assume the position of God and are joined in partnership with God in the creation of an ideal man, family and universe. By taking on the role of God and having the same mission and purpose as God, Adam and Eve inherit the nature and authority of God, that is, God's life, love and lineage. Thus, they are to become "rulers" of the universe. When they become "one" with the Lord, the joy of God and man is the exhilarating joy of a common victory.

Freedom

It is not really freedom to have liberty and then always walk backward, or just do anything you like. In the same way it is not natural to use just one eye, or to plug one ear and listen with the other. Freedom which does not satisfy the Principle is not really freedom. Will freedom be obtained by fulfilling necessary conditions, or does it just come along?

Is freedom necessary for its own sake, or in order to fulfill the ideal? Is freedom itself the ideal? No. It is valuable only because it is necessary for fulfilling the ideal.
Rev. Sun Myung Moon, "The Necessity of Prayer", June 22, 1980

Freedom outside the realm of principled action is not really freedom. It is licentiousness. As Reverend Moon points out, true freedom has a godly purpose. Paul also explains:

Galatians 5:13

You, my brothers, were called to be free. But do not use your freedom to indulge the sinful nature; rather, serve one another in love.

Many Christians believe that man fell because of freedom, or man's "free will agency." He simply chose evil. How could a being of goodness corrupt himself? How can corruption enter into goodness?

Adam and Eve had the potential to be corrupted because they were not yet one with God. They were born flawlessly but not in the state of maturity. Adam and Eve had to grow to gain the qualification to eat from the Tree of Life. The Tree of Life is a symbol of the ideal of the unchanging, eternal state of relationship with God. It is indicative of perfection or maturity. Because Adam and Eve were to ultimately become one in love with God, they had to grow in love, to become givers of love.

To become givers of love, Adam and Eve must dwell in an environment that incorporates creativity, freedom and free choice. Implicit within a free environment are particular responsibilities. Freedom is conditional relative to the degree one adheres to the moral laws that define the limits of freedom. Without taking an active role in self-government (discipline) no being can maintain freedom. For example, the speed limit is posted, but it is the responsibility of the driver to apply that standard to his driving decisions.

By giving Adam and Eve the commandment, God was positioning them to play an active role in their own government and completion toward perfection. The fundamental reason God gives Adam and Eve the responsibility to achieve faith in the commandment was so that in fulfilling that condition they could form the moral foundation for freedom and the life of love. Because the experience of love for Adam and Eve was meant to be a genuine experience, their responsibility to apply the moral law, likewise, had to be genuine.

For their responsibility to be genuine, then, the possibility of failure had to be a potential in the role of responsibility. The potential for failure is present not so that it would be substantiated, but rather, to give definition and authority to the role of responsibility. It is the shadow that gives clarity to a lighted form. It is in this potential for failure that the possibility exists for the corruption of Adam and Eve. Although that outcome was a potential, its substantiation would stand in total contradiction to God's purpose for them.

With regard to free choice, as was mentioned; freedom for Adam and Eve is conditional. That is, Adam and Eve can enjoy the benefits of freedom and free choice as long as free choice is subjected to the standard of righteousness (in the garden, it was the commandment). As Reverend Moon and St. Paul point out, the purpose of freedom is so that sacrificial love can be exchanged. Adam and Eve would have to maintain the condition of faith (their responsibility) in order to maintain the environment of freedom and love.

If they lose faith in the commandment, they will automatically lose the environment of freedom. The loss of freedom results in the rise of uncontrollable excessive desire. This is the character of sin. The cause of sin, then, is not free choice but rather the loss of freedom resulting from losing faith in the commandment. It is why all sin has the nature of habit and addiction, making sinners "slaves to sin."

In other words, man fell not because of freedom but because of the loss of freedom and the rise of inordinate, uncontrollable desire. We lose freedom when we break the condition upon which our freedom rests: faith in the word. In **Romans 6:17-18, 20** Paul teaches,

> *But thanks be to God that, though you used to be slaves to sin. . . . You have been **set free** from sin and have become slaves to righteousness. When you were slaves to sin, you were free from the **control of righteousness.***

James 1:13-15 gives us an even clearer perspective:
When tempted, no one should say, "God is tempting me." For God cannot be tempted by evil, nor does he tempt anyone; but each one is tempted when, by his own evil desire, he is dragged away and enticed. Then, after desire has conceived, it gives birth to sin; and sin, when it is full-grown, gives birth to death.

2 Corinthians 3:17 indicates that freedom is a by-product of closeness to the Lord.

Now the Lord is the Spirit, and where the Spirit of the Lord is, there is freedom.

The truth is that when we maintain the conditions for freedom (faith in God's word), the Lord's presence becomes an integral part of our experience with freedom. In fact, God created us and set up the conditions for us to live in freedom. We need freedom, not for sin to take place, but rather for building the ideal of love.

On this foundation we can begin to understand why God did not unconditionally control man and prevent the fall. Humans fulfilling their God-given responsibility is the essential condition for them to be able to rise to the position of descendant of God. Thus, we can begin to find an altruistic motive for God not to alter or intervene in man's role and portion of responsibility. Reverend Moon explains that God does not intervene in human responsibility:

Does God really love me or not? When you look at how hard I have worked and how I have been persecuted, don't you think God might have done something more on my behalf? You say that God really loves me, but I might argue with you and say, "If God loves me, what has He ever done for me?" At no time in my entire mission have I ever had a peaceful moment. Wherever I have gone, I was not readily welcomed at first; it was only after I had given much and taught many things that people would begin to understand. I have had to fight continuously to gain ground for God—inch by inch.

If God were to give me the power to work miracles and somehow retaliate against those who persecute us unrighteously and show them dramatically how wrong they are, they would not continue to mistreat us. Why does God allow these unrighteous things to continue? When Jesus was crucified, God was certainly watching the scene. Did God not have the power to stop the Roman soldiers and rescue Jesus from the cross? Jesus was God's own son. What kind of a father could bear to see his own son's blood being shed in such an unrighteous way and not do something? Can we call such a God a God of love and justice? Where was God's justice then? When my court case was over and the judge pronounced my sentence, why didn't God do something? Was it because God did not have the power to do anything? Why did God seem to pretend not to know about it? That is a riddle. In this common yet very important issue comes the understanding of the human portion of responsibility.

Man's portion of responsibility is a cosmic truth. Great discoveries have been made in science, such as Einstein's theory of relativity; however, the discovery of the law of human responsibility is the greatest of all. Without understanding this principle, the most fundamental issues in life remain as a puzzle. "Why do righteous people always have to suffer? Why is a great man's name only resurrected after his death?" The answers to these questions hinge upon the principle of human responsibility.

Have you accomplished your portion of responsibility or not? The heaviest consequence of this principle is the requirement that humans make effort to indemnify sin. How long the human indemnity period will last is not known by anyone—not God, not spirit world, not me, not anyone. We may keep asking why the misery in life must go on, but it is a fact that as long as there is sin in the world, we must take responsibility for it. If anybody, including God, were to remove the human burden of indemnity, people could no longer have the dignity of responsible beings. This is not to deny the reality of God's grace, but even grace comes for the purpose of assisting people in fulfilling their portion of responsibility. Therefore God did not intervene when Adam and Eve committed the fall. God did not intervene because he would not violate man's portion of responsibility.

"God's Warning to the World" (Part 2)

The topic "Why God did not intervene in the fall" is an explanation of what Reverend Moon refers to as "the principle of human responsibility." God graciously intervenes in human affairs, but He does so in a specific and principled manner. There is a principle by which God intervenes in human affairs. God will not dehumanize us by treating us like helpless victims. Thus, a central component of that principle is that man must cooperate with God by fulfilling a portion of responsibility. It then affirms that God, as a God of principle, would not intervene in a way that would violate His own principle or render us dependent victims. By explaining the parameters of what would constitute an unprincipled intervention, we establish a foundation for understanding what, then, would constitute a principled intervention. This process of principled intervention is, in fact, what we refer to as "The Principle of Restoration through Indemnity." Thus, the issue of why God did not intervene in the fall is a natural prelude to the explanation of the Principle of Restoration through Indemnity.

Understanding the Principle of Restoration requires a clear understanding of the reasons God did not intervene in the fall. In the same way, understanding the reasons God did not intervene in the fall requires a clear understanding of the principles that govern the relationship of God and man.

The Principles of God's Relationship with Man

Let's look at three components that are essential in understanding the relationship of God and man. These points are the essential elements that would be violated if God were to intervene in the fallen action.

God exerts direct, unconditional control over perfect beings only.
God controls man through love directly and unconditionally only after his perfection. God is perfect and complete. "The Lord is one".

Mark 12:29 Therefore for man to become one with God, we must accomplish "oneness" on the individual level. By uniting mind and body we achieve "perfection". **Matthew 5:48** Our perfection is the perfection of love. **1 John 4:12**

God controls growing, immature beings indirectly and conditionally through the condition of principled action.

As we mentioned, God is one with perfect entities. God is one with His Principle. God's relationship with immature, growing beings is indirect through Principle. This means, in the growing period, immature beings must produce conditions of principled action. Centering on those conditions God can have a direct control over the result of principled action. Thus, man's relationship with God is personal and intimate, but *conditional* during this period.

Adam and Eve's responsibility is to keep faith in the commandment.

As long as they fulfill that condition they remain in the sphere of God's control and freedom. If they fail to produce that condition, they will fall outside the realm of God's control and freedom.

Remember, Adam and Eve's "portion of responsibility" is a portion of God's responsibility. Fulfilling it is the pathway to become "co-creators."

In summary:

There is a perfection realm where relationship with God is unconditional.

Before Adam and Eve achieve perfection, they are to go through a growing period where their relationship with God is conditional.

The process of growth entails man fulfilling a responsibility: to produce the condition of faith in God's word.

With this understanding, let's review the reasons why God didn't intervene and stop the fallen action.

1. In order to maintain the perfection and absoluteness of His Principle

God's wanting to maintain the perfection of Principle was done completely in the interest of love and in the interest of mankind. Sometimes the confusion is generated by the incorrect impression that Adam and Eve were little, helpless children.

The analogy that comes to mind and is often cited is of a small child walking to the end of a pier with the parent fifty feet away sitting on a blanket. It wouldn't be reasonable for a parent, who has already warned his child not to go near the water, to conclude that by jumping up and grabbing his child before he plunges headfirst into the drink, he would be in violation of a principle. This analogy often comes to people's minds, even ministers, as we teach this particular section. It is very important to understand the flaws in this example.

Adam and Eve were not "little children. They were maturing adults. God was not ignoring His children; He was relating to them based on trust, responsibility and love.

The important point is that Adam and Eve were not helpless toddlers. They were maturing young adults. Also, the responsibility with which they were grappling was not some mundane instruction regarding personal safety, but rather was their core responsibility in the path toward co-creatorship.

God doesn't violate His own Master Plan, His Principle. This means that His Principle remains viable and active. Thus, the Principle prescribes the path to our full restoration. Although we fell, the goal of the Principle of Restoration is the full and complete recovery of the original purpose defined by "The Master Plan."

2. In order not to recognize Satan as the creator

This does not mean that God is oblivious to the existence of Satan. In the book of Job, for example, God carries on a dialogue with Satan.

God does not intervene in Satan's activities. God did not impede Satan from attacking Job. It is Job's faith in God that is the key element that forces Satan to relent. This illustrates the basic law of restoration that man must fulfill a responsibility to separate from Satan. God does not recognize Satan as creator and ruler. This does not mean that God isn't aware of Satan's existence.

Obviously, God "recognizes" Satan as an existing entity of evil. The point is that if God were to engage in an unprincipled intervention in the fallen action, it would result in a type of empowerment being imputed to Satan. God would be violating His own Principle by directly controlling immature beings who were without the condition of principled action.

This "new principle" would, therefore, incorporate the existence and co-creatorship of Satan, who instigated the action that precipitates God's reaction. Satan's existence would gain an unconditional foundation. In other words, if God could control immature man directly without a condition, then Satan could, likewise, invade man at will regardless of man's own condition. If this were the case, there would be no way for man to separate from Satan.

The effect of God not changing His Principle means that the basis of Satan's existence remains conditional and not absolute. Thus, even though man has fallen and is in sin, Satan cannot unconditionally claim man. Through the condition of the original sin, Satan has a claim over man as god and ruler; however, for Satan to exert that claim, man must accommodate through a condition.

Conversely, it opens the door for man, likewise by condition, to unbind or reverse the claim of Satan. This is the basis of restoration through indemnity. The bad news is that man made the conditions that empowered Satan. The good news is because man made those conditions, man can play a key role to unbind (indemnify) those conditions and thus be liberated from Satan's claim.

That is why the chapter on the Fall of Man is so important. Through exposing the conditions that led to the fall and the establishment of Satan's sovereignty, we can begin to understand the course to remove that sovereignty. What was Satan's essential motive in maintaining secrecy with regard to the main conditions of the fall?

If man never discovers Satan's secret crime, then he can never know what are the conditions upon which Satan's sovereignty is established. As long as we remain ignorant of the conditions of the fall, we will not be able to reverse those conditions. Satan strives to maintain secrecy, to hide the conditional nature of his claim over man. Secrecy makes obscure the path of reversal that man must go. By the way, this is very directly related to why "confessing my sin" is so important and so hard to do. (More on that later.)

The beginning of the end for Satan is when man finally unlocks the nature of the events of the fall. That is why the chapter on the fall is so important. To maintain man's potential to separate from and subjugate Satan, God did not want to "recognize," that is, empower, Satan as creator. Therefore, Satan's position as "god and ruler" over man is conditional. Because it is conditional, it can be removed. That is why the hope of salvation is the full restoration of all things.

3. In order to give humans dominion

God intended man to have dominion over all things, as expressed in the third blessing. To do that, man must inherit the authority and creativity of the Creator by playing a role in the work of creation. God gave man responsibility to produce the condition of principled action through maintaining faith in the commandment. By fulfilling this responsibility, man plays a role in the completion and perfection of his own creation. Through his own perfection, he likewise perfects his family and the universe via the three blessings.

This inheritance is the essence of humanity, human dignity and the potential to build an enduring culture. It is the direct inheritance of God's life, love and lineage. Without it, man is nothing more than a higher animal, subject to natural law and carnal desire.

If God overlooks man's area of responsibility and "takes over," God will have severely limited man's potential.

For these reasons God did not engage in an unprincipled intervention in the fallen action. God's non-intervention was done in man's interest. God sacrificed Himself in order for His children to maintain their potential to inherit God's life, love and lineage.

A Father and Son

A more descriptive analogy for understanding God's non-intervention in the fall.

A better analogy would be a father and his 16-year-old son with a new driver's license, asking to borrow the car for the first time.

The son quietly approaches the door of his parent's room, his newly issued driver's license clutched tightly in his hand. His father is a stern figure. The son loves him, deeply respects him and also fears him. He pauses at the door for a moment then softly knocks.

"Dad, may I come in?"

The boy's father is standing at his desk; he turns and answers, "Yes, come in, son. What's up?"

The son enters and approaches his father's desk and pauses. His father is reviewing some papers, moving things on his desktop, opening drawers, closing drawers. The son just waits patiently and quietly for his father to finish his activity.

"What's up," the father asks again, realizing his son was standing there waiting for him.

"Well . . ." the boy begins, a tightness forming in his throat, "I got my license today." He holds out the license for his father to examine.

"I see." He reaches out and takes the card. He can see it has his son's photo and name on the front. He looks it over for a few moments while collecting his thoughts and attempting not to look surprised or startled.

"Good, good son, good." He starts to hand the license back. He recognizes the expression on his son's face. He is expecting something more. "Well, let's arrange some practice with the car, perhaps we can plan when your mother gets home."

The son thinks to himself, "He's trying to blow you off, don't let him blow you off."

"Well, Dad, you know, I did all the practicing last year when I got my permit. This is my driver's license. That means, well, I can drive, you know, legally."

"Oh, I see." Dad now knows where this is going.

"Dad, in fact, I was kind of hoping that I could use the car occasionally."

"Uh-huh, well, we'll see. Now if there is nothing else, I've got to get these files together, son; perhaps we could take it up at another time."

The voice inside the son's head is now a shout: "GO FOR IT!"

"Dad, do you think it would be all right if I took the car for a little while, like, uh, now?"

The father looks up from his desk and slowly removes his glasses. He pauses for a moment, leans back in his chair and just gazes at his son. Slowly, his hand crawls into his pant's pocket and locates his car keys. As if in a dreamlike trance, the father just sits there staring and jingling the keys between his fingers.

The son watches his father closely and thinks to himself. "What's he doing?"

"What's wrong with that bike?" the father finally blurts out.

"Huh?" The son answers, confused.

"I said, 'What's wrong with your bike?' Do you know how much I spent on that? And of course, you had to have the ten-speed and the titanium frame. . .So now what, the bike gets thrown in the garage to rust away because now you're going to be driving the car everywhere?"

"Dad, what are you talking about, I just want to practice my driving."

"Well, where do you have to go?" Dad asks pointedly. "It's almost 5:30, it's getting dark."

"I just want to take the car for a spin." As soon the word "spin" leaves his mouth, the son wishes he had an auto-retrieve button on his tongue like one of those fancy tape measures.

The father's eyes widens like a quarterback watching his wide receiver break free across the middle.

"Spin?" the father repeated, his voice dripping with all the incredulity he could muster. "SPIN! Oh, no, no, no, noooo sir. We aren't SPINNING anything. A car is to drive."

"Son, sit down over here," the father directs his son to sit in the chair next to him.

"Oh no," the son thinks to himself, "here comes the 'this car is not a toy' speech."

"Son, this car is not a toy."

The father starts a several-minute dissertation on the potential dangers in driving an automobile. He intersperses his comments with examples, statistics, and vivid images of watermelons dropping off twenty-story buildings, which was supposed to depict what happens to the human body when a car hits a wall at thirty-five miles per hour.

"So you see son, driving a car is a huge responsibility and, well, I'm just not sure you're ready." Dad is moving onto the dangerous turf where words wound young sons.

"Well, the State of Virginia thinks I'm ready; otherwise they wouldn't have given me a license," the son pleads.

"Well, I'm your father and I'm not so sure."

"In other words, you don't trust me." The son stands up and begins to walk away. "Forget it, I'm sorry I asked."

"Son, wait up," the father calls after his son. "Son . . .," but by the time the father gets to the door his son has rounded the corner and is gone.

Has this happened to you yet? What does this story have to do with God not intervening in the fall? It illustrates the challenge of a parent giving his son responsibility. The father wants to give his son responsibility, but he is hesitant. He realizes that in handing over the keys, he places a huge responsibility in his son's hands. He knows that the son is of legal age and has the physical capability to drive a car, but he still hesitates.

What's his problem?

It is fear of the potential for failure and the adverse consequences that would result. It is made even more pronounced by the practical reality that Dad is probably a much better driver than the inexperienced son. Giving responsibility to his son opens the door for tragedy and pain. What if there is an accident, injuries, or worse? The father has done all that he can do to protect his family from pain; that is his mission and responsibility. What if the son is not as serious about his responsibility as the father has been with his?

The father falls into the trap of instinctively withholding responsibility from his son. He pretends in his own mind that he has valid reasons, that the timing isn't right and the risks are too great. Once that conclusion is made it becomes very easy for the father to convince himself, in the interest of the child and the family, he should postpone the giving of responsibility.

His true motive is stealthily hidden behind a mask of denial. It is the fear of losing control and being faced with the consequences of a tragedy he did not cause. The destructive nature of this path is that it directs the father toward an inordinate focus on his child's faults in order to justify withholding responsibility from his child. Behind the mask of denial, the father, unwittingly, imposes upon the son a subconscious sense that he is neither trustworthy nor capable of handling responsibility. The son, thus, never feels validated or worthy.

In this way, the father creates the very monster that rises up to defy him. He can be guaranteed that he will have a son who will be a rebellious terror on the highway. The cycle of denial is complete when the son's behavior justifies the father's initial decision to withhold entrustment of responsibility. Denial will allow both the father and his son to spend a lifetime of blaming others for the consequences of the son's behavior. The simple truth, however, is that the father's *sense of his own responsibility* for the well-being of his family has become so overpowering, so all encompassing that he refuses to ever run the risk that is inherent in bequeathing responsibility to another. Whenever it comes time for Dad to show trust, he habitually balks.

Other fathers try another fruitless approach. They pretend to trust while only giving a hollow responsibility stripped of any real authority. "Son, here are the keys to the car, but I'm coming with you!" Dad piles in the back seat and begins to bark orders into his son's ear, "too fast, slow down . . . turn left . . . put your signal on, I SAID SLOW DOWN!!!" This is equally ineffective. The son never grows, never matures and finally, frustrated, the relationship breaks down.

All fathers must understand, God gave responsibility to Adam and Eve not based upon an assured positive timely outcome. He gave it because in having responsibility man gains the potential to complete his growth and to achieve full maturity. In many cases, the very act of entrusting a child with responsibility is the element that turns him toward maturity. Without that entrustment, all fearful predictions of doom will surely come true.

God gave a real responsibility to Adam and Eve. It is proven by the fact that Adam and Eve had real authority over their role. Even God respected that authority. As a result, their success or failure bore direct consequences for God's purpose and destiny. The consequences of the fall were overwhelmingly personal consequences experienced by God. Consider Reverend Moon's speech, "The Pinnacle of Suffering:"

> *What is the pinnacle of God's suffering? There is no question that the fall of God's children, Adam and Eve, is the focal point of His difficulty. Their separation from God was a very pitiful and tearful situation. God is the Father of mankind and Adam and Eve are His first children, the ancestors of fallen mankind; when these children fell, the consequences had a direct impact on God and caused Him incredible suffering. Because the fall was a physical act, God lost His connection with the physical world, and in addition, He endured suffering of the mind and suffering of the soul. The seeds of man's suffering throughout history were planted by Adam and Eve being corrupted at the beginning of human history, and from that time on suffering was handed down from generation to generation.*
>
> *The fall of man brought three consequences: God lost His children and He lost His temple, because man was to be the dwelling place of God. Furthermore, God lost the only home in which His love could be manifested; Adam and Eve were not only to be the children of God but to be the recipients of His love. With the fall of man God lost everything He had hoped for in the love of His own children, the love between husband and wife, and the love between parent and child.*
>
> **"The Pinnacle of Suffering", June 26, 1977**

How abundantly clear that God placed himself in jeopardy for mankind's sake.

Chapter Four

The Principle of Restoration Through Indemnity

Job 1:6–12

One day the angels came to present themselves before the LORD, and Satan also came with them. The LORD said to Satan, "Where have you come from?" Satan answered the LORD, "From roaming through the earth and going back and forth in it."

Then the LORD said to Satan, "Have you considered my servant Job? There is no one on earth like him; he is blameless and upright, a man who fears God and shuns evil."

Does Job fear God for nothing?" Satan replied. "Have you not put a hedge around him and his household and everything he has? You have blessed the work of his hands, so that his flocks and herds are spread throughout the land. But stretch out your hand and strike everything he has, and he will surely curse you to your face." The LORD said to Satan, "Very well, then, everything he has is in your hands, but on the man himself do not lay a finger." Then Satan went out from the presence of the LORD.

Fallen Man Is in the Midway Position

The story of Job illustrates man's fallen position. Fallen man must contend with two competing sovereignties, each with a legitimate claim, each attempting to establish an exclusive claim over man.

Notice the difference between God and Satan's viewpoint of Job. God is proud of Job and expresses faith in him. God sees Job's goodness and exalts it.

Satan, on the other hand, has a very pessimistic opinion of Job. Satan questions Job's sincerity. He tells God that Job's devotion is merely a result of Job pursuing his own interest. Satan has no faith in Job and wants to convince God of Job's unworthiness.

Both God and Satan can legitimately see themselves in Job. This is the substance of fallen man in the "midway position" between God and Satan. Both God and Satan have a legitimate claim. Both God and Satan can, likewise, see themselves in each fallen person. How did this come to be?

One major result of the fall is that we came under two lords, or two subjects. If we had only one subject and one lord, it would not be such a problem to restore everything and return to the original state. If God were still the only subject, every creature could become harmonized with Him and there would be nothing to oppose such harmony. But there is another subject, whose direction is totally the opposite of God's. That being took the subjective position by rejecting God. As a result of the fall, the opposing power of love that pulls man away from God became much stronger than the power that leads man back to his original source. Thus, the power of love came to be divided into opposing camps of internal and external. Satan is connected to the world of love centering upon external power and God is connected to love centering on internal power. So two subjects came to stand over one object, man. Satan became the external subject, while God became the internal subject.

Rev. Sun Myung Moon, "Total Indemnity," April 3, 1983

God maintains a claim over man. Even though man fell, this does not undo God's status as the true Creator and origin of man. However, due to the fall, Satan established an equal claim over man. Though God created man, this, likewise, does not undo Satan's status as "god."

Matthew 6:24
No one can serve two masters. Either he will hate the one and love the other, or he will be devoted to the one and despise the other. You cannot serve both God and Money.

This is fallen man's plight: We have two masters, each with a legitimate claim. However, we are dwelling in a universe that allows for the exclusive dominion of a single master. God's decision to "not recognize Satan as creator" means that God would not change that principle of exclusive dominion. That decision has a direct imprint on the nature of restoration. The principle by which God has created is applied to the work of restoration or "re-creation" of man.

This means that, although God has a claim over man, He will not exercise dominion over man until He can establish an exclusive claim. The benefit for fallen man, in terms of restoration, is that Satan must follow the same principle. Therefore, Satan cannot exercise dominion without establishing exclusive claim.

The Book of Job shows us that Job walks the course to affirm a single sovereignty. Job, by his actions, will have to negate the claim of one master and affirm the claim of the other. Through Job's conditions, exclusive dominion is established. This exemplifies the essence of man's responsibility in the course of restoration.

Good Conditions: Believe the Word and Act Upon It

Thus, for God or Satan to exercise exclusive dominion, a condition must be established. In order to accomplish this, God sends His word. If fallen man, in the mid-way position, makes the condition to receive the word, believe it, and put that word into action, he will have then set up the condition for God to claim man and stand as exclusive master.

In the Old Testament Age, God would send His word, i.e., the laws, decrees, and commandments of God. If the chosen people would make the condition of receiving the word, believing in it, and putting it into practice, then God could lead them with "a pillar of cloud by day and a pillar of fire by night." He promised them "blessings" if they adhered to that course. Of course, this was not salvation in substance, even so it did clearly foreshadow, as a model course, the process by which salvation would be accomplished.

In the pattern for salvation through Christ, Jesus comes as "the word made flesh." If we make the condition of faith in Christ, receive Christ as the living word, believe and put his words into practice, we will be "judged" and brought to God's side.

John 12:48

*There is a **judge** for the one who rejects me and does not accept my words; that very word that I spoke will condemn him at the last day.*

Matthew 7:24–25

Therefore everyone who hears these words of mine and puts them into practice is like a wise man who built his house on the rock. The rain came

down, the streams rose, and the winds blew and beat against that house;
yet it did not fall, because it had its foundation on the rock.

Bad Conditions: Believe Satan's Word and Act Upon It

It would be nice if we could conclude at this point and say, "Henceforth, make only good conditions centering on God's word." That would be very good advice; however, it would not be the whole story.

The rest of the story involves the reality of another "god" who, likewise, is seeking exclusive claim. This other god follows the same principle in attempting to set up an exclusive dominion. He also sends his word. Satan's word is a counterproposal to the Word of God.

For example, in the Garden of Eden (**Genesis 3:3**), God instructs Adam and Eve not to eat the fruit for on the very day they eat, they "will die." Satan, in contrast, tells Eve, "you will not surely die." **Genesis 3:4** Before Eve can accept the word of Satan, she must, first, make the conscious decision to **reject the Word of God.** This is the beginning of the loss of freedom and, therefore, the consequential rise of inordinate, uncontrollable desire. Man maintaining faith in God's Word is the condition by which God invokes the "control of righteousness" upon growing, imperfect beings. **Romans 6:20**

Satan cleverly mimics God in sending his word. His first objective is for man to reject the God-given basis of his own freedom and authority: the Word of God. This is how Satan gains authority and control over man. Without man's voluntary submission and cooperation, Satan could never exert his claim as god. Therefore, if man receives Satan's word, believes it, and acts upon it, then Satan can exert his will to have exclusive dominion over man. Such a person goes to "Satan's side." This commission of a "bad condition" is what we refer to as sin. Therefore, sin is any thought or action in violation of God's Word that makes a base for Satan to have exclusive dominion over me.

What are the characteristics of being on "Satan's side" or on "God's side"? "God's side" or Heaven is the place of perfect freedom. You will not have a desire for anything that will sever your relationship with God. No desire will emerge that will destroy our primary relations of love because all desire will be one with the universal value of living for others. Therefore, in heaven, our deepest and strongest desires will always adhere to the path of God. In heaven, as a result, we don't need "faith" any longer. Desire and action are one. Therefore, fulfillment is constant in Heaven. That means we will always be joyful and stimulated there. Subject and object will always engage, interact and produce joy. The realm of perfect freedom is the realm where my desire can be realized.

2 Corinthians 3:17

Now the Lord is the Spirit, and where the Spirit of the Lord is, there is freedom.

Freedom without purpose is licentiousness. Paul describes the purpose of freedom. It is not so that we can do as we please, but rather, that we may live in love.

Galatians 5:13–14

You, my brothers, were called to be free. But do not use your freedom to indulge the sinful nature; rather, serve one another in love. The entire law is summed up in a single command: "Love your neighbor as yourself."

Conversely, to be on "Satan's side" is characterized by the loss of freedom. Jesus describes sinners as "slaves."

John 8:33–34

They answered him, "We are Abraham's descendants and have never been slaves of anyone. How can you say that we shall be set free?" Jesus replied, "I tell you the truth, everyone who sins is a slave to sin."

All sin has the nature of habit. I can't stop committing the sin. I do it over and over, and each time I do it, a little more of my freedom is taken away. As I lose more freedom, the desire to sin grows stronger in direct proportion to the loss of freedom. Again, Paul describes this nature perfectly:

Romans 7:16–24

And if I do what I do not want to do, I agree that the law is good. As it is, it is no longer I myself who do it, but it is sin living in me. I know that nothing good lives in me, that is, in my sinful nature.

For I have the desire to do what is good, but I cannot carry it out. For what I do is not the good I want to do; no, the evil I do not want to do, this I keep on doing. Now if I do what I do not want to do, it is no longer I who do it, but it is sin living in me that does it.

So I find this law at work: When I want to do good, evil is right there with me. For in my inner being I delight in God's law; but I see another law at work in the members of my body, waging war against the law of my mind and making me a prisoner of the law of sin at work within my members. What a wretched man I am! Who will rescue me from this body of death?

If the purpose of freedom is so that we may "live in love and live in God," it stands to reason that the consequence of sin is the hardening of our hearts. We lose the God-given ability to love and feel joy in our life. This is death as a result of sin. Paul affirms this consequence:

Ephesians 4:18
They are darkened in their understanding and separated from the life of God because of the ignorance that is in them due to the hardening of their hearts.

As does James, the brother of Jesus:

James 1:13–15
When tempted, no one should say, "God is tempting me." For God cannot be tempted by evil, nor does he tempt anyone; but each one is tempted when, by his own evil desire, he is dragged away and enticed. Then, after desire has conceived, it gives birth to sin; and sin, when it is full-grown, gives birth to death.

Through the condition of sin we lose our position and status on God's side. Satan invades our life and gains dominion over us. We lose true freedom and become slaves to uncontrollable desire for more sin. As a result, our hearts harden and we lose the motive of life: to live in love. Because of the loss of motive, we lose the joy of life and finally, because of this growing void in our souls, we seek, ever increasingly, more sin to replace the real experience of God's love. Once the cycle is complete, sin produces more sin, more death, more habit, more emptiness, more desire for cheap replacements for true love. Indeed, who will save us from this body of death?

Confession

Once a condition of sin is made and Satan gains dominion, he begins the process to expand that base of sin. Satan begins to accuse us for the very sin only moments before he was enticing us to commit. The very same Satan! Does he have a split personality?

Satan is exhorting us toward commission of a particular sinful act. He assures you it is okay to do it. He reminds you of all those who have done the same. He provides ample justifications to assist you over the hump of your conscience. "I know how you feel," he says, "I've felt the same way myself, but I have found that once you go ahead and do it, it's not so bad." Satan perfected the "feel, felt, found" technique of sales. Has anyone noticed, before the condition of sin, Satan is so sympathetic and understanding?

Once the condition is made, however, the tables turn. Now he is quite shocked and disturbed that you would do such a heinous thing. He questions your right to continue to think of yourself as a child of God. He reminds you, repeatedly, that your sin is the most shameful act he has witnessed in quite some time. Now he is wringing his hands over the terrible crime you committed.

If you try to pray, he'll try to stop you. He will point out how ludicrous it would be for a pure God to relate to you, especially after what you did to Him. You remember what you did, don't you? If you continue to listen to Satan, he'll keep talking until you're thoroughly convinced that you have irrevocably damaged your relationship with God. Isn't Satan considerate to be so concerned about our relationship with God? We would do well to be very suspicious of his intentions.

Why does he do this? Why does Satan accuse the sinner?

The reason has to do with Satan's need for secrecy. For example, haven't you ever noticed that before he sins the sinner engages in extensive "rubbernecking"? The sinner surveys the terrain. He wants to make sure that when he sins, no one will see him. Why the need for secrecy? If, indeed, I'm only doing "what everyone else is doing" or "I'm only doing it once, so it's okay," why do we hide?

It is because Satan's sovereignty is conditional. As long as a condition has been laid, Satan can claim man. However, if man faces his sin, begins to understand the nature of those conditions and moves toward taking responsibility by reversing those conditions, he will remove the basis of Satan's authority over man. Such a path separates that man from Satan.

If all people are separated from Satan, then Satan will have no foundation to be "god and ruler." It is of paramount importance, therefore, in order for Satan to maintain his position, that man never discover or take responsibility for the conditions he has made.

Satan accuses us for our sin and, at the same time, tries to convince us that God will never forgive us. If we believe this, we will have no recourse but to repress our sin. This means we will justify our sin and by so doing we are, in effect, hiding the sin from ourselves. We will displace the problem onto something or someone else. As long as we hide the sin from ourselves, we can never change. By that condition of sin, Satan is able to maintain his dominion over us.

When God attempts to bring us to the light with the hope that we will admit our sin and take responsibility, we instead feel the rise of fear in our soul, believing that God will only condemn us. We turn from the light because we think that we have overstepped the bounds of God's love.

The dividend for Satan is that, as long as we continue to avoid facing our conditions of sin, he is able to maintain his position of authority over us. He has tricked us, through fear, into avoiding, at all costs, facing the conditions we have made. In this way, the basis upon which he exerts his authority over us remains intact. He is very clever! He is "wise as a serpent."

The act of confession requires us to relinquish the justification of our sin. Justification of sin is the lie provided by Satan so that I may conveniently repress my sin and avoid taking responsibility to purge the conditions by which Satan is controlling me. Common justifications are:

"It's okay, everybody's doing it!" (No, they aren't.)

"Oh, well, nobody's perfect." (But everyone should be growing.)

One of my favorites: "Go ahead, once won't hurt." (All sinful habits started with a "once" that wouldn't hurt.)

And this one: "Go ahead, you have the rest of your life to repent. What could happen in the meantime?" (How about your funeral for starters?)

Confession is reaching into your soul, gathering your sins into your hands, and boldly holding them to the light. When your sins are bathed in the light of truth, you can see clearly the heinous nature of your actions. You can see how your sins have hurt others, your family and those who look up to you and depend on you. You can see how your sins have a strong tendency to expand into the lives of your most precious loved ones and become a problem for them, as well. You can see how your sins are hurting God and deeply disappointing Him. You can see how your sins are ultimately robbing you of your destiny and greatest potential.

Confession sheds light onto my conditions of sin. Confession also forces me to confront my belief about God. Is God truly a God of love who will forgive me or is He a God who will have lost patience and condemn me? The scripture encourages the sinner by revealing God's nature of forgiveness and His desire to restore us to our former glory.

1 John 1:8–9

If we claim to be without sin, we deceive ourselves and the truth is not in us. If we confess our sins, he is faithful and just and will forgive us our sins and purify us from all unrighteousness.

Through confession I place myself in a position to trust God's love and His ability to forgive. I move in a direction that is 180 degrees opposite to the direction paved by Lucifer when he rejected God's love. Having gained a deeper sense of my sin, through confession, I am ready to move to phase two of the restoration process: repentance.

Repentance

Luke 15:10

In the same way, I tell you, there is rejoicing in the presence of the angels of God over one sinner who repents.

Repentance must come from the heart. Real repentance only happens as a result of really seeing our sin and becoming fully cognizant of its implications. Without confession, it is hard to have genuine repentance. Repentance means turning around and changing my direction. I turn my back on my sinful past and face the direction that leads me back to God's side. Satan hates repentance. He hates that which he cannot do. It is not in his nature to repent.

What is his nature? It is called the original nature of the fall, or, fallen nature. Fallen nature is actually another term for Satan's personality. Simply put, the most common element of Satan's personality is the insistence that he is never wrong. It is always someone else's fault. He always blames others and never considers his own shortcomings.

The process of the fall was precipitated by Lucifer's refusal to acquiesce to Adam's position and authority as the Son of God. Thus, the course of repentance requires the position of a living Adam who can receive our repentance and who has the authority on earth to forgive our sin. Whereas there have been many great prophets and people of God, Jesus was the first to accomplish that authority.

Therefore, the person who stands humbly in front of the living Adam and says, "God, I am at fault, please forgive me," is a man who takes a position that Satan cannot reach. Satan will flee from the repentant sinner because Satan cannot repent himself. The best and surest path to separate from Satan is to perform the task that Satan cannot do.

I have heard people say, many times, that they confessed and repented over and over again, but they still had the same problem. "It didn't work," they say. Well, there is a very important component that must be included in the process of repentance.

Lay an Indemnity Condition

The way for salvation is to pay indemnity and then restore the way. Indemnity means you climb through the path by which the fall happened. Then go the opposite way.

—Rev. Sun Myung Moon

Through confession and repentance we turn from our sin; however, we still are in Satan's area because of our condition of sin. Who produced the condition of sin? We did, by our own actions. That's the bad news. The good news is that because we produced that condition, we have the ability to reverse the condition of sin. This is the purpose of a condition of indemnity.

Through the condition of sin, I lose my position and status on God's side. Conversely, through the condition of indemnity, I restore my position and status. By setting up a condition, we remove ourselves from the territory of Satan's control.

An indemnity condition is a reversal of the pattern of the condition of sin. Primarily, sin involves reversal of original order. For example, I sacrifice others for myself. I tip the balance of mind and body toward the interest of the flesh over the spirit. I disregard public, for private. I nullify absolutes with relativism.

By following this pattern, the sinner walks into Satan's territory and is invaded. He becomes a slave to uncontrollable desire. He justifies his actions with a lie. His heart hardens and no life is found in him. He feels empty and in need. He seeks replacement for his lost life of love. Typical replacements for God's love are drugs, alcohol and other intoxicants, aberrant, illicit sex and pornography. He struggles with depression and anxiety.

Indemnity is the reverse course of sin. Therefore, indemnity is the opposite way of the usual desires of the flesh. That is why fasting, giving up sleep, doing what I don't want to do is the typical pathway of indemnity. Through the process of confession, repentance and laying an indemnity condition, fallen man restores his position and status with God.

Indemnity is a reversal of the process of the condition of sin. Therefore, conditions of indemnity run parallel to the process of sin, yet are moving in the opposite direction upon an opposite motive. "He who has suffered in the body is done with sin". **1 Peter 4:1**

Even though they are headed in opposite directions, sometimes the closeness of their parallel tracks creates confusion. This means that conditions of indemnity can, on the surface, appear to be sin. The story of Tamar in the 38th chapter of Genesis is an exact example of this confusion. To this day, Christians are baffled by Tamar's behavior. It seems like sin, pure and simple. From the standpoint of indemnity, however, Tamar's actions reveal most noble motives.

Restoration and Biblical History

Let's now examine the historical biblical record of God's providence of restoration. In its most simple expression, we could say that the goal of God's historical restoration plan is to resurrect the Adam who died. In that death for Adam was death for all, in the "Last Adam," Christ, all will be made alive. Restoration history consummates in the coming of a new Adam. The new Adam begins the original, intended history.

In the history of the chosen people, we can see that God is setting up the process of sanctification in order to lead His people to make a foundation for Christ to come.

Leviticus 26:40–43
But if they will confess their sins and the sins of their fathers—their treachery against me and their hostility toward me, which made me hostile toward them so that I sent them into the land of their enemies—then when their uncircumcised hearts are humbled and they pay for their sin, I will remember my covenant with Jacob and my covenant with Isaac and my covenant with Abraham, and I will remember the land. For the land will be deserted by them and will enjoy its sabbaths while it lies desolate without them. They will pay for their sins because they rejected my laws and abhorred my decrees.

2 Samuel 14:14
But God does not take away life; instead, he devises ways so that a banished person may not remain estranged from him.

The way that God makes use of "so that a banished person may not remain estranged" is the way of payment for sin, or indemnification of sin. The conditions of sin are reversed through conditions of indemnity payment. In the principle of re-creation, just as in the principle of creation, man must fulfill a portion of responsibility.

We can find many examples where God utilizes the "Principle of Re-creation" in order to recover His chosen people who had gone astray.

The Incident of Worshipping the Golden Calf
The Israelites committed the sin of idolatry by worshipping the golden calf during the time Moses was praying and fasting for 40 days on Mt. Sinai. See how Moses deals with the circumstance of a people whose "bad condition" has moved them to Satan's side. Through conditions of indemnity, he restores their former position and status:

Exodus 32:20, 34–5
And he took the calf they had made and burned it in the fire; then he ground it to powder, scattered it on the water and made the Israelites drink it . . . ."However, when the time comes for me to punish, I will punish them for their sin." And the LORD struck the people with a plague because of what they did with the calf Aaron had made.

Through the bad condition of worshipping the golden calf, Satan could claim the Israelites to his side. Through the process of atonement and punishment the Israelites indemnified their sin of idolatry. Thus they could return, sanctified, to God's side.

Incident of Rebellion at the Border
Our next example is at the border of the Promised Land. Moses sent the spies for forty days of spying in the Promised Land. Upon their return and report, the people grumbled mightily against Moses, Joshua and Caleb. God pronounced a punishment course of forty years of wandering:

Numbers 14:33–35
Your children will be shepherds here for forty years, suffering for your unfaithfulness, until the last of your bodies lies in the desert. For forty years, one year for each of the forty days you explored the land, you will suffer for your sins and know what it is like to have me against you. I, the LORD, have spoken, and I will surely do these things to this whole wicked community, which has banded together against me. They will meet their end in this desert; here they will die.

Through the sin of rebellion, the Israelites lost their position and status on God's side. Satan could dominate them exclusively. God could not deal with them until after they performed a condition of indemnity. At the end of this period of indemnity, the Israelites were returned to their former position and status. Did you notice that the forty years of wandering were meted out on a one day = one year basis? They regained the qualification to enter into the Promised Land by indemnifying the forty-day spying period. This is why the wandering period was forty years.

This is not, however, to be misconstrued to mean that they could accomplish their own salvation or regeneration through a personal course of atonement.

The essence of the principle of restoration is that the conditions of sin that were made by man must be reversed. They are to be reversed through man's conditions of indemnity. It is the course of reversal of the process of sin.

Can sinful man achieve, independent of relationship with Christ, a process of "auto-salvation"? We will see in the fundamental course of salvation that important issues preclude self-salvation and, thereby, make essential the role of Christ in the work of salvation.

One of those determining factors is that sinners did not commit the original sin. Instead, we inherited the consequences of original sin via our ancestral connection to the dead Adam. That is, our experience with original sin has been through the process of inheritance. Therefore, the principle of restoration specifies that we cannot indemnify the original sin, independently, through personal conditions.

Instead, the inheritance of sin and death, wrought by the fall, must be reversed through the Messiah. Sinners, therefore, must establish an inheritance of life and salvation. Sinners cannot save themselves.

Sinners' fundamental problem is a result of an ancestry that links to the "dead Adam." Thus, we must come out of this lineage of death. We cannot just sever our connection to one lineage without, simultaneously, being engrafted to another lineage. Sinners need a new lineage that connects to life. This requires the appearance of a "new Adam." The process of restoration through indemnity requires the sinner to change his blood lineage from the dead Adam to the living Adam. This "change of blood lineage" is the process of rebirth.

1 Corinthians 15:22
For as in Adam all die, so in Christ all will be made alive.

John 3:3
In reply Jesus declared, "I tell you the truth, no one can see the kingdom of God unless he is born again."

The Principle of Restoration through Indemnity, therefore, deeply affirms the centrality of Christ's role.

A New Adam Must Come

In order to reverse the condition of the original sin, we must understand the process by which that sin was linked to us. Sin came to us via the lineage of our birth. Our lineage goes back to a dead Adam. The dead Adam resulted by way of conditions he established that "corrupted his body." We are born as the extension of this corrupted body. Thus, as we have indicated, Adam's descendants did not commit the original sin; they inherited it. This process must be reversed in order for man to be saved.

History did not begin with a dead Adam. History began with a living, sinless Adam. Adam had been, for a time, a "living Adam." Adam had been born, without sin, as the living Son of God. Later, he committed certain conditions of sin that transformed him from a living Adam into a dead Adam. This demonstrates that the dead Adam emerged on a *foundation of conditions*; he didn't just appear without discernible reasons. This "pre-history" of the dead Adam are the events and conditions that transformed the living Adam into the dead Adam.

Mankind needs a new ancestor, a new Adam, into which we can change our lineage. By doing so, we "inherit" salvation and life.

Hebrews 1:14

Are not all angels ministering spirits sent to serve those who will inherit salvation?

When will that new Adam appear? What determines the circumstances for his arrival? Just as the dead Adam did not emerge without a foundation based upon specific conditions, likewise the new living Adam will arrive on the foundation of established conditions. This is why Jesus did not appear until 4,000 years after the fall. Jesus would only appear on the foundation of established conditions. It took 4,000 biblical years to achieve them. We seek to understand what those conditions were.

History began with a living Adam who then performed bad conditions that transformed him into a dead Adam. According to the Principle of Restoration through Indemnity the pathway of reversal of those conditions will lead to the reemergence of a new living Adam. This means before the new living Adam can appear, conditions of indemnity must be laid. Those conditions must reverse the bad conditions that changed the original living Adam into the dead Adam. The pre-history leading up to the birth of Christ is the Providence of God to establish those conditions as the foundation for the emergence of Christ, the new living Adam.

The foundation for the dead Adam was accomplished in a short period of time, possibly one afternoon. However, to reverse those conditions successfully, as mentioned, required 4,000 years of restoration history. The returning path from darkness into light is far more arduous than the primrose path going from light into dark. Although the durations are vastly different, these two trends are directly linked. The genetic code of the 4,000 years of God's providence is the providence to reverse the conditions laid down in the pre-history of the dead Adam. The appearance of Christ on earth will stand on that foundation.

Therefore, in order to understand the ebb and flow of the history leading up to the emergence of Christ, we must have a clear understanding of the "pre-history" that led to the emergence of the dead Adam. That is, we must have a clear understanding of the conditions that were performed by Adam that led to his demise. The reversal of those conditions will serve as the Foundation for the Messiah.

Thus, when we examine biblical history, we assert that there is a common cause that links all events leading up to Christ. That common feature in every providential age is the requirement to reverse the bad conditions committed by Adam. This is the mission of Abel, this is the mission of Noah, the mission of Abraham, Isaac and Jacob. It will be the mission of Moses on the national level, and, it will be the foundation to understand more fully what is the mission of John the Baptist. To accomplish that foundation is man's responsibility in restoration. Just as God would not intervene in Adam and Eve's responsibility laid down in the principle of creation, God will not intervene in fallen man's responsibility in the principle of re-creation.

Each "central figure" of his respective age stands as a "second coming," as it were, of the dead Adam. His mission is to reverse through indemnity the conditions that transformed a living Adam into a dead Adam. If the central figure is successful in his responsibility to establish those conditions, then that victory will serve as the Foundation for the Messiah, i.e., the new living Adam.

If that central figure is not successful, God will re-create, at a later time, the circumstances for the accomplishment of that mission. That means a new central figure will come with the same mission, responsibility and objective as his predecessor. Thus, parallels form over the course of time. The root cause of "historical parallels" is that each central figure in each age is addressing the "common cause," the same set of circumstances, the same role and responsibility, the same objective. Thus, the providence to bring Christ into the world is a "co-creatorship" project. Much in the same way God and Adam were to "co-create" his universe, God and fallen man are to conditionally partnership in establishing the foundation for Christ to come into the world.

This is why certain events in providential history reflect events from previous ages. For example, there is a direct link between the providence centering on Jacob with Moses and even Jesus. Jesus indicated this:

John 5:19

Jesus gave them this answer: "I tell you the truth, the Son can do nothing by himself; he can do only what he sees his Father doing, because whatever the Father does the Son also does."

Likewise, Moses, speaking of the coming Christ, said:

Deuteronomy 18:15

The Lord your God will raise up for you a prophet like me from among your own brothers. **You must listen to him.**

In chapter six on Moses, we will cite eight examples of parallels shared by Jacob, Moses and Jesus. For example, Jacob had 12 sons and 70 family members, Moses had 12 tribes and 70 elders and Jesus had 12 apostles and 70 disciples.

Another clear example is the pattern of the relationship between the elder and younger:

- Cain and Abel
- Ishmael and Isaac
- Esau and Jacob
- Zerah and Perez
- Manasseh and Ephraim
- Aaron and Moses
- John and Jesus

The Foundation for the Messiah

As was mentioned in the previous section, in order to understand the ebb and flow of the history leading up to the emergence of Christ, we must have a clear understanding of the "pre-history" that led to the emergence of the dead Adam. That is, we must have a clear understanding of the conditions that were performed by Adam that led to his demise. The reversal of those conditions will serve as the Foundation for the Messiah.

What is the composition of Adam's bad conditions? In chapter two on the fall, the fall of man was described as a process. In the process of the fall, there is a series of interlinked actions that result in the transformation of Adam and the reversal of order. In other words, Adam not only dies but falls under the authority of a new emerging "god" and "ruler."

Foundation of Faith

What good conditions did God intend for Adam to accomplish? What was Adam's portion of responsibility? First, Adam was supposed to adhere to the word of God. In previous chapters we explained that Adam receiving the Word was, in fact, God's effort to share His role with man. God gave man a five percent portion of His responsibility as creator. Application of the Word, the role of self-governing, was the position that Adam would have gained through faith in the Word. This is the basis of understanding the Foundation of Faith. If Adam had made a faith foundation with the Word, he would then have accomplished the key component of his responsibility during the maturing process of his growth period.

Foundation of Substance

The second element of Adam's role involved his position to have dominion as co-creator. In previous chapters we explained God's intention to rule by love through Adam. As a result, Adam must accomplish the position of dominion over all things, including the angels. Adam having achieved dominion would have been the foundation for God's dominion. This is called the Foundation of Substance. God would have incarnated substantially in Adam. Adam would have received God's nature, His love and spirit. Through perfected Adam, God's dominion over the substance of creation would have been achieved.

We can best understand Adam's failure in relation to his stated role. First, he lost the Foundation of Faith by rejecting God's Word through the temptation of Eve. God's Word was for Adam not to eat the fruit. Eve tempted Adam; however, it was Adam who had to make the decision to relinquish his relationship with the commandment, the Word of God. By doing so, Adam lost the tool of dominion and control. The force of principle, a lesser force, could not control the force of love. Thus, he became a slave to the force of unprincipled love.

Second, by receiving the word of the archangel, Adam made Satan substantial as "god" and "ruler" over him. Lucifer took the position of god by giving the word, "you will not die." However, if Adam had not received that word, believed it and acted upon it, Lucifer could not have gained substantial dominion as "god." This means Adam and Eve are responsible for the dominion of Satan. They in substance gave birth to this false god and false dominion. Through this false god, they inherited his nature. Thus, the Foundation of Substance was lost to Satan.

On a deeper level, it means that Satan claimed "the elder son birthright." God set up Adam in order to transfer His seed. That means, from Adam, the birth of God's lineage was to take place through the expansion of Adam's seed, the descendants of Adam.

When Adam received the word of the archangel, however, Satan claimed that precious birthright. As a result, all the descendants of Adam are born under this claim with the nature of "their father."

Restoring the Foundation of Faith

Having faith in God's Word was the foundation for Adam to inherit God's dominion over all things. Therefore, the loss of God's Word must be reversed. That is why the biblical central figures were asked to accomplish an arduous task of faith. Abel had to make a faithful offering of the finest things he owned, Noah had to build the Ark for 120 years, Abraham had to offer his only son. All central figures in biblical history begin their mission by exercising the muscle of faith in God's Word. The Biblical history cites three requirements to restore the lost foundation of faith:

1. *A central figure.* Since the fall of Adam, all people are the extension of the dead Adam. Ideally, Adam himself should reverse his own bad conditions. However, because all fallen men are the extension of the dead Adam, they can serve in his role. Fallen Adam's role in restoration is to unbind the conditions that transformed him from a living Adam to a dead Adam. The "central figure" in biblical history is the figure given the providential responsibility to reverse through indemnity the lost Foundation of Faith and Foundation of

Substance. This is the mission of Abel, Noah, Abraham, Isaac, Jacob, Moses, the kings, prophets and, finally, John the Baptist.

2. *A conditional object of faith.* Until the law covenant is instituted, roughly 2,400 biblical years after the fall, fallen man had lost all contact with God's recorded Word. The providence of God in the Book of Genesis shows that fallen man would come to God through offerings of faith. The offering of faith, such as the animal offering, was a conditional replacement for the Word that was lost. In Genesis, the central figures offered substance from the natural world. Abel offered animals, Noah constructed a wooden ark and Abraham offered a heifer, ram, goat, dove and pigeon. Adam was to dominate all things through faith in God's Word. Therefore, when man lost God's Word, man also lost all things of creation. That is why Paul reports of the "creation groaning in travail." Thus, via the way of indemnity, the pathway back to God's Word began with offering the things of creation. This was the character of the first 2,000 years of God's providence recorded in Genesis.

3. *A time period to establish faith.* "He who endures to the end, shall be saved." **Matthew 24:13** The victory of faith must be established over a set course of time. We can observe specific time requirements associated with conditions of faith. Jesus fasted for forty days, the Israelites were sent into exile in Babylon for seventy years or became sojourners in land not their own for four hundred years.

Once the central figure had successfully completed his condition of faith over the prescribed time period, he moved on to the next phase of the restoration course.

Restoring the Foundation of Substance

If Adam had kept faith in God's Word and had achieved perfection, he would have inherited God's nature of love and God's authority over all things. Instead, Adam fell under the dominion of Satan and inherited the satanic fallen nature. Jesus indicated: "You are of your father the devil and your will is to do the will of your father." **John 8:44**

Reversing the fallen nature means reversing the process of the fall. The fallen nature is also referred to as " The Original Nature of the Fall." This is because the process of the original sin established the process of all subsequent sin. All sin follows the same process and motives of the archetypical sin, the original sin. Just as a stone dropped into calm waters produces a wake that ripples out to the distant shore, the pattern of the original sin is reflected in the sins committed today. The fallen nature is the nature within us that resonates with that fallen archetype. It is as if the process of the original sin was transformed into a nature or personality and then was inherited by all fallen men. It is a nature that is predisposed toward producing conditions of sin.

The fallen nature and the process of the fall involved the change of the order of dominion of the angel over Adam:

1. The archangel could not love Adam from God's viewpoint.

2. The archangel left his proper position: he refused to receive God's love through Adam.

3. The archangel reversed dominion over Adam, becoming god and ruler.

4. Sin multiplied from Eve to Adam to all Adam's descendants.

This process and nature involves the interplay of two positions: Adam and the archangel. Thus, in the process of indemnity, two positions are established to "reverse the fallen nature and process of the fall."

Those two positions and the course to reverse the process of the fall are the basis of the biblical pattern of elder brother and younger brother. In each instance, the younger is shown favor over the elder. This begins in Adam's own family with his two sons, Cain and Abel.

God reverses the natural order. He bypasses the older for the younger. He places the younger in the position of the elder. Then he challenges the elder to "do what is right." That is to reverse the fallen nature.

Genesis 4:6–7

Then the LORD said to Cain, "Why are you angry? Why is your face downcast? If you do what is right, will you not be accepted? But if you do not do what is right, sin is crouching at your door; it desires to have you, but you must master it."

Remember, the "fallen nature" is the process of the fall as a nature; it is Satan's own personality. If Cain and Abel had reversed the fallen nature, Satan would have separated from them. In effect, to reverse the fallen nature is to negate Satan.

God re-creates the circumstances faced by Adam and Lucifer. This is so the fallen pattern can be reversed. Therefore, Cain must:

1. Love Abel from God's viewpoint. This will reverse Lucifer's

refusal to love Adam from God's viewpoint.

2. Receive God's love through Abel. This will reverse Lucifer's act of leaving his proper position and rejecting Adam as the channel of God's love.

3. Accept Abel's authority. This will reverse the pattern by which Lucifer changed the dominion of angels and man.

4. Multiply goodness at Abel's direction. This will reverse the multiplication of sin that spread from Lucifer to Eve to Adam to all their descendants.

It is important to stress that although God has shown favor to Abel, He loved Cain just as much and wants Cain to walk the correct course that will negate Satan's claim and separate Satan from them.

Just as Satan elicited man's voluntary cooperation in producing the conditions of sin, Cain must walk the course that will, likewise, elicit the voluntary submission of Satan. The only way to elicit Satan's voluntary submission is for fallen man to walk the path that negates the foundational components of Satan's personality. This is why God sets up the circumstances to reverse the fallen nature.

Also, Cain was the firstborn of Adam and carried the "elder son birthright." If Cain could have reversed the fallen nature by uniting with Abel, then the elder brother's birthright would have been restored back to God's side, as well. This is why the completion of the Foundation of Substance establishes the Foundation for the Messiah. God could have restored the first son's birthright and could fulfill his commitment to bring a new living Adam into the world. That new living Adam is the Christ. In this way, God "intervenes" in the fall.

Based on this, we can understand why God encouraged Cain so lovingly to "do what is right." Had Cain heeded God's call and united with his brother Abel, the foundation for the new living Adam would have been established immediately. The problem of sin, at this point, was the problem of a single family. God did not want to see the expansion of a sinful legacy from family, tribe, nation and world over the course of thousands of years.

However, when Cain pummeled his brother to death, he ensured that there would be no timely solutions to the tragedies wrought in Adam's family. Those dire consequences expanded from Adam's family over the next 10 generations and 1,600 years. When God observed those results, **Genesis 6:6–7** reveals a God whose heart "was filled with pain." God even repented that He had made man on earth.

Chapter Five

Noah and Abraham

Noah's Family

God's purpose was to be fulfilled by a central family. However, when they sinned, that central family was required to take responsibility for their sin. Before sin evolved to a world-level problem, it began as a problem for a single family. When Cain killed his brother Abel, however, the family of Adam lost its opportunity to reverse the conditions of the fall. As the family of Adam expands from a central family to a multitude of families and tribes, the legacy of sin expanded as well. This ensued over the course of the next 10 generations and approximately 1,600 years.

By the time of Noah, the earth had become filled with violence and corruption. **Genesis 6:6–7** reveals God's grief at the corruption of humanity. His heart "was filled with pain." God even expressed regret about his initial decision to create mankind. It seemed that everything had gone horribly awry.

A single family stood apart from the degradation and became the object of God's attention. This was the family of Noah. In **Genesis 6:9** Noah is described as "a righteous man, blameless among the people of his time and he walked with God."

Noah's family took up the responsibility of Adam's family. Because of the expansion of 10 generations of sin, however, Noah had to also contend with those corrupted multitudes. Noah is referred to as "a preacher of righteousness" in **2 Peter 2:5**. During the 120 years Noah toiled to build the ark, he also warned the people of an impending doom.

Noah's Foundation of Faith

After Cain killed Abel, God sought to maintain the successful foundation of faith accomplished by Abel before his tragic murder. God chose the youngest of Adam's three sons, Seth, and his line of descendants with the hope to expand the foothold of righteousness.

By the time of Noah, however, righteousness was a rare quality. Thus, the entire cosmos stood on the side of Satan. There was no condition for God to intervene and begin a providence on such a defiled earth. Instead, God announced a condition of indemnity to sanctify the earth and bring it back to His side. In **Genesis 6:13** God said, "I am going to put an end to all people for the earth is filled with violence because of them. I am surely going to destroy both them and the earth."

The people and earth that were to be destroyed were the unrepentant people and the defiled earth under Satan's claim. It is Satan's dominion that God was seeking to destroy. That is why God had Noah preach for 120 years. God did not want to destroy the people per se, but rather He wanted to separate them from Satan. Likewise, God did not want to "destroy" the earth, i.e., the literal planet, but rather the earth under Satan's conditional claim. He would destroy that earth by setting up a condition of indemnity.

As we learned, "God seeks a way for a banished person to not remain estranged from him." The way that God devised to reestablish His claim on earth was the flood judgment.

"Judgment" is different from "punishment." Judgment is the defining and separating of good and evil. The evil people would not have been "destroyed" had they repented in response to Noah's word of warning. In lieu of repentance the sinful people were separated from Noah's family via the flood. The floodwaters that rained down for "40 days and 40 nights" separated Noah's family in the ark from the defiled earth. Let's consider the spiritual significance of the ark.

The Ark

Certainly the ark was structured around practical survival needs. The Lord's design was perfect with regard to those needs. To this day modern ship designers frequently comment on the ark's unique design, a design that provided utmost stability in volatile seas.

The ark also bore significant spiritual meaning in much the same way as the structure of the temple related to the figure of Christ. The ark could be thought of as a symbolic new cosmos. Built out of cypress wood, it had three decks where food, the animals, and the eight members of Noah's family could be contained. The number three is very significant in God's creation and is a common number throughout the Bible. For example, Jesus had three main apostles, Adam had three sons, as did Noah, Jesus rose "on the third day," in the natural world there are three primary colors, earth is the third planet from the Sun, it takes three points to establish a stable foundation. God is a God of the number three as in the Trinity. God is "one" on the foundation of the union of two.

By toiling faithfully for 120 years in building the ark, Noah established the indemnity condition for the Foundation of Faith. Noah never doubted God's unusual command to build a huge ship on dry land and without a cloud in the sky. Imagine the scorn and ridicule that was heaped upon Noah, day after day. Yet, Noah remained steadfast. Not only was he building an ark, he was restoring, as the new central figure, the Foundation of Faith that was lost when Adam rejected God's word.

Having restored the "father of faith" position and after preaching righteousness for 120 years, the floodwaters came. The flood judgment divided the two worlds: the fallen earth and the new symbolic cosmos of Noah's ark. The flood's lasting for 40 days and nights also reflected the purpose of sanctification. The number 40 is often linked to conditions of sanctification. For example, Jesus, John, and Moses fasted for 40 days. The Israelites wandered in the wilderness for 40 years. The reigns of Saul, David and Solomon were each 40 years. The number 40 is associated with judgment and indicates the purpose of purification. For 40 days and nights, the symbolic cosmos composed of Noah's family within the ark was separated from the cosmos under Satan. When the waters subsided, Noah's family returned to a sanctified earth made ready for God's providential intervention. He could reengage His providence on earth and move toward the next objective.

Before leaving the ark, Noah sent out the raven from the ark. This seemed to reflect the symbolism of purging evil from the newly sanctified cosmos. Noah then sends out a dove, but a little while later the dove returned. After a time, Noah sent out another dove.

This second dove also returned, but this second dove returned with an olive branch in its mouth. This indicated that the waters were receding. A third dove was released and did not return, indicating that the waters had fully receded and it was time for Noah's family to emerge from the ark.

As sending forth the raven entails spiritual meaning, the three doves, likewise, deserve close attention. The first dove sent out and returned could represent God sending his son, Adam, into the world with specific hopes. However, God's purpose in sending Adam, like the first dove, was returned to Him unfulfilled. The second dove was sent out and, this time, returned with an olive branch. This could symbolizes God's second Adam, Jesus. The olive branch could reflect God's will to "graft" fallen mankind back into God's lineage as described by Paul in **Romans 11:17**. The third dove that settled on dry land could represent the return of Christ to complete the mission of Adam and establish God's dominion upon the earth.

The Foundation of Substance

Noah led his family out of the ark. It was a fresh new start for the providence of God. Noah made an offering of faith on the altar of sacrifice. He offered clean animals and birds. God was moved and reaffirmed to Noah's family the original three blessings first given to Adam's family. Finally, God placed a rainbow in the sky as a sign of His covenant with man. God promised that He would never again judge man by the waters of a flood. It was such a hopeful moment for God. It seemed the years of violence, grief and pain had drawn to a close as a bright new beginning emerged within Noah's family.

But first, Noah's family had to complete the providence to establish the Foundation for the Messiah. Noah was not the messiah but, rather, was standing in the position of fallen Adam who was walking the course of repentance and restitution. Noah's role, as central figure and "father of faith," was to indemnify Adam's bad conditions. Having successfully laid the Foundation of Faith, Noah had then to complete the condition to indemnify the Foundation of Substance. On that successful foundation, the new Adam, the messiah, would appear. He would be arriving to a world that had been thoroughly sanctified for his coming.

In Adam's family, this required the first son, Cain, to come to

God through the second son, Abel. In order for that to be accomplished, the fallen nature had to be reversed. In Noah's family, the elder son was Shem and the second son was Ham. When we read the story of Noah, however, there is no indication of any mounting tensions between the two brothers that reflect the struggle we observed in Adam's family.

Before Ham could take up the position of Abel, he had to inherit Noah's victory in the Foundation of Faith. In Adam's family, Abel himself established the Foundation of Faith, but in this case, it was Noah who established the Foundation of Faith. Therefore, in order for Ham to assume the position of Abel, he had to establish a bond of unbreakable faith with Noah.

This is why the story of Noah now shifts focus to this very issue: the relationship of Noah with Ham. **Genesis 9:20–25** takes a sudden dark turn that greatly contrasts with the bright hope expressed when Noah's family first left the ark. There was a mighty breach in the relationship of Noah and Ham. That tragic break brought to a close the bright new beginning for humanity.

The story explains that Noah plants a vineyard and apparently, after harvesting the fruit of the vine, he prepared and partook of a substantial amount of wine. In fact, Noah was feeling no pain, as it were, and was so inebriated that he forsook his clothing and fell asleep "au naturel."

Next, Ham, his second son, happened along. Ham observed his father in his rather embarrassing state of nakedness and intoxication. The circumstance required Ham's most acute sense of protocol and diplomacy. It was Ham's duty to protect his father's honor. Not to excuse Noah's behavior, but after 120 years of building the ark and successfully leading his family to safety, Noah was still worthy of Ham's respect, patience and understanding.

Unfortunately, Ham reacted in the worst possible way. He felt ashamed of Noah. This shame of nakedness relates to the shame of the fall. It indicated that Ham was becoming a channel for Satan's intervention back into the world. When Noah cast out the raven from the ark, this represented that Satan had been conditionally separated from Noah's family and, subsequently, from the world. However, the raven kept flying back and forth. This indicated that although Satan had been separated, he would be diligent in attempting to find a way of return. That way was established by Ham's bad condition in his relationship with Noah.

Rather than protect his father's honor, Ham left his father's tent and reported to his brothers about their father's nakedness. Ham was multiplying his wrong view. Ham's two brothers entered Noah's tent. Walking backward and averting their eyes away from the "shameful" scene, they dropped a garment over their father.

Noah awakened in a fit of anger. "Cursed be Canaan!" he shouted. In fact, nearly one thousand years later, when Joshua was ordered by God to drive the Canaanite tribes from "the promised land," the Canaanite tribes would still be paying the price for Ham's providential failure. This was not a minor mistake on the part of Ham. It meant that Ham would not be able to assume the younger son's central position in establishing the Foundation of Substance. Thus, the providence to establish the Foundation for the Messiah and bring the new Adam at that time came to a sudden and sorrowful conclusion.

God had prepared the entire world for a great new beginning, but in the final moment, man could not fulfill his portion of the mission. Thus, restoration history moved on in search of the next central figure. God will began the work of re-creating the providential circumstances and, when the time was right, the next central figure would appear. In this way, man was given another chance to fulfill his responsibility in the work of re-creation.

Abraham's Family

Ten generations and 400 years pass by in the providence of God. At the conclusion of this period, God chose his next central figure. His name was Abram and he was the son of Terah, an idol-maker.

Four hundred years is a long time. Four hundred years ago was around the year 1600. The King James version of the Bible had not been written, the *Mayflower* had not set sail. It was 400 years from Noah to Abraham, and it was a new era for mankind, as the year 2000 is when compared with the year 1600. Sometimes when we review the span of biblical history we skim through ages without considering the expanse of time that each age entails. It may appear to many that Noah came on Monday, Abraham on Wednesday, and Jesus over the weekend. We tend to lose sight of the lengthy duration between key providential moments in God's restoration plan. Thus, we lose sight of the magnitude of struggle and endurance within

God's course. The providential moment stands as a pinnacle moment born of hundreds of years of toil and pain replete with the blood sacrifice of generations of suffering antecedents. It arrives as the conclusion of an exhaustive course and stands out as a lonely island of opportunity, resolution, and change in a sea of violence and pain. It is the moment for which humanity hopes.

All suffering and pain can be erased, however, if only those select individuals fixed within that moment can understand the implications their actions will bear for past, present and future generations. All failures can be wiped away or, conversely, all unfulfilled responsibility can be extended into the future to be taken up by future generations in a prolonged course of darkness.

The failure of Ham in Noah's family was extended to those ensuing 10 generations over the next 400 years. Noah's family was to accomplish the foundation for the coming Christ. Ham's failure meant that this moment of opportunity would be extended to a future age, to be taken up by a future family. That family was Abraham's family. Thus, Abraham's mission would be to restore the lost Foundation of Faith, and then his sons would take up the mission to restore the Foundation of Substance.

God chose Abraham to fulfill Noah's mission. The 400 years and 10 generations between Noah's era and Abraham's suggests 10 forty-year periods. We see at the time of Moses, God indemnified a 40-day condition of spying through a single 40-year period of wandering in the wilderness. The 40-day flood judgment was lost by Ham's breach of faith with Noah. It was being indemnified by 10 generations each enduring a 40-year period reflective of the 40 years the Israelites wandered in the wilderness. This was the foundation of time upon which Abraham emerged.

In each age, the central figure was called by God to make a symbolic offering of faith. For Abel it was the animal sacrifice, for Noah it was building the ark. God calls Abraham to make a unique, three-stage offering of a dove and pigeon, a ram and goat and a heifer. Just as there was deep spiritual meaning related to Noah's releasing the raven and the three doves, Abraham's three-level offering is likewise replete with providential meaning.

As mentioned, the number three has a very frequent appearance related to the work of God. There were three central families in Genesis: Adam's, Noah's, and Abraham's. Abraham's offering of three stages is reflective of that providential sequence.

Abraham's offering came on the foundation of a very significant meeting with the King of Salem, Melchizedek. This meeting was the culmination of Abraham's battle with King Kedorlaomer. Kedorlaomer had taken Abraham's nephew Lot into captivity. After Abraham had recovered his nephew Lot, his household and all his possessions, Melchizedek shared bread and wine with Abraham and extended his blessing to him. This, of course, reflects the coming Christ, as explained in the seventh chapter of Hebrews.

In the same way, Abraham's three-stage offering reveals more than meets the eye. The offering of the dove and pigeon represents the Old Testament era. When John the Baptist baptized Jesus, he observed a dove descend and remain on Jesus. This indicated that Jesus was the fulfillment of the Law and Prophets and that the era of the Old Testament had come to a close. The next stage of Abraham's offering was the ram and goat. This represents the New Testament era, with Jesus standing as "the lamb of God" and referring to all believers as "his lambs." The final stage of Abraham's offering was the heifer. The heifer represents the wife or bride of Christ prepared for him at his return. "Heifer" symbolizes the wife. In **Judges 14:18**, Samson metaphorically refered to his wife as a "heifer."

Also, the three-level offering reflects that Abraham's family was the third family in the providence of restoration. All that was lost in Adam's family and Noah's family would be symbolically restored through Abraham's three-stage offering of faith.

Abraham Makes the Offering Recorded in Genesis 15:9–13

Each element to be offered is to be cut into two, with one half of the carcass placed opposite the other. Again, this portends significant spiritual meaning, and therefore it is extremely important that the central figure offer each element properly.

The cutting of the animal into two represents the dividing of good from evil. As we explained previously, fallen man stands in the midway position. Dominion over fallen man and his lineage is contested between God and a false god, both with a claim. God will, therefore, only relate to someone or something once it has been cleansed from Satan's claim. This is why God divided Adam into Cain and Abel, representing good and evil. Next, he asked Cain to come to him, but only through Abel. At the time of Noah, the earth was divided into two through the flood judgment. This dividing into two is fundamental to the sanctification process. Cutting the offering in two represents this very process of sanctification.

Also significant is the shedding of the bad blood. The satanic blood lineage is the lineage of death. Draining the blood from the offering, then, represents the need, ultimately, for fallen man to be cut off from Satan's bloodline in order to be fully saved.

For some inexplicable reason, Abraham does not offer the dove and pigeon in the proper manner. He did not cut the birds into two. Perhaps after offering the heifer, the ram and she-goat, Abraham felt that a mere dove and pigeon was not worth the effort. This was a huge mistake. We see evidence in terms of what takes place.

Genesis 15:11 reports that "birds of prey" descended upon the offering. This indicates that Satan was able to invade the offering. Also we see later that night that "a blazing torch appeared and passed between the pieces." **Genesis 15:17** The birds not being cut, however, precluded them from this meaningful holy phenomenon.

When Abraham fell asleep, a very deep and disturbing dread came upon him. It is at that moment that God revealed to Abraham that his descendants would be sojourners in a land not their own and that they would experience a life of slavery for a period of 400 years.

Remember, God built a 400-year foundation of time from Noah to Abraham. When Abraham stumbled in his offering in the Foundation of Faith, this 400-year period had to be restored through a condition of indemnity. That was why Abraham's descendants found themselves enslaved in Egypt for 400 years.

Abraham's mistake in the Foundation of Faith also bore implications for the Foundation of Substance. The positions of Cain and Abel were going to be re-created by Abraham's sons, Ishmael, the elder, and Isaac, the younger. Ishmael was the son of Sarah's maid-servant, Hagar. Isaac was the son of Sarah. However, we never witness the Cain and Abel dynamic between these two brothers. Instead, Ishmael and Hagar were sent away. From the line of Ishmael comes the world Islamic culture, just as from Isaac emerges the Judeo-Christian world culture.

Could conflicts in our world today be linked to an unfulfilled responsibility of old?

This first course of dispensation centering on Abraham came to an unfulfilled close. As we have seen in the past, when a central figure is unable to fulfill his role, his mission is extended to another central figure far into the future. In this case, however, God enacted a new twist to the providential pattern. He called Abraham again. Given Abraham's initial failure, new and more challenging requirements would be foisted upon him. Having stumbled in an offering of faith, God set up an alternative course that, if successful, could still provide a contemporary victory. It required Abraham to make an offering that far exceeded that of a mere dove and pigeon. God called Abraham to offer his only son Isaac on the altar of sacrifice.

In this way, God was shooting for the most unlikely of victories. It is like going for it on fourth and 20 from your own 1-yard line with the clock winding down in a game in which your team has only accumulated 30 yards of total offense.

God has to believe that the man who could not offer a dove and pigeon could now find the intestinal fortitude to offer his only son. God also had to have faith that Isaac would remain faithful throughout this test of faith. But how reasonable was it to expect that from Isaac, given the poor example of Ham's display of faith in his father Noah 400 years before? In fact, Isaac's show of faith, in that regard, would have to surpass even that of his father Abraham. After all, Isaac certainly had much more to lose as a result.

Generally, the odds favor the house in predicting man's faith. Satan will take those odds every time and lay down the bundle that man will not cover the point spread. In fact, Satan has become quite a "player" betting against the human capacity to maintain faith.

But this time, a stunning condition of faith would dramatically turn the providential table.

How shocked and broken-hearted Abraham must have been to receive from God those fateful instructions to put away his only son. To be called to do the work with his own hand must have made the task that much more unbearable. Isaac was so beloved by his father. The birth of Isaac was a most unexpected blessing for Abraham and Sarah. The name "Isaac" literally means "he laughs." This name was given because when Sarah was told that she would give birth at her advanced age, she laughed thinking it was ludicrous. The most unexpected blessing always becomes the most precious.

Abraham struggled for three days as he journeyed with Isaac to the region of Moriah, the place of offering. During this journey, Abraham did not let on to Isaac the purpose for going there. Perhaps

Abraham was wrestling with himself about when and how he would explain his intentions to his young son or whether he should explain anything at all. How could he? How could Isaac possibly understand? Perhaps he should just do the deed while Isaac quietly slept and in that way spare the boy undue torment.

Or better, perhaps, he should just turn around and forget the whole thing. Such was the course of Abraham on his way to Moriah.

Upon their arrival at the site of the offering, we can see that Isaac is still unaware of his impending fate.

Genesis 22:7–8

Isaac spoke up and said to his father Abraham, "Father?" "Yes, my son?" Abraham replied. "The fire and wood are here," Isaac said, "but where is the lamb for the burnt offering?" Abraham answered, "God himself will provide the lamb for the burnt offering, my son." And the two of them went on together.

Isaac wasn't aware that he was the burnt offering being provided by the Lord.

The Words have not been invented that can properly express the intensity and heart involved in the event that took place there. As Abraham lifted his son upon the altar, how deeply touched he must have been by the degree of innocence and trust displayed by his only son. How it must have reminded him, in that moment, of the perfect quality of Isaac's loving response to all his papa's love, always. How Abraham battled, utterly flinging himself over the precipice of self-denial as a thousand screaming voices came crashing down against him like angry waves upon the rocky shore, all echoes of his own mind pleading for him to stop.

It was not just an only son that Abraham was sacrificing, but rather was also the promise and potential contained within the one beating heart.

Genesis 15:4–5

". . . a son coming from your own body will be your heir." He took him outside and said, "Look up at the heavens and count the stars-if indeed you can count them." Then he said to him, "So shall your offspring be."

As Abraham raised the dagger, the sunlight sparkling on the blade, he placed his other hand across the neck of Isaac, turning his head away from the impending blow. Abraham could feel Isaac's soft pulse throb between his fingers and his gentle breathing that displayed no resistance to his fate.

This was the moment and the very circumstance that brought Abraham to a place of resonance with the heart of God. Unbeknownst to Abraham, in that moment he was feeling what God had always been feeling. God, who had created in order to see own Godly offspring, had lost all in the fall of man. He had been grieving alone all the while with a heart that was "filled with pain."

God had been relegated to a place of suffering through no fault of His own. Now He had found a man who, willingly and faithfully, was ready to join God in that same place of misery and lost love. God must have been so deeply moved to know that Abraham was willing to bid farewell to his life's greatest love, even without fully understanding, only because God had asked him.

Hebrews 11:17–19
By faith Abraham, when God tested him, offered Isaac as a sacrifice. He who had received the promises was about to sacrifice his one and only son, even though God had said to him, "It is through Isaac that your offspring will be reckoned." Abraham reasoned that God could raise the dead, and figuratively speaking, he did receive Isaac back from death.

It was not only Isaac who had resurrected, but Abraham as well. In that sense, in their unity of faith, they had become one, died, and were resurrected. Isaac was resurrected not as himself alone, but as Abraham, with Abraham's mission. In this way, though Abraham had failed initially in his mission, God could indemnify that failure and still work for a contemporary fulfillment without another prolongation of hundreds of years.

Together, they find a ram stuck in a thicket. The symbolic offering of faith is made. The Foundation of Faith is finally accomplished. Isaac now stands in Abraham's position as the new central figure and "father of faith." Just as Abraham was to have two sons, elder and younger, to carry out the Foundation of Substance, that destiny passes to Isaac.

Jacob and Esau

Had Abraham been successful in his initial offering of heifer, ram, goat, dove and pigeon, Abraham's younger and elder sons, Isaac and Ishmael, in the positions of Abel and Cain, would have carried out the Foundation of Substance. Instead, that mission was passed to Isaac's younger and elder sons, Jacob and Esau. Just as Cain was to come to God through the position of Abel, God instructed Rebecca that her elder son must "serve the younger."

The story of Jacob and Esau is significant, of course, because it is Jacob and Esau that accomplish the first Foundation to Receive the Messiah. Jacob's course becomes the model course reflected in Moses' course and in Jesus' course. Thus, the history of Israel from Jacob's victory leading up to the coming of Jesus will reflect the 2,000 years from Adam to Joseph recorded in Genesis.

The story of Jacob is significant in another sense in that biblical scholars generally take a dim view toward areas of Jacob's behavior. He appears to be a deceiver. He stole his brother's birthright. He fooled his father into giving him the elder son's blessing. You will find very few sermons extolling the virtues of Jacob.

On the other hand, Jacob stands as the root of the chosen nation and of the lineage that brings the Lord into this world. Perhaps we are taking a worldly view of Jacob and overlooking the deeper meaning of the significant events in his life. First, we should clear the record with regard to some of the common accusations leveled against Jacob.

Accusation 1: *Jacob stole his brother's birthright.*

Did he? Not so. Jacob did not "steal" his brother's birthright; he purchased it for the price of lentil stew and bread. Later Esau accused Jacob of "stealing" his birthright; however, it was Esau who initially approached Jacob and readily agreed to the terms of exchange.

Genesis 25:32–34

*"Look, I am about to die," Esau said. "What good is the birthright to me?" But Jacob said, "Swear to me first." So he swore an oath to him, **selling** his birthright to Jacob. Then Jacob gave Esau some bread and some lentil stew. He ate and drank, and then got up and left. **So Esau despised his birthright**.*

Accusation 2: *Jacob deceived his father Isaac.*

Jacob did? Again, not so. It was not Jacob's idea to replace Esau and, through surreptitious means, usurp his brother's blessing. It was his mother Rebecca's idea. Rebecca ordered Jacob to get the blessing. In fact, Jacob was dead-set against it and even protested!

Genesis 27:5–7

Now Rebekah was listening as Isaac spoke to his son Esau. When Esau left for the open country to hunt game and bring it back, Rebekah said to her son Jacob, "Look, I overheard your father say to your brother Esau, 'Bring me some game and prepare me some tasty food to eat, so that I may give you my blessing in the presence of the LORD before I die.'"

Genesis 27:8–13

*"Now, my son, listen carefully and **do what I tell you**: Go out to the flock and bring me two choice young goats, so I can prepare some tasty food for your father, just the way he likes it. Then take it to your father to eat, so that he may give you his blessing before he dies."*

*Jacob said to Rebekah his mother, "But my brother Esau is a hairy man, and I'm a man with smooth skin. What if my father touches me? I would appear to be tricking him and would bring down a curse on myself rather than a blessing." His mother said to him, "My son, **let the curse fall on me**. Just do what I say; go and get them for me."*

"Let the curse fall on me!" Rebecca is extremely confident, isn't she? In fact, no curse ever befell her. Her confidence was based upon what God had told her so many years before. She had a good reason to make sure the younger son received the blessing:

Genesis 25:22–23

The babies jostled each other within her, and she said, "Why is this happening to me?" So she went to inquire of the LORD. The LORD said to her, "Two nations are in your womb, and two peoples from within you will be separated; one people will be stronger than the other, and the older will serve the younger."

The Lord said the elder must serve the younger! One very important element of Jacob's model course is the aspect of mother-son cooperation. Rebecca set a fine standard in two major areas. She maintained faith in the vision that God gave her pertaining to Jacob's future even before Jacob was born. She remained faithful to that vision, and it was the reason she made sure that Jacob received the blessing. This pattern was followed by the mother of Moses, who helped to maintain Moses' allegiance to the God of Abraham, Isaac and Jacob during their 40 years of life together in Pharaoh's palace.

The second important implication of mother-son cooperation is that it prevents Cain from being able to murder Abel. Satan could not claim Jacob because of the foundation between Jacob and Rebecca. With this pattern, we will have a new measure to examine the circumstances affecting Jesus' ministry.

Jacob's Victory

It is also very essential to understand the basis of Jacob's victory. Jacob accomplished some very important objectives in his mission.

1. *Restored elder son's birthright*

He restored the elder son's birthright back to God's side. Notice that Esau's hunger was the basis of the process by which Jacob procures the birthright. Later, at the time of Jesus, Satan attempted to reclaim the birthright by the exact same circumstances. Jesus was fasting, is hungry and Satan tempted Jesus with bread. However, unlike Esau, Jesus valued the birthright as the first Son of God.

2. *Received the blessing from Isaac*

This was similar to the same moment that God received Abel's offering and rejected Cain's. This demonstration of vertical favor is what establishes the position of Abel and Cain. As soon as Jacob was established in the position of Abel, Esau found himself in the position of Cain. Thus, all the circumstances of Cain and Abel were re-created. This re-creation of circumstance is so that the new central figures can reverse through indemnity the failures of the past. This phenomenon could be referred to as "parallel providential periods". In this way, Esau became the "second coming" of Cain and was immediately filled with Cain's emotions. Esau attempted to murder Jacob.

3. *Mother-son cooperation*

Because of mother-son cooperation, Esau did not kill Jacob. Instead, Jacob fled to Haran for his 21-year course of exile and return.

4. *Won the blessing of the angel*

Of all the events of Jacob's course, this is the most important. Winning the blessing of the angel represents the restoration of man's dominion over the angel. Lost dominion to the angels is, of course, the core of the fall.

5. *Esau united with Jacob*

After years of separation, God told Jacob to return to his elder brother Esau. Jacob softened Esau's heart by sending ahead all manner of gifts. He literally poured out his wealth and blessing upon his brother. Esau was finally moved and released the angry heart of Cain. Jacob bowed before him and tells Esau "When I see your face, I see the face of God!"

As Esau embraces Jacob, the Foundation of Substance is achieved. The Foundation for the Messiah is firmly established centering on Jacob, now newly renamed: Israel.

Israel

Jacob became "Israel" and we see, in essence, the birth of the "chosen people" and nation. Sometimes, even Christians have had a vague notion of the "chosen nation." It was almost as if God had some sort of lottery and just reached in the bin of nations and, somehow, for undetermined reasons, just "picked" Israel.

Through reversing the conditions of the fall, Jacob established a family and tribal base that was separated from Satan. Therefore, upon that base, God could "intervene" and begin the effort to expand that foundation toward a nation, world, and cosmos.

Jacob, renamed Israel, had 12 sons. The tribe of Israel became 12 tribes of Israel. The 12 tribes became the foundation of the nation of Israel. From Israel through the line of Judah, 40 generation later, was born the new living Adam.

The significance of this foundation is clearly expressed in the words of Jesus:

Matthew 10:5–7
*These twelve Jesus sent out with the following instructions: "**Do not go among the Gentiles or enter any town of the Samaritans**. Go rather to the **lost sheep of Israel**. As you go, preach this message: 'The kingdom of heaven is near.'"*

Matthew 15:24
*He answered, "**I was sent only** for the lost sheep of the **House of Israel**."*

Chapter Six

Moses

The History of Israel from Moses to Jesus

Jacob successfully accomplished the Foundation for the Messiah. Thus, Israel would be the central tribe upon which the Christ, the new Adam, would appear. However, in actuality, the book of Genesis draws to a close with the tribe of Israel transplanted to a land not their own. Joseph, thrown into a well by his jealous brothers and left to die, had overcome those circumstances and rose in Egypt to a position second only to the Pharaoh. A great famine swept Canaan, forcing the family of Israel southward in search of grain. A most unlikely reunion ensued. Joseph and his brothers reconciled. These were the conditions that ultimately led the tribe of Israel to Egypt to begin a settlement that would last for 400 years.

Where was the messiah? If the foundation had been laid in Jacob's family, why did Christ not appear at that specific time?

The answer brings us back to Abraham and his initial offering of heifer, ram, goat, dove and pigeon. Abraham failed to properly offer the dove and pigeon. "The birds of prey" descending upon the offering indicate its unacceptable status to God. At that time God expressed His displeasure by revealing to Abraham that his descendants would have to endure a period of exile as "sojourners in a land not their own" lasting 400 years.

The requirement of 400 years was reflective of the 400 years from Noah's time to Abraham. In other words, because Abraham was called on the foundation of 10 generations and 400 years, his initial failure would require a subsequent course of indemnity equal to those 400 years upon which he stood.

At the conclusion of this period, God begins a new dispensation for the Israelites, now a teeming population under the bondage of an oppressive Egyptian regime. The new central figure of that dispensation is Moses.

Moses is not the Christ. Why, then, does a Moses appear and a new dispensation begin if the foundation for Christ already exists via Jacob's victory?

Moses' unique mission is to expand Israel's foundation from the tribal to the national level. During their 400 years of bondage, the satanic world had advanced from a world of tribes to a world of nations. The tribes of Israel were enslaved under the dominant sovereignty of an oppressive national regime. This territory and nation had not received the providential sanctification to be separated from Satan. Thus, God had to lead the tribes of Israel out of Egypt and into a land from which a national foundation could be erected. This land had to, likewise, be conditionally separated from Satan. Moses' mission was to build this sanctified nation.

The path and principle of sanctification is the same on the individual, family, tribal, national and cosmic levels. It involves the course to reverse the conditions that transformed a living Adam into a dead Adam. It is the dispensation of establishing a foundation of faith and a foundation of substance. Thus, Moses' course to sanctify a national Foundation for the Messiah will be an extension of Jacob's course to establish the tribal Foundation for the Messiah. As a result, Moses' course will reflect Jacob's course. In the same way, Jesus' course, as the world's messiah, will be an extension of Moses' national course. As a result, Jesus' course will reflect Moses' course in the same way Moses' course reflects Jacob's.

This means that God has established Jacob, Moses and Jesus under a common plan and purpose. It is why Jesus said, "The Son of Man can do nothing of his own accord but that which he sees the Father doing," and why Moses had predicted that "God will raise up from among your own brothers a prophet like me. . .you must listen to him."

The evidence of this link is expressed in the phenomenon of the similarity of events and circumstances faced by Jacob, Moses, and Jesus. God set up this pattern in order to help the chosen people recognize their messiah when he came.

Parallels Linking Jacob, Moses and Jesus

We can find several examples of events that are parallel in the lives of jacob, Moses and Jesus. Each was confronted with a test of faith from God:

In **Genesis 32:25–28** at the ford of Jabbok, Jacob wrestles the angel and subjugates him. At the fall of man, the angel Lucifer overcame Adam and usurped his position. Jacob reversed that condition through his victory over the angel. This victory is implicit within the name "Israel."

In **Exodus 4:24-26**, Moses endured a similar battle with God when God attempted to kill Moses. Zipporah took a flint knife and cut off the foreskin of her son and touched Moses' feet with it. Then "the Lord let him alone."

In **Matthew 4:1–11**, Jesus was led into the wilderness to be tempted three times by Satan. Jesus, as messiah for the world, subjugated the angel (Satan) and thus stood with the authority, on earth, to forgive sin and lead humanity into the Kingdom of Heaven.

The next important parallel involves the flesh and spirit that was lost to Satan at the fall. Satan claimed the spirit and body of man through the condition of the fall. As sinners we are born in sin. We acquire our fallen nature through our defiled spirit and body that are linked to the dead Adam.

In **Genesis 25:34**, Jacob made a dramatic recovery of the birthright from Esau. By offering "bread and lentils," which symbolized the defiled spirit and body, Jacob brought the birthright back to God's side. This was the internal value of "Israel." Israel carried a condition by which God could return a living Adam born in spirit and body under God.

In **Exodus 16:13**, God fed the people with manna and quail, also symbolizing flesh and spirit. Through this provision the rebellious fallen nature of the people was quelled and they, in Cain's position to Moses, were able to unite with Moses who stood in Abel's position. This served to reverse the fallen nature on the national level.

In **John 6:49,53**, Jesus said, "Your fathers ate the manna in the wilderness and they died. . . . I say to you, unless you eat the flesh of the Son of man and drink his blood, you have no life in you."

In this way, Jesus indicated this important condition came on the foundation of Moses. However, Moses was merely foreshadowing the substance of Christ. Jesus emphasized that we need to be linked to Jesus in flesh and in spirit in order to reverse and remove our fallen nature. Eating his flesh and drinking his blood restores our birthright.

Another interesting parallel involves the natural body.

In **Genesis 50:3** Jacob's body was sanctified through a 40-day condition of ritual purification. At the time of Moses, a dispute between the archangel Michael and Satan over the body of Moses is reported in **Jude 1:9**. At the time of Jesus, in **Matthew 28:11–15**, a dispute over his natural body likewise ensued. The chief priests claimed the disciples stole his body, with the disciples testifying to Christ's resurrection.

There are other important parallels of events, periods and circumstances.

When Jacob began his journey, in **Genesis 31:22**, from Haran to Canaan, there was a three-day period before Laban was notified of his absence. At the time of Moses, in **Exodus 5:3**, there was a similar three-day period before Pharaoh and his army began to pursue Moses and the Israelites on their way to Canaan. This foreshadowed the worldwide journey into spiritual Canaan through the resurrected Christ that was preceded by Jesus' three-day period in the tomb.

Jacob had 12 sons and 70 family members. Moses had 12 tribes and 70 elders. Jesus had 12 apostles and 70 disciples.

Another very significant parallel is the common pattern of mother and son cooperation. A perverse mother and son cooperation took place at the fall. Eve's sin established Satan as god and ruler, and this bore its first fruit when Cain killed Abel. Thus, in the reverse pattern of indemnity, God's providence advances when the central figure establishes a partnership with his mother

In **Genesis 27:5–10, 42–45**, we see that Rebecca was instrumental in establishing Jacob in the Abel position. She was told by God before Jacob's birth that the "elder must serve the younger." She went to unprecedented lengths to make sure that her vision was realized.

Likewise, Moses' mother, in **Exodus 2:2**, was the key figure in Moses' rise. She protected him. Pharaoh had ordered all boys born to be thrown into the Nile. Later, by God's design, she was able to raise Moses in the Pharaoh's palace for 40 years. During that time she educated him well in his Hebrew heritage.

In a very similar way, Mother Mary protected Jesus who, as an infant, was under the threat of death as Moses had been. Together, Joseph and Mary took Jesus and fled to Egypt.

Jesus' return from Egypt to Galilee reflects Moses' journey from Egypt to the promised land of Canaan and Jacob's journey from Haran.

There are many more examples we could cite. All of these parallels indicate a common thread of purpose and providence. Whenever the people called by God fulfill their responsibility to reverse through indemnity the conditions of the fall, God's providence advances toward its ultimate fulfillment.

Thus, Moses' mission can best be understood within the matrix of Jacob's course. We can see on the national level the hand of God structuring His providence toward the re-creation of circumstances that require a central figure to reverse the conditions of the fall, that is, on the one hand, restoring faith in God's word and, on the other, reversing the fallen nature through the relation of younger and elder.

This is the pattern of Foundation of Faith and Foundation of Substance that stands as the inner workings of the Foundation for the Messiah. In other words, no matter what level—family, tribe, nation or world—the pattern is the same. This is the reason the course of Jacob, Moses and Jesus all reflect one another.

Moses' Course

The providence of restoration led by Moses was the extension of the Foundation for the Messiah established by Jacob in Abraham's family. This still required Moses himself to lay the Foundation for the Messiah by restoring through indemnity the Foundation of Faith and the Foundation of Substance. As God's providence expands to greater social levels, new circumstances and unique requirements emerge that are specific to that social level.

Although the Foundation for the Messiah has unique elements on each level of the family, tribe, nation and world, we will still be able to observe the common thread of the providential task to reverse the wrongful conditions of Adam's fall. That is, to establish on each level the Foundation of Faith and the Foundation of Substance.

At the conclusion of the 400 years of slavery resulting from Abraham's initial mistake, Moses was called as the central figure to restore the Foundation of Faith. A Foundation of Faith had to be laid anew to begin the course to return to the promised land of Canaan.

As the descendant of Jacob, who had established the Foundation for the Messiah, Moses could serve as the central figure for the national-level dispensation. Moses also stood on the foundation that Joseph had laid when he entered Egypt. Joseph's life, too, foreshadowed that of Jesus. As the son of Rachel (Jacob's wife representing the Abel side) and the younger brother of the sons of Leah (representing the Cain side), Joseph stood in the position of Abel.

He narrowly escaped his older brothers' scheme to kill him, and when he was sold off to merchants, he entered Egypt as a slave. Yet he rose to a rank second only to the pharaoh by the age of 30. Eventually, his brothers and father came to Egypt and humbly bowed before him, fulfilling a prophetic dream he had as a child.

Based upon this providential victory, the Israelites entered Egypt and commenced a period of struggle as predicted by God to Abraham. Joseph's course foreshadowed the course that Jesus would later walk. In the same way Joseph emerged in Egypt, Jesus was born into a satanic world, endured a path of hardships, and emerged as the King of Kings at the age of thirty. He was to bring all of humanity, including his forefathers, into submission, cut all their ties to the satanic world, and restore them to God's realm.

Moses' Offering as the Central Figure in the Foundation of Faith

Moses was in a different position when compared to earlier central figures entrusted with laying the Foundation of Faith. Moses did not need to make a symbolic offering such as the animal sacrifice of Abel or Noah's task of building the ark. Rather, he could restore the Foundation of Faith through obedience to God's Word over a prescribed time period related to the dispensation of the number 40 (for the separation from Satan).

After the sin of Adam, man fell into total depravity and darkness. God would not send His direct word into a realm so controlled by Satan. Instead, God called for symbolic offerings from man, such as animal sacrifices. These "conditional objects" were symbolic substitutes for the Word.

The historical period from Adam's family to Abraham's family (concluding with Joseph), documented in Genesis, is the era in which sacrifices, as conditional objects, had been offered. Centering upon the victory in Abraham's family, however, a fundamental separation from Satan was accomplished. We can see evidence of that separation in **Luke 16:19–31**. Jesus refers to "Abraham's side," which is separated from hell by a great chasm in the spirit world.

Thus, after the Israelites complete the 400-year slavery course, a new providential era begins. We refer to that new era as the Old Testament Age. It will feature a return of God's Word to man upon the sanctified base established by Israel.

Moses and the Foundation of Substance

We recall that Abel made the symbolic offering from the position of a parent in place of Adam and was thereby entitled to stand in the providential position of the younger son in relation to Cain in establishing the Foundation of Substance. Likewise, Moses stood in the dual positions of parent and younger son. When he restored through indemnity the Foundation of Faith, he would be in the position of Adam, or parent. When he restored the Foundation of Substance, he would be in the Abel position, or younger son position, as a forerunner of Jesus, "the everlasting Father."

Once Moses had established the position of Abel, the Israelites, standing in the position of Cain, were supposed to fulfill the national indemnity condition to reverse and remove the fallen nature through their obedience to Moses. By doing so, they would establish the national Foundation of Substance. In other words, the model course for the Israelites' relationship with Moses is patterned after Esau's relationship with Jacob. In the same way the Foundation for the Messiah was accomplished on the tribal level by the union of Jacob and Esau, Moses' relationship with the Israelites would be the determining factor in extending that tribal foundation to the national level.

Moses Accomplishes the Foundation of Faith

For Moses to become the central figure to restore the Foundation of Faith and be qualified to lead the Israelites out of Egypt, he had to establish a condition of faith via the number 40, which related to the separation from Satan. To achieve this purpose, Moses was brought into the Pharaoh's palace, the center of the satanic world, where he spent 40 years, as documented by **Acts 7:23.**

While in the palace, Moses was educated by his mother, who, unknown to anyone, was hired to be his nurse. She secretly imparted to him the consciousness and pride of his heritage. Despite the comforts of palace life, Moses maintained unshakable loyalty and fidelity to the lineage of Israel. After 40 years, he left the palace. **Hebrews 11:24–25** testifies to his successful condition of faith:

By faith Moses, when he had grown up, refused to be known as the son of Pharaoh's daughter, choosing rather to share ill-treatment with the people of God than to enjoy the fleeting pleasures of sin.

Hence, during the 40 years of his life in the pharaoh's palace, Moses fulfilled the dispensation of 40 for the separation from Satan and thereby restored the Foundation of Faith.

Moses Attempts to Establish the Foundation of Substance

When Moses accomplished the Foundation of Faith, he established himself in the position of Abel for the Foundation of Substance. The Israelites, who were in the position of Cain, would have to follow and obey Moses in faith. By doing so, they would fulfill the national indemnity condition to reverse and remove the fallen nature and lay the national Foundation of Substance. The Israelites were to lay the Foundation of Substance by following Moses from the time they left Egypt until they entered the blessed land of Canaan. During that course, Satan would try to deter them by inflaming their fallen nature against Moses in the same way Cain was inflamed against Abel and Esau against Jacob.

Remember the fallen nature entails four major components:

1. Lucifer could not love Adam from God's viewpoint.
2. Lucifer left his proper position and could not receive God's Word from Adam.
3. Lucifer reversed dominion over Adam.
4. Lucifer multiplied evil conditions.

Thus, the Israelites in reversing the fallen nature and separating from Satan, must maintain the following standards:

1. They must love Moses from God's viewpoint.

2. They must receive God's Word through Moses.
3. They must not judge Moses and thereby reverse dominion.
4. They must multiply goodness in obedience to Moses.

The providence to establish the Foundation of Substance started in a very unusual and dramatic way. Seeing one of his brethren being mistreated by an Egyptian taskmaster, Moses was incited by his burning love for his people; he struck and killed the man.

The Israelites, upon witnessing Moses' act of killing the Egyptian, should have recognized that although Moses had been in the palace of pharaoh for all his 40 years, his heart remained with the God of Abraham, Isaac and Jacob. They should have been deeply inspired by his love for Israel, as was God.

Had they felt this way, they would have respected Moses, trusted him and followed him faithfully. Then, through Moses' leadership, God would have brought them directly into the land of Canaan, where they would have established the Foundation of Substance.

In fact, they would not have had to cross the Red Sea or wander through the Sinai wilderness, but would have taken the straight route to Canaan by way of the land of the Philistines. That ideal course could have been as short as 21 days, and would have shown relationship to Jacob's 21 years of exile and return from Haran.

We can see, 40 years later, when finally the people were ready to follow Moses, God led them toward the much more lengthy route. **Exodus 13:17** indicates God's reasons for doing this:

When Pharaoh let the people go, God did not lead them by way of the land of the Philistines, although that was near; for God said, "Lest the people repent when they see war, and return to Egypt."

This longer course was clearly not His first choice. God led the people across the Red Sea and in a detour through the wilderness because He had reason to believe they might turn faithless and return to Egypt without completing their journey.

Sadly, in this first attempt to lead the people toward the promised land, the Israelites were unresponsive to Moses.

Exodus 2:13–15

When he went out the next day, behold, two Hebrews were struggling together; and he said to the man that did the wrong, "Why did you strike your fellow?" He answered, "Who made you a prince and a judge over us? Do you mean to kill me as you killed the Egyptian?" Then Moses was afraid, and thought, "Surely the thing is known." When Pharaoh heard of it, he sought to kill Moses.

Thus, this first effort to establish the national-level Foundation for the Messiah came to an unceremonious close. Moses lost everything. He lost his position in the palace and he failed to achieve his providential position in front of Israel. Just as Jacob had his father's blessing but had to flee to Haran to escape Esau's wrath, Moses under the threat of death quietly stole away into exile in the Midian wilderness.

The Second Attempt to Establish the National Foundation for the Messiah

When the first course to establish the national Foundation to Receive the Messiah had failed, Satan claimed the first Foundation of Faith established by Moses' 40 years of faith in Pharaoh's palace.

Therefore, to establish a second national Foundation of Faith, Moses had to renew a condition of faith related to the number 40. This would restore through indemnity his lost 40 years in the palace.

The Second Attempt to Establish the Foundation of Faith

This was the purpose of Moses' 40-year exile in the wilderness of Midian. During this 40-year period (confirmed by **Acts 7:30**), the Israelites' living conditions in Egypt became even more miserable. This was the penalty for their disbelief in Moses.

Moses went through this second dispensation of 40 years of faith to establish the condition of indemnity for the separation from Satan. There he restored the Foundation of Faith needed in order to begin the second attempt to erect the national Foundation for the Messiah. God then appeared before Moses and said:

Exodus 3:7–10
"I have seen the affliction of my people who are in Egypt, and have heard

their cry because of their taskmasters; I know their sufferings, and I have
come down to deliver them out of the hand of the Egyptians, and to bring
them up out of that land to a good and broad land, a land flowing with
milk and honey, to the place of the Canaanites . . . and now, behold, the
cry of the people of Israel has come to me, and I have seen the oppression
with which the Egyptians oppress them. Come, I will send you to Pharaoh
that you may bring forth my people, the sons of Israel, out of Egypt."

The Second Attempt to Establish the Foundation of Substance

Once Moses restored the Foundation of Faith in the wilderness of Midian, he returned to the providential position of Abel. Thus, as before, if the Israelite people in the position of Cain believe in and follow Moses faithfully, they will be able to enter the promised land. In so doing, they would fulfill the indemnity condition to reverse and remove the fallen nature and as a result, accomplish the Foundation of Substance.

Think of Moses' real situation. He was 80 years old. He had just spent the last 40 years of his life taking care of goats and the like. I'm sure Moses must have felt that his better years were well behind him and that now he was to merely live out his remaining years in the Midian wilderness.

Sometimes, I'm sure, he reminisced on those "days gone by," back in the day when he was in his prime in the palace at the age of 40. Why, he was even in line to be the next pharaoh at the time.

"Now, look at you!" I'm sure he must have said to himself. If he even attempted to convey to his Midian friends his illustrious past, they would just laugh at him and call him a crazy old man. So after several attempts to explain his life, he was just quiet and tried to find solace in simply tending to his animals.

Sometimes, though, when he was alone with his flock on a high hill, he would still whisper to the Midian wind, "I could have become pharaoh. . ."

How unexpected it was for Moses that he would be called to Horeb and from within a burning bush God would instruct him to carry out the undone task of 40 years before. Even Moses recognized that people might doubt him if all he could cite was a voice from within a burning bush. He asked God for authoritative signs that would compel the people to follow him.

In Moses' first effort to lead Israel 40 years before, God worked the dispensation to start the first national course to restore Canaan when Moses killed the Egyptian. This was a "sign" to the Israelites that although Moses had been in the Pharaoh's palace for 40 years, his heart belonged to the God of Abraham. This course was aborted, however, when the people distrusted Moses.

In this next dispensation to start the second national course, God granted the Israelites the three signs and ten plagues.

The three signs that God provided for Moses and Aaron to perform foreshadowed the work of Jesus. The first sign was Moses' staff turning into a snake. God commanded Moses to cast down his staff, and it became a snake. **Exodus 4:3–9** When Aaron later performed this sign before the pharaoh at Moses' command, the pharaoh summoned his magicians and had them cast down their staffs, which likewise turned into snakes, but Aaron's snake devoured their serpents in **Exodus 7:10–12**. This sign symbolically foreshadowed that Jesus would come as the Savior and destroy the satanic world.

The second sign was given when God commanded Moses to put his hand into his bosom. When he withdrew his hand from his cloak it had become leprous. Then God commanded him to put his hand into his bosom a second time. This time when he removed his hand it had been healed. **Exodus 4:6–7** This miracle foreshadowed symbolically that Jesus, as the next Adam, would perform the work of redemption.

In the third sign, God told Moses to pour water from the Nile on the ground and it would turn to blood. **Exodus 4:9** Water symbolizes the unrighteous, spiritually dead people.

Revelation 17:15
"The waters that you saw, where the harlot is seated, are people, multitudes, nations and tongues."

Also in **Jude 1:13**, we see that unrighteous men are called "wild waves of the sea." Therefore, "waters" is a symbol of unrighteous, unsanctified people. Water being transformed into blood, therefore, represents the transformation from death to life.

The symbolism of this sign lies in water, an inorganic substance, being transformed into blood, the substance of life. Thus, this sign foreshadowed that Jesus and the Holy Spirit would come and resurrect fallen humanity, devoid of life, to become the living children of God.

God had Moses and Aaron perform these three signs in order to fulfill symbolic indemnity conditions upon which Jesus and the Holy Spirit would later come to Israel as the True Parents to give rebirth to all humanity as their children. They would restore the original True Family ideal that had been lost to Satan.

In a similar way, through the 10 plagues, God had Moses liberate the Israelites from Egypt. This, too, foreshadowed that in the future Jesus would come with miracles and signs to save God's chosen people. The most telling of all the 10 plagues was the last, the plague of death. In this plague, we see the mighty saving power of the lamb's blood causing the spirit of death to "pass over" that household so sanctified.

When Jacob was suffering 21 years of hardship in Haran, his uncle Laban cheated Jacob 10 times and did not give him his due wages. **Genesis 31:7** Likewise, in Moses' course, which was patterned after Jacob's course, the Pharaoh not only continued to afflict the Israelites beyond the preordained time period, he also deceived them 10 times with the false promise that he would release them. As punishment for this, God struck the Pharaoh with the 10 plagues.

Finally, after the 10 plagues and with the death of pharaoh's own son, he relented and allowed the Israelite to leave under the pretense of a three-day journey into the wilderness to make sacrificial offerings.

When the Israelites witnessed these miracles, they came to believe that Moses was truly sent by God as their leader. They believed and followed Moses, the Abel figure who had established the national Foundation of Faith. As a result, the Israelites could begin the providence to unite with Moses from the position of Cain. If they could have remained united with Moses, reversing and removing the fallen nature all the way to Canaan, then the national Foundation of Substance would be accomplished.

Thus, the Israelites began a wilderness course following Moses as their leader. This time God directed them away from the land of the Philistines and toward the lengthier course of crossing the Red Sea (or Reed Sea).

The Israelites, who numbered some 600,000 according to the Bible, departed from Rameses on the fifteenth day of the first month by the Hebrew calendar. **Exodus 12:37, Numbers 33:3** After three days, they arrived at their encampment at Succoth. It was then that God gave them the grace of a pillar of cloud by day and a pillar of fire by night to guide their way. **Exodus 13:21** The pillar of cloud that led the Israelites by day represented the coming messiah, Jesus, who would one day lead the people of Israel on worldwide level. The pillar of fire by night represented the Bride of Christ as the Holy Spirit, who would guide them from the position of True Mother.

At the shore of the Red Sea, God commanded Moses to stretch out his staff and part the waters; then he led the Israelites across on dry ground. The Egyptians chasing them in chariots were drowned when the waters closed up and engulfed them. **Exodus 14:21**

After crossing the Red Sea, the Israelites' first stop was at the bitter waters of Marah in the desert of Shur. **Exodus 15:22–27** Here the people grumbled, for they were thirsty and the waters of Marah were undrinkable. Moses took a piece of wood that was given him by the Lord and threw it into the bitter waters. Suddenly the waters were transformed to sweet drinkable water. This miracle clearly foreshadows the work of Christ. It also reflects the third miracle of turning the waters into blood that was performed for the pharaoh.

After Marah, they came to Elim, where there were 12 springs and 70 palm trees. This, of course, reflects the foundations of Jacob, Moses and Jesus. Jacob had 12 sons and 70 elders, Moses, 12 tribes and 70 elders, and Jesus, 12 apostles, and 70 disciples.

The Israelites next arrived at the wilderness of Sin on the fifteenth day of the second month. From then until the day they arrived at habitable land, God fed them with manna and quail. **Exodus 16:13–35**

The Israelites then left the wilderness of Sin and arrived at Rephidim. Once again, the people complained because of a lack of drinking water. God commanded Moses to strike the rock at Horeb. He promised that water would spring forth from it. Moses struck the rock and water poured forth. **Exodus 17:6**

1 Corinthians 10:4 affirms, "the rock was Christ." Accordingly, the water from the rock foreshadowed that Christ would save all humanity with the water of life. This is why Jesus would say, "Whoever drinks of the water that I shall give him will never thirst".**John 4:14** The two tablets of stone Moses received on Mt. Sinai symbolized Jesus and his would-be Bride. The rock, which was the root of the tablets of stone, symbolized God. When Moses struck the rock and gave the people water, this laid the foundation upon which Moses could receive the tablets of stone and build the Ark of the Covenant and the Tabernacle.

Later, the Amalekites came and attacked the Israelites at Rephidim. Joshua led the Israelite army against them. Whenever Moses held up his hands, the Israelites prevailed; however, when Moses allowed his hands to drop, the Israelites would falter.

Aaron and Hur had Moses sit on a pile of stones and held his hands up on the left and the right. As a result, Joshua was able to lead the Israelites to victory over the king of the Amalekites and his troops. **Exodus 17:10–13**

This was also very portentous of Christ's role on the world level. Joshua symbolized the believers; the Amalekites symbolized the satanic world. Aaron and Hur represented Jesus and the Holy Spirit. Aaron and Hur holding up Moses' hands and empowering Joshua to defeat the Amalekites foreshadowed that faithful people who worship the Trinity of God the Father, the Son, and the Holy Spirit, will defeat any satanic force that confronts them.

The Providence to Receive the Tabernacle

After their victory over the Amalekites, the Israelites journeyed to the wilderness of Sinai, arriving there in the third month since their departure from Egypt. **Exodus 19:1** God called Moses to the mountain and revealed to him His vision and intention for this new nation he was seeking to build:

Exodus 19:3–6

Then Moses went up to God, and the LORD called to him from the mountain and said, "This is what you are to say to the house of Jacob and what you are to tell the people of Israel: 'You yourselves have seen what I did to Egypt, and how I carried you on eagles' wings and brought you to myself. Now if you obey me fully and keep my covenant, then out of all nations you will be my treasured possession. Although the whole earth is mine, you will be for me a kingdom of priests and a holy nation.' These are the words you are to speak to the Israelites."

So Moses returned to his people and set before them all the words that God commanded him to speak. The Israelites, upon hearing, fully affirmed their commitment to follow the words of the Lord.

The 24th chapter of Exodus records a significant new providence at this point that unfolds within the macro providence of the second course of national restoration. God instructs Moses to come to Mt. Sinai with the 70 elders. Only Moses was called to the summit of Mt. Sinai, where he remained for 40 days and nights. During the 40 day period, Moses received God's instructions for the construction of the ark of the covenant and the tabernacle. **Exodus 25:10-22, 26: 1-37** When the 40-day period was over, Moses received two tablets of stone, inscribed by the finger of God with the Ten Commandments. **Exodus 31:18** The Israelites were to receive the tablets of stone, the tabernacle and the ark of the covenant.

However, when Moses came down from Mt. Sinai with the two tablets of stone and went before the Israelites, he found them worshipping a golden calf that had been fashioned by Aaron at the request of the people. Foolishly, they proclaimed that this was the god who had led them out of Egypt. Moses' anger burned hot when he saw this. He threw down the tablets of stone and broke them at the foot of the mountain. **Exodus 32:1–19**

What did this all mean? As we have been able to observe in the entire course of Moses, virtually every event is declaring a deep spiritual meaning beyond the surface of practical circumstances. The providence to bring the tablets of stone, the ark of the covenant and the tabernacle is very important and directly reflective of the very coming of Christ that would fulfill their destiny.

It was previously explained that if Adam and Eve had not fallen and had become perfected, they would have stood as the incarnations of the Word. Instead, they lost God's Word when they received the false word of the archangel.

Moses received the two tablets inscribed with the Word, the Ten Commandments, at the conclusion of a 40-day period for separation from Satan. This represented the symbolic restoration of Adam and Eve as incarnations of the Word. Thus, the two tablets symbolized restored Adam and Eve.

Who are to be the restored Adam and Eve? This is, of course, the coming Christ, the next Adam, and his bride who will stand as the True Parents of rebirth. In **Revelation 2:17**, Christ is symbolized by a white stone, and in **1 Corinthians 10:4**, Paul declares, "The Rock was Christ."

The tabernacle, likewise, is a symbol of Christ. In **John 2:19–21** Jesus compared his body with the temple. Likewise, Paul tells us that believers are "God's temple," in **1 Corinthians 3:16**. The temple was a precursor of Jesus who stood as the substantial temple.

The tabernacle was a precursor of the temple. If the Israelites had quickly united with Moses 40 years previously and had accomplished the dispensation in one course, then they would have immediately built the temple in Canaan. Because the providence had been prolonged, however, God set up the tabernacle as an interim procedure. Like the temple, the tabernacle was a representation of Jesus. When God commanded Moses to build the tabernacle, He said, "And let them make me a sanctuary, that I may dwell in their midst." In the same way, Jesus was Emmanuel in substance. "Emmanuel," of course, means "God with us."

The value of the tabernacle was incalculable. It was composed, as would be the temple, of an outer holy place and an inner "most holy place" representing the spirit and body of Christ. Within the most holy place would be the ark of the covenant that contained the two tablets of stone.

It was as if Christ himself were in their midst leading them in the wilderness. It meant that even if Moses faltered in faith, whoever revered the tabernacle containing the ark of the covenant and the two tablets of stone would become the new Moses to lead Israel toward its destiny.

In fact, we can see evidence of God's intent for the coming Christ in the way that God instructed and trained the Israelites in their conduct toward the tabernacle. For example, they were to camp around the tabernacle, three tribes on each side. **Numbers 2:1–31** This foreshadowed that Christ was to be the center of the nation. Whenever God placed a cloud above the tabernacle, it meant the Israelites were to encamp at that location. Whenever the cloud lifted the Israelites were to set out. **Numbers 9:15–20** This was God's way to train the Israelites to follow Christ unequivocally. For this reason, Moses implored his people about the coming Christ,

Deuteronomy 18:15; Acts 3:21–22

The Lord your God will raise up for you a prophet like me from among your own people; you must listen to everything he tells you.

In order for the Israelites to receive the messiah, they had to establish a Foundation of Faith and a Foundation of Substance. This same principle holds true toward receiving a representation of the messiah, the tabernacle. God would not just hand over the two tablets of stone, the ark of the covenant and the tabernacle, all symbols of

Christ, without the Israelites first establishing the proper condition to receive them.

This is why Moses found himself called to the top of Mt. Sinai for a period of 40 days of faith. It was also why the Israelites would not be able to receive the tablets of stone, the ark and the tabernacle unless they could unite with Moses, their "Jacob," as Esau had united with Jacob.

They clearly failed in the first attempt to receive the tabernacle. When Moses saw their faithless revel and worship of the graven image of a golden calf, he threw down the two tablets of stone. Moses recognized that there was no foundation to receive them. This would also serve as a warning to future generations of Israelites that they would have to fulfill a proper condition of faith in order to receive the coming messiah.

The Second Attempt to Receive the Tabernacle

God appeared again to Moses and told him to carve another pair of stone tablets identical to the first pair, promising that He would inscribe the Ten Commandments on them again. Moses presented himself before God on the mountain and this time fasted, without food or water, for 40 days. God instructed Moses to write on the tablets the words of the covenant, the Ten Commandments. **Exodus 34:1, 27–28** Moses took these tablets and went before the Israelites again. This time they honored Moses. In obedience to his directions, they built the ark of the covenant and constructed the tabernacle.

By remaining faithful while Moses was fasting on the mountain, and then obeying his instructions to build the tabernacle, the Israelites fulfilled the indemnity condition to remove the fallen nature. This laid the Foundation of Substance for the tabernacle, and hence the foundation for the tabernacle.

The tabernacle was built by the first day of the first month of the second year. **Exodus 40:17** However, in order to complete the Foundation of Substance in this second course of national restoration, the Israelites, as was mentioned earlier, would have to remain faithful all the way until they entered the promised land.

In fact, from now on, God will be much more discerning and strict with His people when they start to deviate from His Word. As mentioned earlier, with the receiving of God's Word for the first time since the fall, mankind entered a new providential era centering on the covenant with God's Word. This providential era we refer to as the Old Testament Era.

On the twentieth day of the second month of the second year, the Israelites set out from the wilderness of Sinai, arrayed in formation around the tabernacle and led by the pillar of cloud. **Numbers 10:11–12** Yet before long, they began to complain about their hardships and murmured against Moses. We can see God's heightened strictness displayed as he destroyed their camp.

However, even after that display of God's burning wrath, the Israelites did not repent. They continued to complain, lamenting that they had nothing to eat but manna. They were resentful toward Moses and longed for the fruit, meat, vegetables and luxuries of Egypt. **Numbers 11:1–6** Thus, the Israelites failed to maintain the second Foundation of Substance for the tabernacle.

This would require a third attempt for the tabernacle. This is why God called them to do another faith condition centering on the number 40 before they could enter the promised land. This was to be accomplished through the 40-day period of spying in the promised land.

The Third Attempt to Receive the Tabernacle
Although Satan defiled the second foundation for the tabernacle, Moses' faith and devotion to the tabernacle remained unchanging. Therefore, the tabernacle stood firmly upon the Foundation of Faith that Moses had laid, while the Israelites still stood upon the foundation of having drunk the water from the rock at Rephidim.

The rock, as mentioned earlier, was the root of the tablets of stone, which was at the center of the tabernacle. Upon this foundation, the Israelites commenced yet another dispensation of 40 for separating from Satan. By obeying Moses, who still honored the tabernacle, they were to restore through indemnity the foundation for the tabernacle in their third attempt. The 40-day mission to spy out the land of Canaan was given as the condition to achieve this.

When they returned, all the spies except Joshua and Caleb gave faithless reports:

Numbers 13:28, 32–33
"The people who dwell in the land are strong, and the cities are fortified and very large . . . [it] is a land that devours its inhabitants; and all the people that we saw in it are men of great stature . . . and we seemed to ourselves like grasshoppers, and so we seemed to them."

As a result of these faithless reports, the people were stirred up against Moses. They sought to find a new leader who would take them back to Egypt.

This was a seminal moment in the history of Israel. It should be noted as a great lesson for all that it was at the very borderline of victory that Israel stumbled and fell.

Thus, Israel could not enter the promised land and build the temple at that prescribed moment. The Israelites had refused to receive the tabernacle properly three times. The consequences of that failure meant that the second course to establish the national Foundation for the Messiah had come to an unfulfilled close.

The Third Attempt to Establish the National Foundation for the Messiah

When the Israelites turned traitorous after hearing the report of the faithless spies, the second national course ended in failure. Moses had established that Foundation of Faith for the second course through his 40 years of faith in the wilderness of Midian.

As a result of the failure of the mission to spy out the land, the people had to wander in the wilderness for 40 years, one year for each day of the 40-day spy mission, until they returned to Kadesh-barnea. **Numbers 14:31–34**

The Third Attempt to Establish the Foundation of Faith

For Moses, this 40-year period was to re-establish the lost Foundation of Faith for the third course. Moses honored the tabernacle with faith and loyalty throughout the entire 40 years of wandering in the wilderness. By the time he returned to Kadesh-barnea, he had completed the Foundation of Faith for the third national course. Accordingly, he once again secured the position of Abel for the Foundation of Substance.

The Third Attempt to Establish the Foundation of Substance

The Foundation of Substance for the second course ended in failure when, due to the people's persistent disbelief, Satan defiled the foundation for the tabernacle. However, at least the Foundation of Faith for the tabernacle remained, preserved by Moses' continued devotion. If, upon this foundation, the Israelites had faithfully followed Moses through the 40 years of wandering in the wilderness, thus establishing the basis for the separation from Satan, they would have set up the Foundation of Substance for the tabernacle and completed the foundation for the tabernacle. If they had then honored and obeyed Moses and entered Canaan in faith, they would have also completed the Foundation of Substance for the third national course to restore Canaan.

For Moses, the 40 years of wandering in the wilderness was the period required to establish the Foundation of Faith for the third national course. For the Israelites, the goal for this period was to accomplish the dispensation to start the third course. They were to do this by establishing the foundation for the tabernacle, thereby returning to the state of grace that they had enjoyed in the second course when they first constructed the tabernacle under Moses' direction.

The tablets, the tabernacle and the ark of the covenant became necessary in the second course only because the Israelites lost faith in the wilderness. Soon after they crossed the Red Sea, they forgot the three signs or miracles that God had granted Moses at the start of the second course. To restore this through indemnity, God tested the people through a 40-day period while Moses was on Mt. Sinai. He then gave them three manifestations of divine grace: the tablets of stone, the ark of the covenant and the tabernacle.

In a similar way, God had granted the 10 plagues, which were to restore Laban's 10 deceptions of Jacob in Haran. Yet when the Israelites lost faith even after witnessing these, God attempted to restore the 10 plagues through indemnity by giving the Ten Commandments.

If the Israelites had renewed their faith by honoring the three manifestations of divine grace and obeying the Ten Commandments, they would have returned to the state of grace they had enjoyed when they left Egypt under the power of these miracles.

Accordingly, in the third course the Israelites should have completed the 40-year indemnity period by following Moses in faith and obedience through the wilderness. After they returned to Kadesh-barnea, they should have stood with Moses upon the foundation for the tabernacle and exalted the tablets, the tabernacle and the ark.

This moment in the third course would have paralleled the moment in the second course when the 10 plagues had been completed and the Pharaoh had reluctantly given his permission to release the Israelites for three days.

As we mentioned before, Jesus was the substantial temple, the temple was the image of Jesus, the tabernacle was the symbol of Jesus, the two tablets of stone within the ark represented Jesus and his bride and, finally the rock and stone itself represented Christ. **Revelation 2:17, 1 Corinthians 10:4**

Therefore, the third national course to restore the Foundation of Substance was to start at Kadesh-barnea, centering on "the rock." In the first course, the sign given the Israelites was when Moses killed the Egyptian. In the second course, it was the three miracles and 10 plagues. In the third course, it was the water of life. Henceforth, had the Israelites honored the tabernacle with faith and devotion and followed Moses into Canaan, they would have fulfilled the indemnity condition to remove the fallen nature required for the Foundation of Substance in the third national course.

How did God intend to start based on the rock? Previously in the second course at Horeb, God told Moses in **Exodus 17:6** to "strike the rock and water will come out of it for the people to drink." This rock had to be struck because it represented dead Adam. Striking the rock with his staff changed a rock without water into a rock with water. This represented reviving the dead Adam back into a living Adam.

The rock at Kadesh-barnea, therefore, did not need to be struck because that rock was already representing Christ. Thus, rather than striking the rock, God told Moses "to speak to the rock."

Numbers 20:8
The LORD said to Moses, "Take the staff, and you and your brother Aaron gather the assembly together. Speak to that rock before their eyes and it will pour out its water. You will bring water out of the rock for the community so they and their livestock can drink."

The implications of striking the rock were very great for Moses:

Numbers 20:12
But the LORD said to Moses and Aaron, "Because you did not trust in me enough to honor me as holy in the sight of the Israelites, you will not bring this community into the land I give them."

Moses, at 120 years of age and after 80 years of providential leadership, had faltered in a crucial moment. His mission would now be transferred to Joshua. In a moment of weakness and temper, Moses had set up a bad condition that suggested a possible future in which the chosen people may be tempted to strike the Christ.

Sadly, God would have to replace Moses for this breach of faith. God chose Joshua to replace Moses. God could call Joshua to replace Moses because Joshua had always been in unity with Moses and, even more important, he had always upheld the tabernacle, the ark and tablets of stone representing Christ to come.

After 40 years, all those who had grumbled and murmured against Moses died in the wilderness. Moses himself "returned to his fathers" atop Mt. Nebo without ever entering the promised land.

Centering on Joshua, a new generation of Israelites followed. That new generation united with Joshua on the national level. This unity on the national level represented the same victory accomplished by Jacob and Esau on the tribal level. Thus, as that tribal-level victory was the foundation for Jacob to become the tribe of Israel, likewise, the national-level victory was the foundation for the tribes of Israel to become the nation of Israel.

Joshua led the Israelites across the Jordan. One of the first things God did was have them renew the covenant He had made with Moses. The essence of that covenant was that God had a plan and destiny for the nation of Israel. It was a destiny that would not just affect them alone, but rather, the entire world.

Chapter Seven

The Law and All of the Prophets

The History of Israel from Judges to Jesus

What is meant by the words "the Old Testament"? It has come to mean all the books of the Bible before the book of Matthew. But its essential meaning is much more specific. "The Old Testament" refers to a contract, or covenant, made between God and his people, the Israelites, centering on Moses, later reaffirmed with Joshua and maintained through the history leading up to Christ. It is stated in **Deuteronomy 26:16–19**

> *The LORD your God commands you this day to follow these decrees and laws; carefully observe them with all your heart and with all your soul. You have declared this day that the LORD is your God and that you will walk in his ways, that you will keep his decrees, commands and laws, and that you will obey him.*
>
> *And the LORD has declared this day that you are his people, his treasured possession as he promised, and that you are to keep all his commands. He has declared that he will set you in praise, fame and honor high above all the nations he has made and that you will be a people holy to the LORD your God, as he promised.*

The agreement between God and Israel requires something on the part of each party. The Israelites must maintain faith in the "laws, decrees and commandments" of God. If they do so, God will make sure that Israel realizes a blessed destiny as the central nation of the world.

Deuteronomy 28:1–7
*If you fully obey the LORD your God and carefully follow all his commands I give you today, the LORD your God will set you high above **all the nations on earth**. All these blessings will come upon you and accompany you if you obey the LORD your God:*

You will be blessed in the city and blessed in the country. The fruit

of your womb will be blessed, and the crops of your land and the young
of your livestock—the calves of your herds and the lambs of your flocks.
Your basket and your kneading trough will be blessed. You will be
blessed when you come in and blessed when you go out. The LORD will
grant that the enemies who rise up against you will be defeated before
you. They will come at you from one direction but flee from you in seven.

The status of this agreement is the core determinate in the course of the unfolding of events in Israel leading up the coming of Christ. The entire 28th chapter of Deuteronomy outlines all the "blessings" if Israel maintains faith. However, God also reveals all the curses "if" they break faith with the laws, decrees and commandments of God.

"IF"

At times, God expresses himself to man in a manner that requires more than a strict, traditional theological view to understand. Many believers become rather uneasy when God uses a word like "if." In the 28th chapter of Deuteronomy, God explains that "if" Israel has faith they will be blessed, but "if" they do not have faith, they will be cursed.

"If"? It seems to be a rather inappropriate word for a God who knows all. **Exodus 4:2** is noteworthy because God asks Moses for information, "What is that in your hand?" He asks. Even more noteworthy, Moses confidently gives God the information He seeks. "A staff," Moses replies. In **Mark 9:21**, Jesus also requests information. "How long has he been like this?" Jesus asked the boy's father. If Jesus was to ask believers today such a question, they might be thrown into a fit of doctrinal anxiety. Isn't the Lord all-knowing?

Certainly God has the power to know all. If God has the power to know all, He must surely also have the power not to know something if He so chooses. That's why God tells Israel "if" they have faith they will be blessed. Using that word is not an expression of an inability on the part of God to know something, but rather is the expression of His decision that Israel will play a central role, via faith, in the accomplishment of God's will for His people.

God is giving the nation a portion of responsibility. It is going to play a central role in the outcome. It is the same parameters that enveloped the relationship of Adam and Eve with God. "If" they had kept the commandment, they would have had life.

God relates to the chosen people in this manner because He has not changed his Master Plan. Thus, their faith in the laws, decrees, and commandments of God is the pathway to the fulfillment of God's Will. That Will must be for a blessed Israel to be realized. An Israel that "is the head and never is the tail."

God's expresses clearly what His will is for Israel in **Deuteronomy 30:19:**

> *This day I call heaven and earth as witnesses against you that I have set before you life and death, blessings and curses. **Now choose life**, so that you and your children may live.*

Deuteronomy 30:19 should dispel any notion that God is indifferent to the course Israel chooses.

The process of restoration places Israel in "the midway position." Thus, they need to set up a condition to stand on God's side. This is the meaning of the laws, decrees and commandments. It is the condition necessary to come to God's side. However, if the Israelites break faith with God, they will have to set a secondary course of indemnity.

This twofold potential centering on Israel's responsibility is what establishes a primary and secondary course in God's providence of restoration. God's primary Will for His people is that they receive His Word and keep faith. God's secondary Will for His people is, "if" they fail, that they set up a course of indemnity to restore their previous position and status (**2 Samuel 14:14**). God does not determine the outcome without man's participation, that is, the fulfillment or failure in his portion of responsibility.

The more we can see the manifestation of this primary and secondary dynamic in the history leading up to Jesus, the more we will be able to recognize Jesus' own ministry within that same matrix.

Thus, "if" Israel fulfills its responsibility and keeps faith, God will be able to lead the nation toward its destiny "to be the head" and not the tail. This is God's primary will. However, "if" Israel rejects the laws, decrees and commandments of God and moves down the path toward curses, God will send a prophet to implore the rebellious people to repent and return to the original path.

No prophet ever appeared when the people of Israel were headed properly to the destiny of "blessing." The secondary (or consequential) path is always less preferred. In fact, it is not preferred at all. Look what God says about that course in **Ezekiel 33:11**

*Say to them, "As surely as I live, declares the Sovereign LORD, I take **no pleasure** in the death of the wicked, but rather that they turn from their ways and live. Turn! Turn from your evil ways! **Why will you die**, O house of Israel?"*

This shows that when Israel turned from its primary destiny, God would intervene through a prophet's voice to encourage repentance and return. God "takes no pleasure" in having to invoke the tragic course of the secondary path of indemnity.

God also indicates that if ever the curse is invoked upon Israel, it will not be because of His "Will" but rather as a result of Israel failing in its role of responsibility. See **Deuteronomy 29:24–25**

All the nations will ask: "Why has the LORD done this to this land? Why this fierce, burning anger?" And the answer will be: "It is because this people abandoned the covenant of the LORD, the God of their fathers, the covenant he made with them when he brought them out of Egypt."

In **Isaiah 5:1–4**, we can see this self-imposed line that God will not cross with regard to man's portion of responsibility:

I will sing for the one I love a song about his vineyard: My loved one had a vineyard on a fertile hillside. He dug it up and cleared it of stones and planted it with the choicest vines. He built a watchtower in it and cut out a winepress as well. Then he looked for a crop of good grapes, but it yielded only bad fruit.

*"Now you dwellers in Jerusalem and men of Judah, judge between me and my vineyard. **What more could have been done for my vineyard than I have done for it? When I looked for good grapes, why did it yield only bad?"***

God did all that He could do and yet He did not get the result of His desire and Will. How could that be? Is God weak? Not at all.

The time of Jeremiah provides us with a clear example of this phenomenon.

Jeremiah 25:4–7

*And though the LORD has sent all his servants the prophets to you **again and again**, you have **not listened** or paid any attention. They said, "Turn now, each of you, from your evil ways and your evil practices, and **you can stay in the land the LORD gave to you** and your fathers for ever and ever. Do not follow other gods to serve and worship them; do not provoke me to anger with what your hands have made. Then I will not harm you."*

*"But you did not listen to me," declares the LORD, "and you have provoked me with what your hands have made, and **you have brought harm to yourselves**."*

God explains clearly that, first, He had been sending prophet after prophet to try to convince them to repent and return to the path of the destiny of blessing. He tells them that if they had listened, "they could have remained in the land." In other words, clearly the secondary course is undesirable to God. He wants it to be unnecessary. It was not God, then, who invoked His Will for the Babylonian exile and prolongation of 210 years. God said, "You have brought harm to *yourselves*."

God "takes no pleasure" in this course because it is a prolongation of the fulfillment of His original will. At the end of that prolongation, the chosen people are placed in exactly the same position with the same responsibility. After 210 years of exile and return, in this case, they returned to the land, rebuilt the temple, reproved the faith, and renewed the covenant. In other words, they were placed in exactly the same position as their disobedient, unrepentant ancestors of 210 years before.

The Law Covenant Is the 'Operating System' of the History Leading to Jesus

As we enter the period of Judges, we can see the direct evidence of this "operating system" between God and His people. God would lead them to their blessed destiny as long as they kept faith in the laws, decrees and commandments. They could defeat any army, rout any tribe, and move steadfastly toward securing the land. When, on the other hand, they stood in violation of their creeds, they were hopeless and ineffective. In fact, at one point, they began to fight among themselves, almost wiping out the entire tribe of Benjamin. Over the course of the next 400 years, we see this vacillation from faith to faithlessness, moving from God's ways to the ways of the Canaanite tribes. Each time we can see the outcome as prescribed by the Covenant.

The Philistine army was a renowned nemesis of the Israelites during this period. In fact, it was the emerging threat of the Philistines that moved the Israelites to repentance centering on the Prophet Samuel. The providence shifted from the nation as an aggregation of tribes to the establishment of the monarchy of Saul, David and Solomon.

With the establishment of the position of king, the status of the king's faith in the laws, decrees and commandments of God will be the new determinate. In this requirement, we see that Saul is deemed unworthy in **1 Samuel 13:13:**

*"You acted foolishly," Samuel said. "You have not kept the command the LORD your God gave you; if you had, **he would have established your kingdom over Israel for all time."***

There's that word "if" again. Samuel tells Saul that had he kept faith, God would have established a kingdom over Israel "for all time." The implications are very great. It is a clear, emphatic statement that God wants to establish a strong, central nation as the foundation for Christ. Again, that is the primary objective "if" Israel (and now the king) maintains the condition of faith in the laws, decrees and commandments of God.

Saul becomes unacceptable to God. Saul's kingship is passed on to David. In **2 Samuel 7:12–16,** God makes a promise (or covenant) with King David:

*When your days are over and you rest with your fathers, I will raise up **your offspring** to succeed you, who will come from **your own body**, and I will **establish his kingdom**. He is the one who will build a house for my Name, and **I will establish the throne of his kingdom forever**. I will be his **father**, and he will be my **son**. When he does wrong, I will punish him with the rod of men, with floggings inflicted by men. But my love will never be taken away from him, as I took it away from Saul, whom I removed from before you. Your house and your kingdom will endure forever before me; **your throne will be established forever.***

This promise, or covenant, is considered to be very significant. The "Davidic Covenant" is thought to pertain to the coming work of Jesus. Indeed, Jesus is the fulfillment of that vision. However, this covenant has an immediate relevance and potential fulfillment.

Consider what God says to David's son Solomon in **1 Kings 9:4–9**

As for you, **IF** *you walk before me in integrity of heart and uprightness, as David your father did, and do all I command and observe my decrees and laws,* ***I will establish your royal throne over Israel forever, as I promised David your father when I said, "You shall never fail to have a man on the throne of Israel."***

There is an important contemporary implication in this promise that is sometimes overlooked because its relevance is thought to only apply to a future Christ. First, God tells David that one of his offspring will establish a kingdom that will never decline. Of course, Christians are aware of this promise in relation to Christ's arrival a thousand years from that time.

However, God explains to Solomon that when He made that promise to his father David, He was referring to him, Solomon. In other words, the unbroken line of kings and unending kingdom was to begin at that time. "I will establish your royal throne over Israel, as I promised David your father when I said, 'you shall never fail to have a man on the throne of Israel.'"

God is telling Solomon that "if" he maintains faith, God will establish Israel as the central nation and dominant empire in the world, Christ will be born on the foundation of an unbroken line of kings to a nation that is supreme in the world. In other words, Jesus should have been born in the palace in an era of Israel's global dominance. This was God's "primary" plan for Christ "if" the condition of faith had been maintained. It was the vision God gave Moses when He told him He would make Israel "His treasured possession, a kingdom of priests and a holy nation."

In fact, initially under Solomon, Israel achieved its "Golden Era." The time of Solomon is the absolute zenith of the history of the nation of Israel. We mostly regard Israel in terms of the last 2,000 years of its history. During the time of Jesus, for example, it was a small land under the domination of Rome. Prior to that, the Greeks conquered it; before them, the Persians, and before the Persians it was the Babylonians. Our image of the nation of

Israel is one of, certainly, spiritual greatness, but modest in terms of practical influence.

This was not the case under Solomon's rule. Under Solomon, Israel's army expanded its territorial control to the level of empire. Not only did Israel possess the strongest military, but it was the dominant economic power of the era. It was the leading culture in terms of art, music, trade and scientific study.

God promised that Israel would be the "head" and never be the tail, as long as the nation maintained faith. Under Solomon, God was carrying out that primary vision. He promised that no empire would ever rise against Israel and take it down. That is unless:

1 Kings 9:6–9

*But **IF** you or your sons turn away from me and do not observe the commands and decrees I have given you and go off to serve other gods and worship them, then I will cut off Israel from the land I have given them and will reject this temple I have consecrated for my Name.*

*Israel will then become a byword and an object of ridicule among all peoples. And though this temple is now imposing, all who pass by will be appalled and will scoff and say, "**Why has the LORD done such a thing to this land and to this temple?" People will answer, "Because they have forsaken the LORD their God,** who brought their fathers out of Egypt, and have embraced other gods, worshiping and serving them—that is why the LORD brought all this disaster on them."*

Did you notice that God repeats the wording of **Deuteronomy 29:24**? If Israel is destroyed, it will not be God's doing but rather, it will be the result of the people (and now the king) forsaking God.

Solomon demonstrates a serious breach in his covenantal relationship with God. Although Solomon could have been Israel's greatest king, he certainly began to run afoul of some of the more important laws, decrees and commandments. See **Deuteronomy 17:17**:

The King must not take many wives or his heart will be led astray.

Solomon showed a total disregard for God's warning.

1 Kings 11:1–4, 10

King Solomon, however, loved many foreign women besides Pharaoh's daughter—Moabites, Ammonites, Edomites, Sidonians and Hittites. They were from nations about which the LORD had told the Israelites, "You must not intermarry with them, because they will surely turn your hearts after their gods." Nevertheless, Solomon held fast to them in love. HE HAD **SEVEN HUNDRED WIVES** OF ROYAL BIRTH AND **THREE HUNDRED CONCUBINES**, AND HIS WIVES LED HIM ASTRAY. *As Solomon grew old, his wives turned his heart after other gods, and his heart was not fully devoted to the LORD his God, as the heart of David his father had been.*

Although he had forbidden Solomon to follow other gods, Solomon **did not keep the LORD's command.**

Solomon erected temples to house the gods of his foreign wives. Thus, Israel turned away from its primary objective and began to move toward the woeful secondary path of indemnity, repentance and delay, all consequential characteristics of this unfortunate and less preferred course.

The kingdom of Solomon is retracted from world dominance and the nation becomes divided into North and South. God began to send prophet after prophet to Israel with the hope that Israel would repent and restore its direction back toward its primary destiny: to be blessed; to be the head and not the tail.

In the ensuing 600 years, we see the emergence of the 4 major and 12 minor written prophets. Their writings reflect the "genetic code" of God's providential relationship with Israel. They also reflect a nation that had a brush with greatness and tasted its true potential. On the one hand, they describe images of "blessing"; that is, a nation that is the head, a nation reflective of the glory of Solomon's era. On the other hand, they also articulate the impending "curse" promised if Israel fails to repent. An unrepentant Israel is doomed to be the "tail," not the head, and is scattered to the four corners of the earth.

Inherent in their twofold message is the image of a new coming king whose own destiny will be determined by the nation's choice. On the one hand, a faithful Israel will welcome a new Solomon-like figure, the "messiah" who will "restore the kingdom to Israel." On the other, a faithless Israel rejects its king, who suffers and dies, bringing on the dark days of utter destruction. Which destiny will be realized? It is Israel's choice.

Imagine then, the enormity, the weighty implications inherent within the single word, "if."

Glory and Suffering: Dual Prophecy

In a previous chapter we talked about oracles and prophecy and their tendency to bear meaning in an immediate as well as future context. Probably no greater element has been brought to bear on the Christian understanding of Jesus. Without understanding the meaning and effect of human responsibility, it becomes nearly impossible to understand the prophet's voice with full clarity.

Many Jewish scholars see prophetic declarations of Israel's destiny to be literal. A king must come, a new Solomon, the messiah, as it were, must fulfill the vision of a "blessed" Israel. For them, this was not Jesus of Nazareth.

Many Christian scholars see prophetic declarations of Israel's destiny to be only foreshadowing a spiritual kingdom of Christ. For them, this was not the literal nation of Israel.

On the one hand, Jewish scholars struggle to come to terms with the idea that Jesus was that hoped-for messiah. On the other hand, Christians struggle to understand Jesus' role as a Jew. Although Jesus' role as messiah was to certainly transcend Hebrew expectations, that messianic role was also to fully incorporate the earthly, Solomon-like dimensions of the Hebraic expectation. Only when this can be clearly understood will the 2,000-year-old rift between Jews and Christians begin to be resolved.

In other words, God's expressed desire for the nation of Israel to "be the head" and not be the tail was expressing God's truest intent for that nation. Jesus' mission is indelibly intertwined with that primary vision.

The issue is: who is responsible for that vision not coming about? Is it God who made Israel to fail, so we Christians could be blessed? Or is there another dynamic at work?

Typically, believers insist that all prophecy must be fulfilled. If not, God is a liar, the Bible is untrue. Thus, most Christians conclude that dual prophecy, that is, predictions of Christ glorified, and predictions of Christ suffering, must all be fulfilled. In their view, the process by which prophecy is fulfilled is in the following manner: All prophecy of a Christ who will suffer is, obviously, referring to Jesus of Nazareth of 2,000 years ago. All prophecy of Christ received and establishing his Kingdom is prophecy pertaining to the returning Christ for whom Christians wait.

Therefore, in the view of many Christians, the phenomenon of dual prophecy reflects a predetermination of God that there will be two comings of Christ: the first to suffer, die and atone for sin, the second to set up His kingdom.

The liability of this perspective is that it potentially obscures the motives of Jesus' "sorrow unto death" in the Garden of Gethsemane. Why was Jesus praying, "let this cup pass," if in fact this cup was all there was for him to accomplish. In other words, we need to be made aware that when Jesus announced, in **Matthew 16:21**, his suffering to come, he was simultaneously closing the door to a primary, original purpose of even greater magnitude. This is the basis to understand his suffering circumstance and his grieving heart.

Comparing Prophecy

The 4 major and 12 minor prophetic books are grouped together in the Old Testament. They are the last 16 books of the Old Testament, beginning with Isaiah and ending with Malachi. This 600-year period of the major and minor prophets begins with the fall of Solomon's kingdom and concludes with Malachi and the beginning of the 400-year inter-testament period. Take some time to review the prophets and see if you can observe the dual nature of each prophet's voice.

With a partial sample, let's compare prophecies of glory with prophecies of suffering:

Glory: Isaiah 2:4–11, Zechariah 8:1–23, Ezekiel 37:15–28, Jeremiah 31:31, Isaiah 60 & 61, Ezekiel 34.

Suffering: Isaiah 53, Psalms 22 & 118:22, Zechariah 13:7, 11:7–14, Jeremiah 32:6–9

Out of this sample, let's select a specific example from Ezekiel and Zechariah.

Ezekiel 37:15–28	**Zechariah 11:7–14**
Chosen people receive king	Chosen people reject king
Judah/Israel united	Judah/Israel divided
No exile ever again	Exiled again (**Zechariah 13:7**)
Covenant established	Covenant broken

The phenomenon of dual prophecy is, of course, not an expression of God's predetermination that Christ will be rejected and die. It is, instead, another reflection of the actual process by which God is fulfilling His will. In other words, human responsibility will bear a direct impact on the expression of prophecy. Let's examine how.

As we have seen, God expressed His primary and secondary Will in **Deuteronomy 28**. All prophecy related to God's primary Will is absolute and must be fulfilled. However, it is not determined *who* will fulfill it. The central person, or nation, must fulfill its portion of responsibility for that prophecy to be fulfilled. "If" they do not do that, the fulfillment of that prophecy will be prolonged to a later time in history, to be taken up by a new central person or nation.

Prophecy related to God's secondary (or consequential) Will is not absolute. It does not have to be fulfilled because it is not an expression of God's original (that is, primary) Will. Therefore, if man repents, God does not have to carry out that secondary course, even if it has been announced.

That is why when Jeremiah announced the beginning of the Babylonian exile in **Jeremiah 25:4–7,** he stated that it would have been unnecessary had they just heeded the prophets and repented. Consider what God says himself about prophecy:

Jeremiah 18:7–10
If at any time I announce that a nation or kingdom is to be uprooted, torn down and destroyed, and **IF** *that nation I warned repents of its evil, then I will relent and **not inflict on it the disaster I had planned.***

And if at another time I announce that a nation or kingdom is to be built up and planted, and **IF** *it does evil in my sight and does not obey me, then I will reconsider the good I had intended to do for it.*

This is the definitive word on prophecy. God is the highest authority and the best theologian.

Prophecy doesn't negate human responsibility. Let's cite some examples in biblical history:

- **2 Kings 20:1–6** God instructs Isaiah to tell Hezekiah he will not recover from his sickness and will die. Hezekiah prays with tears, God relents and adds 15 years to his life.
- **Jonah** God tells Jonah to tell the people of Nineveh that they will be destroyed in 40 days. The people repent and God does not destroy Nineveh.

- **Matthew 11:23** Jesus affirms that Sodom would not have been destroyed "if" they had repented.

These three examples pertain to the first part of **Jeremiah 18:7–10**:

> *If at any time I announce that a nation or kingdom is to be uprooted, torn down and destroyed, and* **IF** *that nation I warned repents of its evil, then I will relent and* **not inflict on it the disaster I had planned.**

That is, God relents in the secondary course because of repentance. Is there an example in history of God relenting in His primary Will, as per:

> *And if at another time I announce that a nation or kingdom is to be built up and planted, and* **IF** *it does evil in my sight and does not obey me, then I will reconsider the good I had intended to do for it.*

Consider this important example with regard to Israel's primary destiny.

Isaiah 65:17–19
"Behold, I will create **new heavens and a new earth**. *The former things will not be remembered, nor will they come to mind. But be glad and rejoice forever in what I will create, for I will create* **Jerusalem** *to be a delight and its people a joy. I will rejoice over Jerusalem and take delight in my people; the sound of weeping and of crying will be heard in it no more.*

This vision for Israel did not come true, not because of God's predetermination but rather because of Israel's lack of faith in Jesus.

Matthew 21:43
Therefore I tell you that the kingdom of God will be **taken away from you** *and given to a people who will produce its fruit.*

Thus, we see **Revelation 21:1–2**
Then I saw a **new heaven and a new earth**, *for the first heaven and the first earth had passed away, and there was no longer any sea. I saw the Holy City, the* **NEW JERUSALEM**, *coming down out of heaven from God, prepared as a bride beautifully dressed for her husband.*

Because Israel failed to recognize its king, Israel lost its mission. However, because God's primary Will was to bring "the new heaven and new earth," God will re-create a "new Jerusalem" to fulfill this absolute prophecy. A new Jerusalem returns to do the mission of the first Jerusalem. Likewise, a new Adam comes to do the primary mission of the second Adam.

Thus, Jesus *had a primary mission* that pertained to the Kingdom of God and finding faith in Israel. Jesus' first two years of his ministry focused on the Kingdom and the hope for faith in Israel, because, that mission *was viable at that time*.

Many doctrines teach that by the time of Malachi, the final prophet, it is already determined that Christ will be rejected and crucified. A second coming is already in the works. However, consider how the final words of Malachi so differ from that assertion:

Remember the law of my servant Moses, the decrees and laws I gave him at Horeb for all Israel. *See, I will send you the prophet Elijah before that great and dreadful day of the LORD comes. He will turn the hearts of the fathers to their children, and the hearts of the children to their fathers;* **or else I will come and strike the land with a curse.**

The contingency of "if" is still in effect. Israel will decide which destiny, blessing or curse, will be invoked based upon the success or failure of the coming Elijah.

When Jesus begins his public ministry with the words, "Repent, now is the time for the Kingdom is at hand," he was indicating a contemporary objective. It was his primary destiny. With this understanding, we will open the door, for the first time, and enter in to the inner sanctum of Christ's deepest sorrows.

Jesus prayed, sorrowing unto death, "let this cup pass from me." This indicates that the Lord may have had another mission before circumstances necessitated his going to the cross. (It is only in understanding the nature of that intended mission that we will be able to understand the substance of that prayer and the pathway to liberate Jesus from his sorrows.)

Chapter Eight

The Change of Blood Lineage
The Lineage of Jesus

The history of Adam, Noah, and Abraham's families, Moses, and the nation of Israel is the story of the building of the "external" Foundation to Receive the Messiah. This chapter, however, is the explanation of the "internal" Foundation to Receive the Messiah. It explains the age-old question of how a sinless living Adam could emerge from a lineage that has its origin in the death and sin of Adam's fall.

The sinless birth of Christ from Mary's womb stands at the very heart of what is probably the most intriguing mystery of faith. It summons extenuating questions pertaining to the relationship between human sexuality, sin, spirituality and the divine.

The spiritual descendants of Abraham (Jews, Christians and Moslems) still grapple with an array of definitions and moral standards that have yet to rid our world of a wide assortment of dysfunctions and troubles.

In reaction to this, many began to challenge religion itself as presumptuous and illegitimate in its role to establish moral sanctions over human sexual desire. The alternative was to unfetter sexual desire entirely. However, such an environment only served to accelerate the demise of culture. The convincing record of history demonstrates that culture "liberated" from all moral constraint will soon decline in a maelstrom of social ills.

Although those religious sanctions were vitally needed, in a sad and tragic irony, it is their imperfect expression and implementation that contributed to secular reactions such as that witnessed in the "sexual revolution" of the modern era. Unclear moral classifications imposed in guilt and shame will always manifest the very monster they fear. This tragic antagonism between the sacred and the secular, with human sexuality hanging in the balance, serves as a significant hidden dimension in the conflict of peoples.

Since the beginning of time, one key goal of secular interest, albeit largely unspoken, has been to "liberate" human sexuality from the moral codes of religion. Actually, Satan himself is the father of that movement. Satan's principal complaint was that God insisted on imposing a code over human sexual conduct. (God prohibiting human-angel coupling was, no doubt, a primary point of contention.)

In the Garden, God's moral code was based upon the precept that Adam and Eve must first achieve a personal standard "to be fruitful" before they could "multiply." Therefore, the moral sanction "Do not eat the fruit" served to bolster Adam and Eve toward this objective. The essential implication of this moral code was this: Adam and Eve must fulfill the qualifications and then elicit God's permission before sexual relations may proceed. Satan, in contrast, wanted sexual experience irrespective of this requirement.

Sexual conduct in Eden proceeded without God's permission. This is the root of sin. Henceforth, the stain on sex, resulting from the fall, pertains to the issue of God's withheld permission. Mankind, in ignorance, has been unaware of the reasons God withholds his approval. It has been withheld because a fundamental purpose of human sexuality is not being accomplished as a result of the fall. This loss of permission has contributed to the confusion of values about human sexuality; even in a monogamous union, children are "conceived in sin" and are born in urgent need of "rebirth." Since the fall, there seems to be no standard that meets with God's unconditional approval.

Thus, most Christian thought tends to promote an inherent sense of alienation between God and sexual function. There is no greater manifestation of this than the assumed link between Christ's sexless conception and his sinless birth. This estrangement between God and human sexual conduct is also linked to the religious value of celibacy: the idea that renouncing sex promotes a deeper fellowship with God.

On the positive side of the ledger, the vital contribution of Judeo-Christian thought, albeit imperfect, has been its efforts to establish provisional consent upon the sexual relation. This has been the historical key in the building of enduring, vigorous culture since it reflects the original paradigm in Eden. It has also been instrumental in the course to imbue love as the prime motive for sexual union. For example, it is not a coincidence that when a culture embraced the idea of premarital abstinence, it likewise embraced and developed around the experience of love in marriage.

This provisional consent within religious culture, though it reflects the original sanction in Eden, is not the full recovery of the original suspended permission resulting from the fall. Thus, the original sin maintains its heritage through the Christian era. Christian culture, though a higher culture, is, therefore, not the final culture for which we wait.

The course to achieve full human potential was set up in Eden. That pathway required that Adam and Eve be placed in a position to exert authority over desire. Of course, sexual desire is the strongest of desire. It is the core of the life force, the force of nature. By displaying authority over this desire, man stands in the position of Lord over nature.

In standing in this position, we share a common protocol with God. Like the main server in an I.T. network of computers, God begins to download all the "Creator 7.0" program drivers and files to man. Man completes this divining process with God through the "co-creatorship" function. On that foundation, Adam and Eve would elicit God's permission to "multiply," that is, begin their sexual life.

In our modern "values free" secular world it has become politically incorrect to assess cultures and assign categories of higher and lower. However, with the clear focus of understanding God's purpose for creating, we can conclude that whenever humans of any culture displayed values that reflected this original archetype, they inadvertently stumbled into the key of cultural development. That is the cultural dividing line separating primitive from higher, transitory from enduring.

Christ comes to restore God's permission for human sexuality. Christ restores sexual relations to its original purpose and potential. Understanding "The Change of Blood Lineage" is instrumental for Christians to understand the truest nature of Christ's mission.

Standing in the way are many theological and traditional beliefs that effectively block the Christian world from understanding the most fundamental of all Christ's roles. The idea that Jesus would take a bride is hard for Christians to consider, given the view of traditional theology.

Christianity and Sex

Mrs. Ruth Smythers was the wife of a Methodist pastor at the turn of the 19th century. In her advice to new wives of that era, she displays the fruit of nearly 2,000 years of Christian thought on human sexuality.

One cardinal rule of marriage should never be forgotten: GIVE LITTLE, GIVE SELDOM, AND ABOVE ALL, GIVE GRUDGINGLY. Otherwise what could have been a proper marriage could become an orgy of sexual lust.

*On the other hand, the bride's terror need not be extreme. While sex **at best is revolting** and at worse rather painful, it has to be endured, and has been by women since the beginning of time.*

Although we may find such an expression to be awkward today, it *was* the widespread mind-set of that time. This oppressive religious domination over a primal human desire is one catalyst that stimulated the reactionary rise of the social sciences as an alternative for human enlightenment. Freud, Margaret Sanger and others laid down the ideological foundation that fueled the explosion of the sexual revolution of the modern era.

As those ideas gained popularity, they gave rise to the notion that sexual regulation is unhealthy and, therefore, moral standards are contrived. Today the battle lines are drawn. The religious side, though not as strident as in 1894, still seeks to exert moral restraints upon sexuality, while the secular world bristles against any such restrictions.

However, neither religionists nor humanists alone can liberate sexuality from its historical chains. On the one hand, Christians remain unable to elicit God's permission to the extent of removing the roots of shame from the sex act. For them, it remains the conduit of sin, death, and need for "rebirth." On the other hand, the humanist reaction only leads society down the primrose path of social destruction.

In the Christian view, a pure messiah must be inexplicably untouched by human sexuality. Jesus conceived by the Holy Ghost and born of a woman unscathed by human sexual intercourse is assumed to be essential for Christ to attain "sinless" status.

The first step away from this position is for Christians to understand that Jesus' sinless status was not just affected by the nature of his conception. Jesus' sinless birth involved more elements and conditions than has ever been previously understood. While affirming that Jesus was born without sin, and that he was conceived by the work of the Holy Spirit, we do not affirm that his sinless state was the direct effect of the *sexless* nature of his conception. In other words, even if the conceiving work of the Holy Spirit had happened to use the vehicle of an earthly father, Jesus' birth would *still* have been without sin.

The expectation that the Messiah would be born of a virgin was set up by **Isaiah 7:14**:

> *Therefore the Lord himself will give you a sign: The virgin will be with child and will give birth to a son, and will call him Immanuel.*

In other words, Jesus' virgin birth is a *sign* and not a necessity with regard to affecting his sinless state. Thus, we need to examine other conditions in order to understand the process that culminates with the birth of Christ without sin.

When we assert that Jesus was born without "sin," it is important that we first establish our working definition of sin:

Sin is any thought or action that makes a base for Satan to have give and take with me. Sin is not a substance; it is **a claim**. Satan has a claim over Adam's lineage, based on a sequence of conditions that result in the extension of his authority.

Therefore, the process to remove this claim of authority means reversing the sequence of conditions upon which that claim is based. This is the process of historical indemnity. Jesus could be born without this claim extended to him because there was a historical process of indemnity in his lineage that reversed the sequence of conditions responsible for the generational passing of sin. Those conditions address directly the circumstances that resulted in the suspension of consent for human sexuality.

By pinpointing this process in Jesus' lineage we are able to answer the question: how could a living Adam come forth from a lineage that was linked, through Mary, to the dead Adam? Again, the mode of conception, i.e., sexless, is not the determining factor. Christian thought leans toward this conclusion because, again, it assumes an inherent estrangement between God and sexual relations.

The actual determining factor is related more, for example, to the reason God chose to impregnate a woman who was already engaged to another. This circumstance placed Joseph in a deeply disturbing position. Why did God choose a woman who was already betrothed to another? By doing so, Joseph was compelled to achieve a lofty standard of faith, not only in God but in Mary as well. It would seem choosing an unattached candidate would be less problematic.

Sexless conception *is a sign* that Jesus is the messiah. The conditions set up for his sinless birth, however, must be conditions of indemnity that reverse the conditions by which Satan extended his claim over Adam's lineage. That is, conditions that address the reason man lost God's authorization for sexual life.

Our objective is not to impose the idea of a paternal function in the conception of Jesus. It is, rather, to begin the process of discovering the original ties between God and human sexuality. This will be the first step toward recovering the permission that was suspended in the beginning and carrying out the original motive expressed in **Malachi 2:15**:

Has not the LORD made them one? In flesh and spirit they are his. And why one? Because he was seeking godly offspring.

The Lineage of Jesus

Jesus' lineage is revealed in two of the Gospels: Matthew and Luke, which have two very distinct differences. You will notice that Matthew's portrayal goes through David's son Solomon, while Luke's goes through David's son Nathan. Another notable difference is that whereas both end in Joseph, the supposed father of Jesus, Matthew identifies Joseph's father as "Jacob" while Luke refers to Joseph's father as "Heli."

One theory to explain the differences is that Matthew's depiction is of Mary's lineage while Luke's is that of Joseph. This theory stands on the fact that it was Hebrew custom to list the wife's lineage culminating in her husband's name.

Most significant in **Matthew 1:1–17** is the mentioning of five notable women in Jesus' lineage: Tamar, Rahab, Ruth, Bathsheba, and Mary. Among these five woman there is a common feature in each of their stories.

Tamar: Had an incestuous relationship with her father-in-law while engaged to another.

Rahab: A prostitute in Jericho

Ruth: Tempted Boaz on the threshing room floor while, technically, engaged to another (a closer kinsman).

Bathsheba: Was involved in an adulterous relationship with David while married to Uriah (gave birth to Solomon).

Mary: Became pregnant out of wedlock while engaged to another; gave birth to the Son of God.

Why would scripture only preserve the names of the women in Jesus' lineage involved in what appears to be decadent activity? Why would an entire chapter of Genesis (Genesis 38) be devoted to the story of a woman deceiving her father-in-law into having sexual relations?

In the chapter on Restoration through Indemnity, we indicated that the way of indemnity is the reverse course of the way of sin. That is, the sequence of bad conditions is reversed.

This creates a type of reflection between the two courses. When one examines the two superficially, they may be indistinguishable from one another. That is, the course of indemnity can appear to be nothing more than the course of sin. The course of sin and the course of indemnity *are* on parallel tracks. They *do* reflect each other. It is why people frequently accuse God's great champions of being criminals and reprobates. Did they not so accuse Jacob? Moses? And even Jesus?

The events in Jesus' lineage can only be fully understood in this light. The superficial view is that we read of sexual acts in Jesus' lineage that do not conform to the parameters of their contemporary age nor to the standards of the present Judeo-Christian age. In that view, we would tend to conclude, therefore, that illicit sex has taken place.

The challenge in understanding its actual meaning is that each and every time there was an instance of sexual activity that could not be defined within the accepted standard, it *was* rightly deemed illicit. It manifested its consequences in social chaos and decline.

In this case, however, scripture records sexual activity taking place outside accepted norms and yet its fruit is interwoven into the fabric of God's providence to bring the Christ. It seems to transcend the normal parameters of prohibition and escape the standard consequences of social decline. We must examine this closely to see if we can ascertain the basis of this unique moral reality.

Another substantial challenge in understanding is that the course of indemnity is not a part of God's absolute and original will. The course of indemnity requires the central figure to do things that *only* he will do. Tamar having sexual relations with her father-in-law is not a standard that God wants the world to emulate. In a similar way, Christ is sacrificed once and for all in our place rather than we ourselves mounting the cross. We must recognize that there is a difference between the path of restoration, with its required conditions, and the ideal.

To transcend the superficial view, we must penetrate to the level of motive and purpose. In order to recognize the fundamental difference between the course of sin and the course of indemnity, one must be cognizant that the parallel tracks are moving in *opposite directions*. The motive and purpose of sin is 180 degrees opposite of the motive and purpose for the path of restoration. Understanding from this perspective opens our eyes to a new level of meaning within the events documented in the lineage of Jesus.

The Pattern Begins In Eden

First, we must pinpoint the conditions by which Satan could extend his claim over the lineage of man. This, of course, is why we study the fall of man. The fall indicates that Satan achieved his position of dominion through an illicit relationship involving the archangel, Eve, and Adam (the spiritual and physical fall).

While Adam and Eve were in their period of engagement, Eve violated her trustful bond with God and Adam, aligning herself instead with the archangel Lucifer and fornicating with him. This is the way of the spiritual fall. Next Eve enticed Adam away from his trustful bond with God and transformed him into a dead Adam, likewise through fornication. This was the physical fall. Thus, Adam died and was reborn as the "son" of Satan.

Restoration is the reverse course. In order for God to resurrect one dead Adam, He had to initiate a dispensation that would reverse the pattern of the fall. We can find that pattern of reversal throughout the lineage of Jesus, including but not restricted to the figures and circumstances of his own conception and birth.

The first instance we find is documented in **Genesis 12:10–20:**

Now there was a famine in the land, and Abram went down to Egypt to live there for a while because the famine was severe. As he was about to enter Egypt, he said to his wife Sarai, "I know what a beautiful woman you are. When the Egyptians see you, they will say, 'This is his wife.' Then they will kill me but will let you live. Say you are **my sister**, so that I will be treated well for your sake and my life will be spared because of you."

When Abram came to Egypt, the Egyptians saw that she was a very beautiful woman. And when Pharaoh's officials saw her, they praised her to Pharaoh, and she was taken into his palace. He treated Abram well for her sake, and Abram acquired sheep and cattle, male and female donkeys, menservants and maidservants, and camels. But the LORD inflicted serious diseases on Pharaoh and his household because of Abram's wife Sarai. So Pharaoh summoned Abram. "What have you done to me?" he said. "Why didn't you tell me she was your wife? Why did you say, 'She is my sister,' **so that I took her to be my wife? Now then, here is your wife. Take her and go!**" Then Pharaoh gave orders about Abram to his men, and they sent him on his way, with his wife and everything he had.

Abram instructs Sarai (before their name-change to Abraham and Sarah) to say that she is his sister. By doing so, Abram and Sarai take the position of Adam and Eve. The Pharaoh is, obviously, in the position of the archangel. Sarai is taken into his palace with the intent that she will become one of the Pharaoh's sexual partners. The Lord informs the pharaoh (through serious diseases) that Sarai is the wife and not the sister of Abram. Pharaoh could have ignored these warnings, had Abram killed, and taken Sarai anyway. That would have been the pattern that would follow the fallen norm. Instead, the Pharaoh releases Sarai without defiling her, does not kill her husband, and allows them to return to Canaan unscathed. This is a very significant reversal of the norm.

The second instance, also involving Abraham and Sarah, is recorded in **Genesis 20:1–17**:

Now Abraham moved on from there into the region of the Negev and lived between Kadesh and Shur. For a while he stayed in Gerar, and there Abraham said of his wife Sarah, "She is my sister." Then Abimelech king of Gerar sent for Sarah and took her. But God came to Abimelech in a dream one night and said to him, "You are as good as dead because of the woman you have taken; she is a married woman."

Now Abimelech had not gone near her, so he said, "Lord, will you destroy an innocent nation? Did he not say to me, 'She is my sister,' and *didn't she also say, 'He is my brother'? I have done this with a clear conscience and clean hands."*

Then God said to him in the dream, "Yes, I know you did this with a clear conscience, and so I have kept you from sinning against me. That is why I did not let you touch her. Now return the man's wife, for he is a prophet, and he will pray for you and you will live. But if you do not return her, you may be sure that you and all yours will die."

Early the next morning Abimelech summoned all his officials, and when he told them all that had happened, they were very much afraid. Then Abimelech called Abraham in and said, "What have you done to us? How have I wronged you that you have brought such great guilt upon me and my kingdom? You have done things to me that should not be done." And Abimelech asked Abraham, "What was your reason for doing this?" Abraham replied, "I said to myself, 'There is surely no fear of God in this place, and they will kill me because of my wife.' "

The pattern carried out in Egypt with the pharaoh is repeated in Gerer with King Abimelech. This time, God gives Abimelech a dream in which Sarah's marital status is revealed.

The pattern continues, this time with Abraham's son Isaac and Isaac's wife, Rebecca. This is recorded in **Genesis 26:1–16:**

Now there was a famine in the land—besides the earlier famine of Abraham's time—and Isaac went to Abimelech king of the Philistines in Gerar. The LORD appeared to Isaac and said, "Do not go down to Egypt; live in the land where I tell you to live. Stay in this land for a while, and I will be with you and will bless you. For to you and your descendants I will give all these lands and will confirm the oath I swore to your father Abraham. I will make your descendants as numerous as the stars in the sky and will give them all these lands, and through your offspring all nations on earth will be blessed, because Abraham obeyed me and kept my requirements, my commands, my decrees and my laws." So Isaac stayed in Gerar.

When the men of that place asked him about his wife, he said, "She is my sister," because he was afraid to say, "She is my wife." He thought, "The men of this place might kill me on account of Rebekah, because she is beautiful." When Isaac had been there a long time, Abimelech king of the Philistines looked down from a window and saw Isaac caressing his wife Rebekah. So Abimelech summoned Isaac and said, "She is really your wife! Why did you say, 'She is my sister'?" Isaac answered him,

"Because I thought I might lose my life on account of her." Then Abimelech said, "What is this you have done to us? One of the men might well have slept with your wife, and you would have brought guilt upon us."

Again, the pattern of the fall is reversed. Abimelech doesn't take Rebecca and allows her and her husband to continue their life as husband and wife.

These three instances in Abraham's family set the scene for us to understand the significance of the 38th chapter of the book of Genesis: the story of Tamar.

Tamar

The story of Tamar stands out as one of the most unusual chapters in the Bible. Certainly, it is the most misunderstood chapter. It is often interesting to examine various Bible commentaries as they attempt to make sense of the story and devise theories as to why such a story would even appear. Consider this typical evaluation given by *The Interpreter's Bible*:

> *To many readers of the Bible, it must seem strange that this story is inserted in the midst of the narrative of Joseph. It is like an alien element, suddenly and arbitrarily thrust into a record that it serves only to disturb. Certainly few people would choose this chapter as a basis for teaching or preaching. Then why is this dark old tale preserved?*
>
> *. . . Even so, in the unlovely narrative there are at least some elements of right purpose emerging like flowers from rank ground. One can see here—twisted though its manifestation may be—the powerful and generally wholesome instinct of the Jewish people that family heritage must be continued. One may see also in Tamar the wistful and pathetic yearning of the woman for motherhood.*

"Twisted though its manifestation may be?" Yet, how could it be that the lineage of Christ was produced from such "rank ground?"

As the 38th chapter opens, we see Tamar married to Judah's eldest son Er. However, Er "was wicked in the Lord's sight" so God puts Er to death. Nothing more is mentioned of Er. In response to this death, Judah gives Tamar to her deceased husband's closest relative. This was in keeping with the Levirate code of that time, which provided that the closest relative of the deceased would take the widow as his spouse. The closest kin of Er was his next oldest brother, Onan.

Onan received Tamar as his wife; however, it seems that Onan was rather reluctant to consummate this new relationship. In **Genesis 38:9**,

But Onan knew that the offspring would not be his; so whenever he lay with his brother's wife, he spilled his semen on the ground to keep from producing offspring for his brother.

God is not happy with Onan's behavior. In the 10th verse:

What he did was wicked in the Lord's sight, so he put him to death, also.

For countless generations, this verse has served as an admonition from God for all those young men who would contemplate spilling seed on the ground. How many guilt-ridden young men lay cowering under their blankets in the middle of the night waiting for the vengeful retribution of the Lord?

However, the meaning of this verse is far more significant than the mere rendering of a personal hygiene advisory.

Truth be known, there have been many "wicked men" in history, yet God did not put them to death as summarily as he did Er. Likewise, there have been countless seed spillers since the dawn of time, yet none of them was put to death as swiftly as was Onan. On the surface, how can you compare Onan's crime with that of a serial killer like David Berkowitz or a ruthless dictator like Fidel Castro?

Obviously, God has a very intense interest in seeing a seed from the tribe of Judah develop in the womb of Tamar. What is the nature of this intense interest? What makes that interest so different than in any other case?

Let's start with the most obvious. From Tamar's womb will come, 40 generations later, the birth of Christ, God's Son. Unbeknownst to the world's theologians, we are seeing the expression of the most primal force within God: His motive to birth His lineage.

Poor Onan. He had no idea of the position in which he was placed. By not cooperating in consummating his relationship with Tamar, he stood in defiance of not just *a* purpose of God, but rather, *the* purpose of God. God's primary Will was to produce His own uncontested lineage. That lineage was to spring forth from the tribe of Judah, *through the womb of Tamar.* Henceforth, all of Judah's men had better take heed: don't interfere with God's plan to place a seed, from Judah's tribe, within the womb of Tamar.

Next in line for Tamar is Judah's last son, Shelah. Shelah is of a young age, so Judah tells Tamar that she will have to wait until Shelah has grown to manhood. However, the 11th verse reveals that Judah is secretly concerned about the fate of his last remaining son. "He may die, like his brothers." Apparently, Judah's suspicion is directed toward Tamar. He is concerned that the death of his sons is somehow Tamar's fault. He, of course, would never consider that his sons were responsible.

After the passing of some time, Tamar realizes that Judah is never going to give his last son to her. This is when she hatches, out of desperation, plan B. Obviously; Tamar's biological clock is ticking. She decides that she has one last chance to receive the providential seed. She also knows that she will have to risk her life because if she becomes pregnant and is found out, she will surely face a horrible and painful death by burning (the prescribed punishment for such an offense).

Tamar disguises herself as a temple prostitute and waits for Judah who is on his way to visit a friend. Judah sees her but does not recognize her because her face is veiled. Judah approaches her and suggests sexual relations with her. Tamar agrees, for a price. She cleverly asks for a payment that will require him to leave some sort of identification until he returns with the payment (a young goat). She asks for his cord, seal, and his staff. This would be the modern equivalent to documents of identification. She said she would hold these until he returned with payment.

After they have relations, Judah leaves and sends one of his friends to bring the goat to her. But by the time he gets there, Tamar is long gone. She had what she wanted: she had his seed and was pregnant by Judah, plus she had a way to positively identify Judah as the father (by his seal, cord, and staff).

Three months later, it is reported to Judah that his daughter-in-law is pregnant. Judah immediately condemns her to be burned to death. Tamar sends a message to Judah: "The man by whom I am pregnant is the owner of these. See if you can recognize whose cord, seal and staff these are." Judah takes a good look at his cord, seal, and staff, and says, "She is more righteous than I, since I would not give her to my son Shelah!" **Genesis 38:26**

The reason Tamar's story is remembered is because no woman had touched God's heart so deeply. There are two fundamental components that stand out uniquely.

First, Tamar was willing to do her mission at the risk of her life, but second and even more important, she was willing to risk her life for God's most fundamental, primary and important purpose: to produce His line. Since the fall, no one had been in the position to attend God on this deepest of levels. The deepest standard of attendance is to identify and attend the most essential purpose and desire of God. Tamar did that at the risk of her life. The most direct and perfect attendance of God, therefore, is to produce His line, His lineage. There is no greater manifestation of the words: God's Will.

Far from being a shameful person, Tamar is setting the example of the life that will most fully console God. That is accomplished by living for the advancement of God's lineage at the risk of one's own life. This is, in fact, the model of the messiah's purpose and virtue.

Thus, the name Tamar will endure throughout the ages despite the indictments of a Judeo-Christian world against her.

"strange"

"an alien element"

"serves only to disturb"

"few people would choose this chapter as a basis for teaching or preaching"

"dark old tale"

"unlovely narrative"

"from rank ground"

"twisted"

"wistful"

"pathetic yearning"

Christian ministers for ages have had to answer questions regarding Tamar's behavior. Many either avoided the question or concluded that it was just a mystery. Church leaders, for centuries, have told their members that the question wasn't important or that such a question expressed doubt toward their faith. Such leaders are too mindful of the possibility that their members would realize that their leaders didn't know everything. The tragedy is that, in such responses, we have lost a key opportunity to understand the Old Testament's deepest example of attendance and heart to God.

Understanding this heart will be a key in understanding what deeply motivates Jesus in his primary mission. It opens the door for us to more fully commune with his sorrow that night before his cross.

Today, armed with the clear vision of the scripture, we are able to bring everything out into the light. We need not fear any knowledge. There is no circumstance that cannot be enlightened through God's word.

The truth of the scriptures not only exonerates Tamar but exalts her to the highest level. Could there be any greater example that demonstrates the need for a deeper, fuller perspective?

Zerah and Perez

While engaged to another (Shelah), Tamar becomes pregnant by Judah. In fact, she is pregnant with twins. The twin brothers, Zerah and Perez, are to be to the internal Foundation for the Messiah, what Esau and Jacob are to the external Foundation for the Messiah.

Zerah sticks his hand out of the womb and a red cord is tied around his wrist to signify that he came out first. Zerah is firstborn and is, therefore, in the Cain-Esau position. Then, in an unprecedented fashion, the two brothers changed positions *inside the womb* and Perez emerged ahead of Zerah. This represents the change of blood order inside the womb of Tamar.

Remember when Jacob restored the birthright back to God's side? The change of blood order inside the womb means that the birthright is restored to God's side inside the womb of Tamar.

Joshua inherited Moses' mission because he was placed in a similar situation and displayed a similar faith as Moses. Elisha received "a double portion" of God's spirit after Elijah. Likewise, if there could be a future woman in a similar situation as Tamar with a similar attitude and heart, she could then become the recipient of Tamar's condition that had sanctified her womb, making a foundation for a living Adam to be born.

Exactly 40 generations later, Mary received the invocation of the Holy Spirit and Jesus was conceived inside her womb. Mary's faith and circumstance mirrored that of Tamar's.

Rahab

After Tamar we see the story of Rahab in the book of Joshua. Rahab is a prostitute in Jericho. The king of Jericho instructs Rahab to keep on the lookout for any Hebrew spies lurking about. Instead, Rahab hides the spies from the king's soldiers. Later, when Jericho is destroyed, only Rahab and her family survive. She eventually becomes Salmon's wife of the tribe of Judah.

Ruth

Next is the story of Ruth. Ruth has her own book in the Old Testament. Ruth is the mother of Obed, the father of Jesse, the father of King David.

Ruth was married to Mahlon, but he died. The story in the book of Ruth explains how she became the bride of Boaz. The significant moment with regard to the restoration pattern is when Ruth approaches Boaz while he is asleep on the threshing room floor. Boaz was the kinsman of Mahlon. By the same Levirate code that was applied to Onan, the closest kinsman of the deceased husband should take his property and his widow.

Ruth takes a shine to Boaz. Boaz is a kinsman of her deceased husband but is not the closest kinsman. She waits until he is asleep and then lays down at his feet. When Boaz wakes, he is surprised to find a woman there with him. She says to him, "spread the corner of your garment over me for you are my kinsman-redeemer." She was making an offer that most men wouldn't refuse. However, Boaz does not accept her offer. He indicates that, technically, he wasn't her kinsman-redeemer because there was a "closer kinsman than I."

Eventually, Boaz meets with the closer kinsman, they come to an agreement and Boaz takes Ruth as his wife. Boaz and Ruth were the great-great grandparents of David.

Bathsheba

Bathsheba is the wife of Uriah, one of David's generals. One day David is on a rooftop and spots Bathsheba in her house taking a bath. He takes great interest in Bathsheba at that moment for obvious reasons.

Reverend Moon explains in his speech on "The Change of Blood Lineage,"

Actually, the mother of King Solomon was Bathsheba, originally the wife of Uriah before King David stole her. Then how could the child from that union become King Solomon? Bathsheba was in the providential position of Eve in the Garden of Eden, before the fall. David was in the position of Adam, and Uriah was in the position of the archangel. The archangel distracted the spouse of Adam with love and stole her away, making her fall. A reversal course is needed in order to indemnify that; therefore a person in the position of the archangel's wife had to be restored to the position of Eve. Therefore, the child who was born on the foundation of that reversal could be born as a child of heavenly love, a child of glory. Solomon was such a child of glory.

Mary

The conception of Christ is set up in the same historical pattern. Joseph is in the position of the archangel, Mary in the position of Eve and the Holy Spirit in the position of Adam.

In the pattern of the fall, while Adam and Eve are engaged the archangel tempts Eve to him, and through sexual relations ultimately Adam dies and is reborn as the "son" of Satan.

Mary, like Tamar, is thought to be guilty of illicit sexual activity. Like Tamar, the penalty of death looms over her for her apparent act of adultery. Until an angel appears to Joseph in a dream, even he believes she has violated her vows of purity. Yet Mary is steadfast and faithful. In the same pattern as Tamar, Mary willingly risks her life in attendance to the most essential Will of God: to produce His lineage.

The conception of Christ follows the reverse course of the fall. While the archangel (Joseph) is engaged to Eve (Mary), Adam (the Holy Spirit) tempts Eve to God's side. Thus, the fruit of Mary's womb is the sinless Adam, the Son of God.

Ultimately this story reveals the unique position and ability of Christ to attend God's deepest and most essential motives. It is the very purpose for which He created. It is the substantial affirmation of His invisible nature as "Father."

John 3:16 proclaimed, "God so loved the world, that He gave His only Son." What is the meaning of "He gave"? What did God give when Jesus was sacrificed on the cross? Does the world know? Do we Christians really know?

Did God really give all that much? Wasn't Jesus going to heaven anyway? After he died on the cross, didn't he go to the right hand of the Father? Then, what did God give up when He sacrificed Jesus on the cross? The life that was sacrificed was the life that could have multiplied the pure lineage of God.

When such a statement is made it will be ridiculed and scorned. Christians will reel in its wake. The secular culture will laugh and scoff. It will be the butt of jokes and snide remarks. But it is true. Jesus gave up his opportunity to be a true husband and true father. This is the full meaning of his cross. It is the root of his deepest sorrow.

God gave up the full potential that would have been achieved through Jesus' own family life.

Jesus' Family Life

Look at those three words together. What does it make you feel? Do you feel a stirring, a disturbing, uncomfortable sense? Do your eyes want to move past it and on to something else? Why is that? Why would the concept of Jesus with his holy bride and lovely holy children create such a reaction?

It is because the entire history of culture meets, clashes and falters under the weight of that mighty concept. There are no existing cultural or religious values, until now, that can sustain it. Therefore, it should be those cultures and religions that are deemed remiss, not the concept of Jesus' True Family.

As a result, the confrontation of the two cultural trends is destined to come to an end. One views man as nothing more than a natural animal subject to natural desires, while the other views man as spirit, yet cursed within the vile sexual desires of temporal flesh. God's True Family Ideal is a part of neither.

Jesus came as the second True Parents of humankind. The original first parents were Adam and Eve. If Jesus had not been killed, the

*unification between Judaism and Israel would have come about cen-
tering upon Eve, the mother position. The Messiah comes in the position of parent and king. The king needs his queen. Jesus stood in the
position of the bridegroom, and his 12 disciples, 72 apostles and 120
elders were all in the position of the bride. Once the bride and bridegroom positions united, then it was possible to return to the original
True Lineage. Israel doesn't realize this. The Christian world doesn't
realize this.*

**Rev. Sun Myung Moon,
"True Parents' Day is My True Son's Day," April 18, 1996**

Psalms 45:10–17

*Daughters of kings are among your honored women; at your right hand
is the royal bride in gold of Ophir. Listen, O daughter, consider and give
ear: Forget your people and your father's house. The king is enthralled
by your beauty; honor him, for he is your lord. The Daughter of Tyre will
come with a gift, men of wealth will seek your favor. All glorious is the
princess within her chamber; her gown is interwoven with gold. In embroidered garments she is led to the king; her virgin companions follow her
and are brought to you. They are led in with joy and gladness; they enter
the palace of the king. Your sons will take the place of your fathers; you
will make them princes throughout the land. I will perpetuate your memory through all generations; therefore the nations will praise you forever
and ever.*

Chapter Nine

Mission of Jesus

We begin this chapter on Jesus on the foundation of an entire historical providence that unfolds in primary and secondary dimensions. This twofold manifestation is a reflection of the centrality of human responsibility in the affairs of God.

We have categorically established that the primary branch of God's dispensation is His original Will, which is predestined to be realized eventually. Because God requires man's cooperation in the fulfillment of His primary Will, however, a secondary route of providence opens as a consequence of man's failure to fulfill that providential role.

The objective of that secondary path is to re-create all the necessary events, circumstances and figures in order to fulfill, at a future time, the primary Will of God. Once that new foundation is established, a new central figure takes up the mission of the predecessor and attempts to once again fulfill God's original Will.

The providence centering on Jesus is likewise established with primary and secondary objectives. Unlike the traditional Christian view that divides Christ's mission into two advents separated by 2,000 years, Jesus seeks to accomplish everything in a single primary mission that requires the faithful response of contemporary Israel.

This primary objective is what is meant by the term "the Kingdom of God."

Jesus Calls for Faith and the Kingdom

Mark 1:15

"The time has come," he said. "The kingdom of God is near. Repent and believe the good news!"

Matthew 4:17

From that time on Jesus began to preach, "Repent, for the kingdom of heaven is near."

John 6:28–29

Then they asked him, "What must we do to do the works God requires?" Jesus answered, "The work of God is this: to believe in the one he has sent."

Clearly the Kingdom was an immediate objective in Jesus' view. He said the "time has come, the Kingdom is near." He is asking them, at that moment, to repent. If they do, the unfolding of the Kingdom will be the consequence of that repentance. How more explicit can it be than the clear answer of **John 6:28–29**? The Will of God is to believe in him, whom God has sent.

Matthew 23:37

"O Jerusalem, Jerusalem, you who kill the prophets and stone those sent to you, how often I have longed to gather your children together, as a hen gathers her chicks under her wings, but you were not willing."

Matthew 23:37 is significant because Jesus is describing the two branches of God's providence. Jerusalem "killing and stoning the prophets" reflects **Jeremiah 25:4–7**. Jeremiah tells Israel that they were inexorably locked on the secondary path; however, they could have remained in the land had they heeded the prophets.

Jesus indicates that the Israelites' rejection of him falls into that same secondary category and is contrary to his own expressed desire "to gather Israel together, as a hen gathers her chicks under her wings." Jesus' desire reflects **Isaiah 65:17**, which stated "a new heaven and new earth" would come to Jerusalem, the primary plan.

Jesus indicates, "You were not willing", that is, Israel was not willing. Jesus wanted it, God wanted it, but it was Israel's responsibility. In failing to respond in faith to Jesus, Jeremiah's admonition of 600 years earlier, "you have brought harm to yourselves," is, sadly, realized once again.

Could it be possible that Jesus had a personal desire that was contrary to the primary Will of God? Could the faithless people be in greater concert with what God really wanted than Jesus himself?

In **John 8:37–42**, Jesus clearly explains the proper conduct of "the descendants of Abraham."

John 8:37–42

*"I know **you are Abraham's descendants. Yet you are ready to kill me**, because you have no room for my word. I am telling you what I have seen in the Father's presence, and you do what you have heard from your father."*

*"Abraham is our father," they answered. "**If you were Abraham's children**," said Jesus, "then you would **do the things Abraham did. As it is, you are determined to kill me**, a man who has told you the truth that I heard from God. **Abraham did not do such things**." "You are doing the things your own father does."*

"We are not illegitimate children," they protested. "The only Father we have is God himself."

*Jesus said to them, "**If God were your Father, you would love me, for I came from God** and now am here. I have not come on my own; but he sent me."*

Jesus establishes that the people *are* the descendants of Abraham, "yet you are ready to kill me." Jesus is affirming that killing the messiah is inconsistent with the purpose for Abraham's descendants. Jesus goes on to explain even more emphatically, "If you were Abraham's children, you would do the things Abraham did; as it is, you are determined to kill me . . . *Abraham did not do such things.*"

Matthew 21:35–37

*The tenants seized his servants; they beat one, killed another, and stoned a third. Then he sent other servants to them, more than the first time, and the tenants treated them the same way. Last of all, he sent his son to them. "**They will respect my son**," he said.*

Here Jesus reveals the motive of God in sending the son, "They will respect my son." In fact, this parable (**Matthew 21:35–43**) borrows from the fifth chapter of Isaiah "Song of the Vineyard" in which God laments "what more could I have done for my vineyard that I did not already do? And yet, when I looked for good fruit, why did I find only bad?" Jesus indicates that the bad tradition of Israel rejecting its prophets is one that God seeks to reverse in sending His son; surely "they will respect my son."

The Kingdom Was Meant to Unfold in Israel

Let us consider scripture that shows the Kingdom could have been established in Jesus' day.

Matthew 21:43
Therefore I tell you that the kingdom of God will be taken away from you and given to a people who will produce its fruit.

Notice that Jesus says, "The Kingdom of God will be *taken away* from you." This indicates that the Kingdom *was* theirs, *was* to be set up at that time and, therefore, all prophecy of "glory" *was* relevant for that time. However, some mitigating circumstance intervened and altered that destiny. What could it possibly be? Perhaps God's warning through Jeremiah is the answer:

Jeremiah 18:9–10
And if at another time I announce that a nation or kingdom is to be built up and planted, and **IF** *it does evil in my sight and does not obey me, then I will reconsider the good I had intended to do for it.*

The contemporary relevance of the Kingdom is also expressed in **Matthew 23:13:**

Woe to you, teachers of the law and Pharisees, you hypocrites! You **shut the kingdom of heaven** *in men's faces. You yourselves do not enter, nor will you let those enter who are trying to.*

Notice, first of all, Jesus' great frustration and sense of loss because of the actions of the religious leaders. Second, notice that he indicates that they are engaged in "shutting" the gates to the Kingdom. This, of course, means that the gates "were open" because now "was the time." Jesus didn't say that their hypocrisy failed to "open" the gates; he indicated, instead, that the gates were already wide open.

Jesus' frustration, then, is that a great potential for good is being postponed. Thus, the Kingdom must be given to others who can produce the fruits in their season, sadly far in the future.

This will give even greater impetus to Jesus' words later when he says, "the harvest is plentiful, but the laborers are few." The problem wasn't "the time" or that the "fruits were not in season." The problem was that "the laborers were few." This will reflect back on the job performance of the man who was to "make a people ready for the Lord" (John the Baptist).

Luke 19:41–44

*As he approached Jerusalem and saw the city, **he wept over it** and said, "If you, even you, had only known **on this day what would bring you peace** but now it is hidden from your eyes. The days will come upon you when your enemies will build an embankment against you and encircle you and hem you in on every side. They will dash you to the ground, you and the children within your walls. They will not leave one stone on another, **because you did not recognize the time of God's coming to you.**"*

Here again, we see Jesus' sorrow and frustration. Notice that he again pinpoints "on this day" the potential of his contemporary age to "bring you peace." Later, we will examine what Jesus means by "peace." Also noteworthy is that Jesus cites a bleak future for Israel as a result of its failure to recognize "God's coming to you."

The Dispensation Turns from 'Primary' to 'Secondary'

Consistent with the covenant-centered flow of history, the providence shifts from primary to secondary whenever Israel fails to respond in timely fashion. Typically, the people are unable to understand and they react defensively to the change of focus from "blessing" to "curse." We see an example of this in the book of Jeremiah. After Jeremiah announces the 70 years of exile, he is considered to be a traitor. They do not understand what he is talking about in **Jeremiah 26:8–9:**

*But as soon as Jeremiah finished telling all the people everything the LORD had commanded him to say, the priests, the prophets and all the people seized him and said, "**You must die!** Why do you prophesy in the Lord's name that this house will be like Shiloh and this city will be desolate and deserted?"*

We see the same phenomenon in the mission of Jesus. After roughly two years of calling for faith and repentance, Israel is unrepentant and unresponsive. As a result of this faithless stance, Jesus announces the dispensational shift from primary to secondary in **Matthew 16:21:**

From that time on Jesus began to explain to his disciples that he must go to Jerusalem and suffer many things.

"From that time Jesus *began."* This is the shift from the Kingdom to the cross, from primary to secondary, from blessing to curse, from glorious destiny for Israel to bleak destiny for Israel, from Lord of Glory to Lord of Suffering. This is six days before the Mount of Transfiguration and roughly the beginning of the last year of Jesus' ministry.

We can also examine the disciples' confusion at this sudden shift of focus.

Luke 18:34

The disciples did not understand any of this. Its meaning was hidden from them, and they did not know what he was talking about.

Why were they so confused? Were they just not paying attention for two years or was this message categorically different from Jesus' teaching of the first two years? We can see evidence that the apostles, even after the crucifixion and resurrection, still clung to the idea that "the Kingdom" was going to be erected in their lifetime. After all, in **Matthew 13:11–16**, Jesus affirms that the "knowledge of the Kingdom of Heaven" had been given to his disciples.

We can see their attitude after the crucifixion of Jesus in **Luke 24:21**. Their faces are "downcast." In the *King James Version*, Jesus asks them, "What manner of communications are these that ye have one to another, as ye walk, and are sad"? Most interesting is the disciples' answer: *"We **had hoped** that he was the one who was going to **redeem Israel**."*

To what were they referring by the term "redeem Israel." It is the vision of the Kingdom with Israel as "the head" and not "the tail." It is the primary work of "the messiah" to restore the glory of Solomon's era. Consider **Zechariah 8:21–23:**

And the inhabitants of one city shall go to another, saying, "Let us go speedily to pray before the LORD, and to seek the LORD of hosts: I will go also."

> *Yea, **many people and strong nations** shall come to seek the LORD of hosts **in Jerusalem**, and to pray before the LORD.*
>
> *Thus saith the LORD of hosts; "In those days it shall come to pass, that ten men shall take hold out of all languages of the nations, even **shall take hold of the skirt of him that is a Jew**, saying, 'We will go with you: **for we have heard that God is with you.'** "*

This vision is what the apostles "had hoped" for. Notice that they describe their hope in past tense. Clearly, Jesus' death closed the door on an expectation laid down in scripture and reaffirmed by Jesus in the first two years of his ministry. Thus, they were saddened and disheartened by Jesus' crucifixion.

Even in their last meeting with Jesus before his ascension into heaven, they ask:

Acts 1:6
*So when they met together, they asked him, "Lord, are you at this time going **to restore the kingdom to Israel**?"*

They just can't fully accept that the providence had turned away from that initial destiny. This is probably one reason Jesus told them, "I'm coming soon." If they had known that they were just beginning a providence of at least a 2,000-year prolongation, they might have been irrevocably disheartened.

From 'Blessing' to 'Curse'

With the shift from primary to secondary, we also see a change in the description of Israel's destiny from one of "blessing" to one of impending "curse."

Luke 23:28–31
Jesus turned and said to them, "Daughters of Jerusalem, do not weep for me; weep for yourselves and for your children. For the time will come when you will say, 'Blessed are the barren women, the wombs that never bore and the breasts that never nursed!' Then they will say to the mountains, 'Fall on us!' and to the hills, 'Cover us!' "

Jesus recites **Hosea 10:8**: "They will say to the mountains, 'Fall on us!' and to the hills, 'Cover us!' " These were the words of sinful Israel carried away by the Assyrians. Jesus is indicating that his rejection and crucifixion represents the same kind of turning point in Israel's destiny as it did in Hosea's time. He is predicting hard times ahead for Israel as a result. This is very significant in relation to God's promise in **Deuteronomy 29:24**: Israel will only be destroyed if it violates the laws, decrees and commandments of God.

In the 34th verse of the same 23rd chapter of Luke, Jesus says, "Father forgive them, they know not what they do."

Of course, the implication is that had they known what they were doing, they would not have proceeded to crucify Jesus.

We also see a gloomy description of Israel's future in Luke.

Luke 19:41–44

As he approached Jerusalem and saw the city, **he wept over it** *and said, "If you, even you, had only known* **on this day what would bring you peace**—*but now it is hidden from your eyes.* **THE DAYS WILL COME UPON YOU WHEN YOUR ENEMIES WILL BUILD AN EMBANKMENT AGAINST YOU AND ENCIRCLE YOU AND HEM YOU IN ON EVERY SIDE. THEY WILL DASH YOU TO THE GROUND, YOU AND THE CHILDREN WITHIN YOUR WALLS. THEY WILL NOT LEAVE ONE STONE ON ANOTHER,** *because you did not* **recognize the time of God's coming to you."**

In fact, in 70 A.D., Rome sacked Jerusalem, the Jews were scattered and were without a nation until 1948.

Jesus and the Old Testament

On the one hand we can find words of Jesus that seem to state that the Old Testament writings declare, solely, that Jesus should die.

Luke 24:25–26

He (Jesus) *said to them, "How foolish you are and how slow of heart you are to believe all that the prophets have spoken!* **Did not Christ have to suffer these things and then enter into his glory?"** *And beginning with* **Moses and all the Prophets**, *he explained to them what was said in* **all** *the scripture concerning himself.*

John 18:36

*Jesus said, "**My kingdom is not of this world**. If it were, my servants would fight to prevent my arrest by the Jews. But now my kingdom is from another place."*

John 12:37–41

Even after Jesus had done all these miraculous signs in their presence, they still would not believe in him. This was to fulfill the word of Isaiah the prophet:

"Lord, who has believed our message and to whom has the arm of the Lord been revealed?"

For this reason they could not believe, because, as Isaiah says elsewhere:

*"**He has blinded their eyes and deadened their hearts, so they can neither see with their eyes, nor understand with their hearts**, nor turn and I would heal them."*

Isaiah said this because he saw Jesus' glory and spoke about him.

We can now understand why we observe what appear to be contradictory assertions about the way Jesus should go. There was a providential shift from primary to secondary, from blessing to curse, as prescribed by the covenant agreement. Thus, we can pinpoint a dramatic change in focus after **Matthew 16:21**. As a result, Jesus' scriptural focus likewise reflects this shift toward the suffering-curse side of the ledger. In the last year of his ministry, Jesus is faced with the approaching course of blood atonement. This does not mean, however, that Jesus will not accept repentance even up to the last minute. Consider, for example, in Jeremiah's time, that even after he has announced the 70-year exile period, God tells him in **Jeremiah 26:3:**

Perhaps they will listen and each will turn from his evil way. Then I will relent and not bring on them the disaster I was planning because of the evil they have done.

In a similar way, even though the cross became the announced objective in his last year, Jesus still maintained a flickering hope that his chosen people would still repent and in the 11th hour fulfill their (and his) original destiny.

This is the substance of his sorrowful prayer in Gethsemane, "if it be possible, let this cup pass . . ." Christians are shut out of

Gethsemane because it is a perfect articulation of Jesus grappling not with a single destiny but rather with primary and secondary purpose. How could the Lord himself express reluctance to go to the cross if that were the only course of action, "from the foundation of the world"?

Many insist that **Revelation 13:8** emphatically declares Jesus' death by reference to "the lamb slain from the foundations of the world." However, upon deeper inspection, the prepositional phrase "from the foundations of the world" is more correctly linked to "all whose names have not been written in the Book of Life" rather than to "the lamb who was slain." The proper rendering of Revelation 13:8 would then be as follows: All the names not written from the foundations of the world in the Book of Life belonging to the Lamb who was slain." This is supported by **Revelation 17:8**.

In the last year of his ministry, Jesus' struggle is rooted in his desire, on the one hand, to maintain his focus on the possibility that the Kingdom could still come at that time. After all, Nineveh repented in the final moment.

On the other hand, faced with the reality of no faith in Israel, he had to also address the providential meaning of his impending death. Most important, the apostles would need to understand the significance of his death, were it to come. That understanding, as well as the understanding of the coming Kingdom, was implicit within the voice of the Old Testament.

In fact, there is a dramatic example of God seeking intervention in the final moment. We see the amazing story recorded in **Matthew 27:19**:

> While Pilate was sitting on the judge's seat, his wife sent him this message; "Don't have anything to do with that innocent man, for I have suffered a great deal today in a dream because of him."

Think of it, on the single day out of the year a Jewish prisoner is to be released, Jesus stands before Pilate to be judged. Pilate's wife, on that very same day, has a dream of Jesus, and his innocence is revealed to her. The reason Pilate is trying to bargain for Jesus' life is because he has been prodded to do so at his wife's insistence. It had already been decided beforehand that Barabbas would be the prisoner to be released. However, Pilate suggests releasing Jesus in order to satisfy his wife's sudden and most irregular request.

As mentioned, after Jesus' crucifixion, his followers were

depressed and disheartened. Jesus had to convince them that what took place was not just a failure or defeat. He had to show them that, though less preferred, the prolongation course of the way of indemnity is also a course that culminates in great hope. And thus, "beginning with Moses and all of the prophets, he explained to them what had been said in all the scriptures concerning himself."

In the first two years of his ministry, however, Jesus' view of the meaning of the Old Testament was quite different.

John 5:39–40

*You diligently study the Scriptures because you think that by them you possess eternal life. These are the Scriptures that **testify about me**, yet you **refuse to come to me** to have life.*

Here Jesus affirms that the intent of the scripture is to convince the chosen people that they *should* come to Jesus. He goes on to express even more emphatically:

John 5:45–47

*But do not think I will accuse you before the Father. **Your accuser is Moses**, on whom your hopes are set. **If you believed Moses, you would believe me, for he wrote about me**. But since you do not believe what he wrote, how are you going to believe what I say?*

When did Moses write of Jesus? It is in **Deuteronomy 18:15:** *The Lord your God will raise up for you a prophet like me from among your own brothers. **You must listen to him.***

How can it be unequivocally asserted that Moses is referring to Jesus? **Acts 3:21–22** recites Moses' words from **Deuteronomy 18:15**

***He (Jesus) must remain in heaven until the time comes for God to restore everything, as he promised long ago through his holy prophets. For* MOSES SAID,** *"The Lord your God will raise up for you a prophet like me from among your own people; you must listen to everything he tells you."*

From this viewpoint, the Old Testament is testifying that Israel should receive its king.

Jesus and Prophecy of Glory

If it were true that all prophecy of glory is only referring to the Second Coming of Christ, then it would stand to reason that we would not observe any evidence of Jesus in Israel linking those scriptures with his contemporary role. It is thought that only prophecy of suffering applies to Jesus in his first coming.

In fact, Jesus makes several references to prophecy of glory and indicates that indeed they pertain to his work in Israel. Let's first examine **Luke 4:16–21:**

> *He went to Nazareth, where he had been brought up, and on the Sabbath day he went into the synagogue, as was his custom. And he stood up to read. The scroll of the prophet Isaiah was handed to him. Unrolling it, he found the place where it is written: "The Spirit of the Lord is on me, because he has anointed me to preach good news to the poor. He has sent me to proclaim freedom for the prisoners and recovery of sight for the blind, to release the oppressed, to proclaim the year of the Lord's favor."*
>
> *Then he rolled up the scroll, gave it back to the attendant and sat down. The eyes of everyone in the synagogue were fastened on him, and he began by saying to them, **"Today this scripture is fulfilled in your hearing."***

Jesus himself chooses to recite Isaiah chapter 61. "The scroll of the prophet Isaiah was handed him. Unrolling it, *he found* the place where it is written." What a perfect time to recite **Isaiah 53**, "by his stripes we are healed." Yet Jesus bypasses **Isaiah 53** (a prophecy of suffering) and goes straight to **Isaiah 61** (a prophecy of glory).

Notice the "blessing" tone of the chapter:

Isaiah 61:4–6, 9
*They will rebuild the ancient ruins and restore the places long devastated; they will renew the ruined cities that have been devastated for generations. **Aliens will shepherd your flocks; foreigners will work your fields and vineyards. And you will be called priests of the LORD, you will be named ministers of our God. You will feed on the wealth of nations, and in their riches you will boast.***

*Their descendants will be known among the nations and their offspring among the peoples. All who see them will acknowledge that they are a people the **LORD has blessed.***

Jesus recites the opening verses of chapter 61 and concludes, *"Today this scripture is fulfilled in your hearing."*

"Today" it is fulfilled. Also significant is the 8th verse mentions the establishment of a new, everlasting covenant. We see mention of a "new covenant" in other scripture:

Jeremiah 31:31–34

*"The time is coming," declares the LORD, "when I will make a **new covenant** with the house of Israel and with the house of Judah. It will not be like the covenant I made with their forefathers when I took them by the hand to lead them out of Egypt, because they broke my covenant, though I was a husband to them," declares the LORD.*

"This is the covenant I will make with the house of Israel after that time," declares the LORD. "I will put my law in their minds and write it on their hearts. I will be their God, and they will be my people. No longer will a man teach his neighbor, or a man his brother, saying, 'Know the LORD,' because they will all know me, from the least of them to the greatest," declares the LORD. "For I will forgive their wickedness and will remember their sins no more."

Jeremiah is describing the unfolding of the Kingdom in Israel "if" Israel receives the messiah when he comes. Because this did not happen, Christians assume this refers to the Second Coming and the eventual salvation of the Jews, with no relevance to Jesus in his first coming.

What it actually reveals is that a "new covenant" was to be set up if Israel accepted Christ when he came. It provided for forgiveness of sins without having to *require his path to the cross*. Remember, his suffering would only be required "if" no faith was found in Israel.

We see another example in **Ezekiel 37:24–27:**

*My servant David will be king over them, and they will all have one shepherd. They will follow my laws and be careful to keep my decrees. They will live in the land I gave to my servant Jacob, the land where your fathers lived. They and their children and their children's children will live there forever, and David my servant will be their prince forever. **I will make a covenant of peace with them**; it will be an everlasting covenant. I will establish them and increase their numbers, and I will put my sanctuary among them forever. My dwelling place will be with them; I will be their God, and they will be my people.*

"The covenant of peace" is the same "new covenant" of Jeremiah 31 and Isaiah 61. Recall Jesus' words in:

Luke 19:41–44

As he approached Jerusalem and saw the city, **he wept over it** *and said, "If you, even you, had only known* ON THIS DAY WHAT WOULD BRING YOU PEACE—*but now it is hidden from your eyes. The days will come upon you when your enemies will build an embankment against you and encircle you and hem you in on every side. They will dash you to the ground, you and the children within your walls. They will not leave one stone on another,* **because you did not recognize the time of God's coming to you."**

"What would bring you peace" = the covenant of peace = the new covenant. It was to be received in Israel through faith in Jesus. It would not require Jesus to suffer and die. Jesus had to suffer and die because "it was hidden" from their eyes and they "did not recognize the time of God's coming to them." Thus, the curse in the law was invoked. The "new heaven and new earth" could not be implemented in Jerusalem. The Kingdom, then, "is taken from them and given to another nation that can produce the fruits in their seasons." A "new Jerusalem" is set up for future fulfillment, a fulfillment that could have been realized at that time.

But the most amazing and explicit of all are Jesus' words in **Matthew 10:5** and **Matthew 15:24.**

Matthew 10:5–7

These twelve Jesus sent out with the following instructions: "Do not go among the **Gentiles** *or enter any town of the* **Samaritans**. *Go rather to* **the lost sheep of Israel**. *As you go, preach this message: 'The kingdom of heaven is near.' "*

Matthew 15:24

He answered, "I was sent only to **the lost sheep of Israel**."

Why did Jesus show such a startling preference toward the blood descendants of the house of Israel? Was it because he only cared for his fellow Jews? Of course not! The reason is simple. It was only the blood descendants of the house of Israel who were given the responsibility in the covenant. In other words, it was only the Jews whose faith in Christ or lack thereof would determine the outcome of the Kingdom or the cross. It was *their* faith or lack thereof that would swing the providence toward primary or secondary.

When Jesus uses the term "lost sheep of the house of Israel," he is alluding to another prophecy of glory in Ezekiel:

Ezekiel 34: 16, 23–28

I will search for the lost and bring back the strays. I will bind up the injured and strengthen the weak, but the sleek and the strong I will destroy. I will shepherd the flock with justice.

I will place over them one shepherd, my servant David, and he will tend them; he will tend them and be their shepherd. I the LORD will be their God, and my servant David will be prince among them. I the LORD have spoken.

I will make a covenant of peace with them and rid the land of wild beasts so that they may live in the desert and sleep in the forests in safety. I will bless them and the places surrounding my hill. I will send down showers in season; there will be showers of blessing. The trees of the field will yield their fruit and the ground will yield its crops; the people will be secure in their land. They will know that I am the LORD, when I break the bars of their yoke and rescue them from the hands of those who enslaved them. They will no longer be plundered by the nations, nor will wild animals devour them. They will live in safety, and no one will make them afraid.

Again, this new covenant, if received in faith by Israel, would transform the world. All prophecy of glory would be fulfilled at that time. Jesus would not have had to go the way of the cross and there would be no need for the return of Christ 2,000 years later. We would all be speaking Aramaic today. The nations would have "beaten their swords into plowshares" many years ago. The "Kingdom" would have been established and the vision of **Zechariah 8:22–23** would have been realized:

Yea, many people and strong nations shall come to seek the LORD of hosts in Jerusalem, and to pray before the LORD.

Thus saith the LORD of hosts; "In those days it shall come to pass, that ten men shall take hold out of all languages of the nations, even shall take hold of the skirt of him that is a Jew, saying, 'We will go with you: for we have heard that God is with you.'"

And **Isaiah 65:17-18**

Behold, I will create new heavens and a new earth. The former things will not be remembered, nor will they come to mind. But be glad and rejoice forever in what I will create, for I will create Jerusalem to be a delight and its people a joy.

This Kingdom would have an earthly manifestation. It would not *just* be an earthly Kingdom but would follow the parameters of "what is sown on earth is reaped in heaven."

This, then, forms the basis to understand the role and method of the Second Coming of Christ. We see this reflected in **Hebrews 9:28:**

Christ was sacrificed once to take away the sins of many people; and he will appear a second time, not to bear sin, but to bring salvation to those who are waiting for him.

Christ returns to the moment, position, and function that Jesus leaves behind when he turns from his primary objective to the secondary course of blood atonement.

Christ returns to accomplish Jesus' primary mission, that is, the bringing of a salvation that will manifest visibly in the world and will not require his shedding of blood. What could that mission entail?

The Need for Blood Atonement

Jesus came to bring the Kingdom and salvation in such a way that it would not have necessarily required him to shed his blood. He could not do this, however, because there was no faith. So the Second Coming will accomplish this goal and without shedding his blood. "He will appear a second time, not to bear sin, but to bring salvation". **Hebrews 9:28**

Let's affirm clearly that we are not seeking to *redefine the root of Christian faith*. Jesus *did* shed his blood and it *was* his shed blood that *did* atone for our sin. Salvation through Jesus Christ *is* valid and *is* what most Christians believe it to be.

We are examining the undone aspect of his mission because this is the true measure of evaluation with regard to the "fruit" of Christian faith, that is, the return of Christ and the nature of that mission.

Christ returns to do that which remains to be accomplished. If we reject out of hand that Jesus had a primary mission other than the way of the cross, however, we will have lost the truest measure by which we can understand the nature of that coming mission.

It is not a coincidence that, on the one hand, most Christians have a vague sense of Jesus' primary mission and, on the other hand, the cause of most divisiveness is the ever-widening array of eschatological issues.

Many cite the reference to Jesus as "the lamb of God" as indicative of a sole destiny to suffer and die. Jesus as the Lamb of God, however, does not absolutely imply the course of blood atonement. You will note that Jesus refers to all believers as his "lambs" in **John 21:15**. The lamb is a symbol of absolute obedience and innocence.

Hebrews 9:22 states that "without the shedding of blood, there is no remission of sin." This seems to suggest that there is no other way of atonement except by blood. The sentence structure of the original Greek text, however, places the word "almost" as a qualifier for the blood. It indicates that blood atonement in the Old Testament is not an absolute tradition or the sole preferred process of atonement.

And almost all things are by the law purged with blood; and without shedding of blood is no remission. (King James version)

A slightly different wording is in the New International Version:

In fact, the law requires that nearly everything be cleansed with blood, and without the shedding of blood there is no forgiveness.

Usually only the latter part of **Hebrews 9:22**, "without the shedding of blood there is no remission of sin," is emphasized. Overlooked is the most important first part that indicates that blood atonement, even in the Old Testament, is not an absolute standard. "Almost" and "nearly everything" is not indicative of an absolute.

We see evidence of this in **Hosea 6:6, Proverbs 16:6, Leviticus 16:10,** and **1 Samuel 15:22**. Nor is blood the sole way of covenant ratification in the Old Testament. Covenants could be ratified in a number of ways: building a monument, having a feast, salting, loosening the shoe, giving gifts, etc.

It should be stressed, we are not arguing against the atoning quality of Christ's shed blood, nor are we suggesting that there is no scriptural basis for Jesus' path to the cross. Christ's blood atoned for sin without a doubt. We are seeking to examine the nature of Jesus' primary plan for salvation because this will be the purpose for which he returns. He is returning, "not to bear sin, but to bring salvation." Again, our focus, in this case, is on the fruit, not to change the root.

The Bible on Atonement

There are many biblical examples of other methods of atonement for sin:

Hosea 6:6
*For I desire **mercy**, not **sacrifice**, and **acknowledgment of God** rather than **burnt offerings.***

In other words, faith supercedes the requirement for blood atonement.

Proverbs 16:6
Through love and faithfulness, sin is atoned.

Faith and Love Accomplish Atonement of Sin

In the Old Testament, another method of atonement that did not involve bloodshed was the tradition of the "scapegoat," as in **Leviticus 16:10:**

*But the goat chosen by lot as the scapegoat shall be presented alive before the LORD to be used for **making atonement** by **sending it into the desert** as a scapegoat.*

Compare this to what Jesus was trying to accomplish in the early part of his ministry:

Matthew 4:1–3

Then Jesus was led by the Spirit into the desert to be tempted by the devil. After fasting forty days and forty nights, he was hungry. The tempter came to him and said, "If you are the Son of God, tell these stones to become bread."

The heart of Christian faith is the "substitutionary atonement" of Christ's death. However, Jesus also established in the wilderness a "substitutionary atonement" through being "tempted in every way just as we are," yet without sinning. (**Hebrews 4:15**) In being tempted and not sinning, Jesus atoned for sin, in our stead, by his love and faithfulness in front of God. Thus **Luke 5:24:**

*"But that you may know that the **Son of Man has authority on earth to forgive sins.**"*

Jesus declares that he has the authority to forgive sins *on earth*! In fact, when anyone linked to Jesus in love and faith, Jesus would apply that authority to forgive them of their sins.

Luke 5:20
*When Jesus saw their **faith** he said, "Friend, **your sins are forgiven.**"*

Luke 7:47
*"Therefore, I tell you, **her many sins have been forgiven**—for **she loved much.** But he who has been forgiven little loves little." Then Jesus said to her, "Your sins are forgiven." The other guests began to say among themselves, "Who is this who even forgives sins?" Jesus said to the woman, **"Your faith has saved you;** go in peace."*

He didn't say, "Your sins will be forgiven after I die." He didn't have to make any sort of blood offering on the spot. He already had the authority via his wilderness course.

Thus, if the whole nation had done "the work of God to believe in him whom He has sent," would not Jesus be able to apply the forgiveness of sin to the nation and world at that time? Would not being prevented from doing that because of Israel's faithlessness cause him an immeasurable "sorrow unto death"?

Faith Is Primary while Blood Atonement Is Secondary

We are going to see a consistent placement of the tradition of blood atonement in a secondary, less preferred context. God's primary requirement is for the condition of faith. Where that condition of faith is established, the need for blood atonement is waived.

Hosea 6:6

*For I desire **mercy**, not **sacrifice**, and **acknowledgment of God** rather than **burnt offerings**.*

1 Samuel 15:21–22

The soldiers took sheep and cattle from the plunder, the best of what was devoted to God, in order to sacrifice them to the LORD your God at Gilgal.

*But Samuel replied: "Does the LORD delight in **burnt offerings and sacrifices** as much as in **obeying the voice of the LORD**? To obey is better than sacrifice, and to heed is better than the fat of rams."*

Micah 6:6–8

*With what shall I come before the LORD and bow down before the exalted God? Shall I come before him with **burnt offerings**, with calves a year old? Will the LORD be pleased with **thousands of rams, with ten thousand rivers of oil**? Shall I offer my firstborn for my transgression, the fruit of my body for the sin of my soul? **He has showed you, O man, what is good.** And what does the LORD require of you? **To act justly and to love mercy and to walk humbly with your God.***

The Mount of Blessing and the Mount of Curses

When the Children of Israel were given the law covenant, God asked them (**Deuteronomy 27**) to divide into two groups. One group was to go stand on top of Mount Gerizim and proclaim all the blessings in the law. The other group was to stand atop Mount Ebal and proclaim all the curses in the law. God asked Moses to erect an altar for burnt offerings on one of the two mountains. Can you guess which one will have the altar? Read the 27th chapter of Deuteronomy and see.

Jesus came to "redeem us from the curse of the law." (**Galatians 3:13**) The curse "of the law" was called up, however, because there was no faith in Israel. In our next chapter on the mission of Jesus we must answer the question: If Jesus was to be received in faith by Israel, what, then, were the actual reasons that the nation was unable to recognize Jesus as the coming Lord? Certainly Israel was in a high state of anticipation for the arrival of the messiah, but something prevented it from coming to Jesus. If it was not the "primary will" of God, then what were the practical reasons Jesus could not be recognized in Israel?

The following is a question asked by a Christian minister in response to the material in this book:

*The Old Testament sacrificial system only has meaning as it finds its fulfillment in the ultimate sacrifice of the lamb of God which takes away the sins of the world. The central theme of the book of Hebrews is the absolute necessity of the cross for: (**Hebrews 1:23**) the purging of sin; (**Hebrews 9:12**) remission of sin; (**Hebrews 9:26**) the putting away of sin by the sacrifice of himself; (**Hebrews 10:19**) the access into the "Holiest."*

*By extension, no cross, then no remission of sin, no purging of sin, no putting away of sin, no access into the presence of God. Jesus was the lamb of God "slain from the foundation of the world." The heart of historical Christian faith is the "substitutionary atonement" of Christ's death. **Rev. R.G., Baptist***

Answer:

The Master Plan fully affirms the atoning work of Christ as the rightful heart of Christian faith and that the cross was the predestined, pre-planned dispensation of God through which sin was cleansed. There are important differences that I would like to clarify. Though we recognize the predestined nature of the cross, we would not agree that the nature of that predestination was absolute. We would see the cross as a limited or conditional predestined providence, which was announced and begun in the last year of the ministry of Jesus.

The limited predestination centers on the condition of faith in Israel toward Jesus. The responsibility to produce the condition of faith is in the hands of the chosen people, and it is for this reason that God uses the word "if" when declaring the ultimate destiny of Israel (in the law of covenant). Though God declares a twofold potential for Israel with regard to its role and destiny, it is the unmistakable primary will of God that Israel fulfill the destiny of "blessing" as expressed in **Deuteronomy 30:19**.

Also, we see that the cross, as a dispensation of God, would only be invoked as a consequence of Israel's faithlessness, and thus, a primary dispensation other than the way of the cross would be fulfilled "if" Israel fulfilled, in faith, toward Jesus. The accomplishment of that primary dispensation is, therefore, the central purpose for which Christ comes. This purpose was promised as a central theme of the law covenant's declaration that blessing would be the destiny of Israel on the condition of faith.

The vision laid out in Old Testament scripture of a "blessed" Israel is one that accepts the king and establishes his kingdom from sea to sea. Jesus calling for faith and repentance, stating that "now is the time, the Kingdom is at hand," indicates that God's primary Will was to establish His Kingdom at that time and not to divide the fulfillment of Christ's coming into two comings separated by some 2,000 years. But, again, to establish His Kingdom providentially required the faithful response of the chosen people towards Jesus.

When that faith was not forthcoming, just as in the time of Jeremiah, the dispensation turns from the destiny of blessing to one of curse, that is, from the vision of the Kingdom to the dispensation of the cross and a future return of Christ and the establishment of His Kingdom. That turn represents, also, a turn from the primary will to the consequential will and plan of God. It was "from that time" that Jesus began to explain his suffering and death to come, as it was "from that time," resulting from Israel's faithlessness toward Jesus, that the cross becomes the determination of God and the only course of salvation.

This would not be inconsistent with the Old Testament sacrificial system, in that God states that the tradition of blood atonement is less preferred and superseded by the condition of faith in Israel. God desires mercy and acknowledgment of God rather than blood, as expressed in **Hosea 6:6** and **1 Samuel 15:22**. Faith in Jesus in Israel would effectively supersede the requirement of blood "under the law" for atonement. Whenever sinners, in Israel at the time of Jesus, fulfilled that condition (**Luke 5:22, 7:27**), forgiveness from Jesus, was bequeathed to them. It is also why **Hebrews 9:22** cannot declare an absolute Old Testament tradition of blood atonement as the sole means of atonement (and thus, "almost" by blood all things are atoned).

We would not see John's declaration of Jesus as "the lamb of God" to be an emphatic prediction of the cross, any more than Jesus' declaration in **John 21:15** that we are his "lambs" is a prediction that believers will shed their blood. The purpose of this teaching is not to change the heart of Christian faith but rather to make clear the nature of the providential failure of the first Israel and the true purpose for which the chosen nation was called.

In that realization comes the acute awareness that Jesus' heart in Gethsemane was broken because of the lost providential opportunity. It is the desire to comfort that heart that is the true power and impetus driving Reverend Moon. Just as the failure of Cain and Abel returned to be unbound by Jacob and Esau, the failures of the first Israel have returned to be unbound by today's generation of Christians.

Chapter Ten

Jesus and John the Baptist

"It is too small a thing for you to be my servant to restore the tribes of Jacob and bring back those of Israel I have kept. I will also make you a light for the Gentiles, that you may bring my salvation to the ends of the earth."

God spoke those words to Isaiah (**Isaiah 49:6**) to indicate that the coming mission of Christ would be a worldwide mission. God sent prophets to Israel to prepare them to recognize and receive Christ. God also sought to prepare the nation to participate in a global mission. The chosen people, therefore, had to be ready for a dispensation that would transcend the borders of the chosen nation.

The 400 years from Malachi to Jesus' birth, the period between the Old and New Testaments, was the period God used to prepare the world for Christ's arrival. By Jesus' time, the world had become polarized between a godless Roman empire in the West and a developing amalgamation of religious cultures in the East. Jerusalem stood in the middle and was a crossroads of sorts between those two worlds. In Jerusalem, one would be just as likely to meet a Zoroastrian sage as he would a Roman centurion.

God obviously had a plan:

Zechariah 8:7-8, 20–23
This is what the LORD Almighty says: "I will save my people from the countries of the east and the west. I will bring them back to live in Jerusalem; they will be my people, and I will be faithful and righteous to them as their God."

This is what the LORD Almighty says: "Many peoples and the inhabitants of many cities will yet come, and the inhabitants of one city will go to another and say, 'Let us go at once to entreat the LORD and seek the LORD Almighty. I myself am going.' And many peoples and powerful nations will come to Jerusalem to seek the LORD Almighty and to entreat him."

This is what the LORD Almighty says: "In those days ten men from all languages and nations will take firm hold of one Jew by the hem of his robe and say, 'Let us go with you, because we have heard that God is with you.' "

Jacob walked the tribal-level course of sanctification to conditionally separate Satan from the tribe of Israel. Moses walked the national-level course of sanctification to conditionally make the nation holy. Their courses foreshadowed the way that Jesus would go in substance.

Jesus' course was the actual course, not just to conditionally separate Satan, but to destroy Satan's sovereignty over the world and to establish God's dominion over all things. However, though walking this worldwide course, Jesus still followed God's model demonstrated in the tribal and national courses.

God had told Moses, "I will raise up for them a prophet like you from among their brethren; you must listen to him." **Deuteronomy 18:15** By "a prophet like you," God was referring to Jesus, who was to walk the same course Moses walked.

Jesus said, "The Son can do nothing of his own accord, but only what he sees the Father doing; for whatever he does, that the Son does likewise". **John 5:19** By that he meant that God had revealed the model course through Moses and that he was following that model on the worldwide level.

Before Jesus, as the messiah in substance, can be received, there must be a worldwide Foundations of Faith and Substance offered. This, then, will be the Foundation for the Messiah on the worldwide level, following the pattern of Jacob and Moses.

This is why the last prophet of the Old Testament, Malachi, proclaimed,

Malachi 4:4–6
Remember the law of my servant Moses, the decrees and laws I gave him at Horeb for all Israel. "See, I will send you the prophet Elijah before that great and dreadful day of the LORD comes.

He will turn the hearts of the fathers to their children, and the hearts of the children to their fathers; or else I will come and strike the land with a curse.

This second coming of Elijah will be the central figure to establish the Foundation of Faith and the Foundation of Substance on the worldwide level. In this way, he will "go on before the Lord," to establish the Foundation to Receive the Messiah by making "a people prepared for the Lord."

If the people don't receive him, God will "strike the land with a curse". That will necessitate a woeful course of atonement in order to "break the curse in the law."

As Moses came on a foundation of 400 years, likewise John the Baptist appears, before Christ, on the foundation of the 400 years from the prophet Malachi.

Preparation in Jesus' Family

The house of Joseph and the house of Zechariah

Even before the birth of Jesus and of John the Baptist, God was working diligently to make sure that the two houses would know clearly the role and mission of their sons. Especially important was the mission of John the Baptist in preparing the way for Jesus' mission. The degree and scope of that spiritual preparation indicates how important it was that all responsible parties be made aware.

The first account of heavenly intervention recorded in Matthew's Gospel is, of course, the conception of Jesus by the Holy Spirit with the Virgin Mary. Yet, when Joseph hears of it, his first reaction is to not believe. In his view, Mary must have been guilty of sexual impropriety. We read in **Matthew 1:19** that Joseph decided to divorce her "quietly." However, that evening an angel appears to Joseph in a dream:

> But after he had considered this, an angel of the Lord appeared to him
> in a dream and said, "Joseph son of David, do not be afraid to take Mary
> home as your wife, because what is conceived in her is from the Holy
> Spirit."

The House of Zechariah

In Luke's Gospel, we find that six months earlier God had begun his preparatory work in the house of Zechariah. In the first chapter, the angel Gabriel announces to Zechariah the coming birth of John. As he is explaining to Zechariah, Gabriel makes a significant and startling announcement:

Luke 1:17
*"And he will go on before the Lord, **in the spirit and power of Elijah**, to **turn the hearts of the fathers to their children and the disobedient to the wisdom of the righteous—to make ready a people prepared for the Lord.**"*

There are three areas of significance in Gabriel's statement. It is very important that Zechariah listen carefully so that he will be able to properly prepare his son for his mission. They are:

1. John is "Elijah." This is an extremely important statement. The Jews were expecting the literal return of Elijah, the prophet of old, before the appearance of the messiah. This expectation was based on the words of the prophet **Malachi 4: 4-6**:

Remember the law of my servant Moses, the decrees and laws I gave him at Horeb for all Israel. "See, I will send you the prophet Elijah before that great and dreadful day of the LORD comes. He will turn the hearts of the fathers to their children, and the hearts of the children to their fathers; or else I will come and strike the land with a curse."

2. Gabriel indicates to Zechariah that the orthodox expectation of Elijah's literal return is incorrect. Zechariah's son John, instead, will serve in a symbolic way as that hoped-for "Elijah."

Gabriel makes this point clear. When he explains that John would be born *"in the spirit and power of Elijah"* he goes on to quote from the very scripture from Malachi that served as the basis for the Jewish expectation of Elijah's literal return. Gabriel says, John as "Elijah" will *"turn the hearts of the fathers to their children."* This reflects **Malachi 4:6** *"He will turn the hearts of the fathers to their children."* It is incumbent upon Zechariah to make this important connection between the existing doctrine of Elijah's return and the reality of Elijah's return via his son John.

3. *"Or else, I will come and strike the land with a curse!"* Malachi's words indicate that "Elijah" accomplishing his mission will determine the outcome of "blessing" or "curse" in Israel. What is John's mission as Elijah? Gabriel states it clearly: *To make ready a people*

prepared for the Lord! John will prepare the Foundations of Faith and Substance on the worldwide level. John is the central figure to prepare the foundation for Jesus.

Mary Arrives

The next significant event is Mary's arrival at Zechariah's house. Mary is now pregnant with Jesus and as she enters the house, Elizabeth, Zechariah's wife (and Mary's cousin), is filled with the Holy Spirit and says:

Luke 1:42–45

Blessed are you among women, and blessed is the child you will bear! But why am I so favored, that the mother of my Lord should come to me? As soon as the sound of your greeting reached my ears, the baby in my womb leaped for joy. Blessed is she who has believed that what the Lord has said to her will be accomplished!

Elizabeth's words clearly indicate that she is fully aware of the significance of Mary's future son. She refers to Mary as "the mother of my Lord."

John's Birth and Zechariah's Song of Praise

The next important event is the birth of John. On the eighth day, Zechariah, who had been struck dumb since his first meeting with Gabriel, suddenly has his voice returned. At that time, Zechariah offers high praises to the coming son of Mary. In this song of praise he also explicitly expresses the nature of his son's relationship with the coming messiah, indicating that he, too, is fully cognizant of Jesus' coming mission:

Luke 1:68–79

Praise be to the Lord, the God of Israel, because he has come and has redeemed his people. **HE HAS RAISED UP A HORN OF SALVATION (JESUS) FOR US IN THE HOUSE OF HIS SERVANT DAVID** *(as he said through his holy prophets of long ago), salvation from our enemies and from the hand of all who hate us, to show mercy to our fathers and to remember his holy* *covenant, the oath he swore to our father Abraham: to rescue us from the hand of our enemies, and to enable us to serve him without fear in holiness and righteousness before him all our days.*

AND YOU, MY CHILD (JOHN,) WILL BE CALLED A PROPHET OF THE MOST HIGH; *for you will go on before the Lord to prepare the way for him, to give his people the knowledge of salvation through the forgiveness of their sins, because of the tender mercy of our God, by which the rising sun will come to us from heaven to shine on those living in darkness and in the shadow of death, to guide our feet into the path of peace.*

Thus, everyone is prepared: Joseph through his dream with the angel, Mary through direct contact with the angel Gabriel. Elizabeth, likewise, clearly knows who the coming Lord is and that her son will prepare his way. Zechariah knows that his son is the Elijah and must make a people prepared for Jesus, the "horn of salvation" raised up in the house of his servant David.

All the key providential figures have been thoroughly prepared by God. Heaven has given all the key figures more than enough information to carry out the mission of preparing their two sons for their great missions. Would it not be reasonable to expect that these two families maintain close contact over the coming years?

But something, for some reason, goes horribly awry.

The Birth of Christ

The first indication is at the birth scene of Jesus. How out of sync with the glorious pronouncements and preparation is the birth of Christ in a stable because there was "no room in the inn"?

Even within a modest frame of reference, Jesus is the King of Israel. Where are Zechariah and Elizabeth? Even though the census required Joseph to register his family in his own hometown of Bethlehem in Judea, shouldn't, then, Joseph's family be available to lend their support at such a critical moment? If this is his "hometown," does he not have at least some friends of the family that could offer some assistance? Where is Mary's family? How could they be so poorly prepared that they would end up in a stable?

In truth, all the circumstances of Jesus' birth indicate that traditional family support was lacking. It shows, even at this early date, many important providential people prepared by God to support

Joseph and Mary were not steadfast in fulfilling their roles.

Juxtapose this sad reality with God's past efforts to bring Christ on the foundation of an unbroken line of kings. The "everlasting kingdom" was to begin, if you'll remember, with Saul, David and Solomon. Christ was to be born in the palace to a nation, an empire of unchallenged supremacy.

Christ's birth scene was, in reality, a filthy animal dwelling enveloped in stench and excrement. It was a breeding ground of festering bacteria and deadly disease. It provided very little protection from the cold Judean winds that blew through the open spaces of flimsy walls. It was hardly the quaint, picturesque setting of our modern nativity scenes.

Jesus' life, even in infancy, is in imminent peril. Israel as a nation had wilted down to a tiny patch of territory that had been conquered by the pagan powers of Babylon, Persia, Greece and, now, Rome. The king of Israel, Herod the Great, a hatefully vicious dictator, will be none too happy to abdicate his throne to this new King Jesus.

It seems that God, in understanding the situation, sends in the Magi, the wise men from the East. Being neither Jewish nor, of course, Christian, they are led to Jerusalem following a star, which, to them, indicated the birth of a great new king.

Their mistake was they went to Herod, whose own plan was to use them to locate and then have the new king killed. After the "wise men" found and worshiped Jesus, they returned home by a different route. Their effort to protect Jesus underestimated the ambition of Herod. He simply ordered the death of all male children under the age of two in the city and vicinity of Bethlehem. The first Christmas ends with Joseph, Mary and the infant messiah fleeing for their lives while leaving behind the weeping and wailing of fathers and mothers whose murdered children had been snatched from their loving arms.

What could be the reason that Mary and Joseph appear so isolated and vulnerable? On the one hand, the Holy Spirit is working so powerfully around them, yet their practical circumstances only become more threatening. Had something gone wrong?

We could consider a possibility. When Joseph first heard of Mary's pregnancy, did he believe her? He concluded that she had betrayed her vows to God and to him. No doubt, he was hurt and deeply saddened. Why did he change his mind and not divorce her? Was it because an "angel of the Lord" appeared? In fact, the angel didn't exactly appear. It was actually *a dream* about an angel. Over time, would Joseph begin to place less stock in the authority of a dream? After all, Mary and Zechariah both received a personal appearance from no less than Gabriel himself.

Consider how challenging it must have been for Joseph to be sustained by this dream for all his life. If, for even a moment, he begins to doubt his dream, in that very second Mary will become, in his eyes, a betraying spouse. What will Jesus then become in his eyes? Don't forget, scripture has already shown us that Joseph is not beyond deciding it is in his interest to "divorce her quietly."

Little consideration is given to Joseph because he is in the archangel position. He had to pay a tremendous price for being in Lucifer's position. For example, Mary's untimely pregnancy no doubt required a change in wedding plans. Plans had to be suddenly altered, schedules moved up. In those days, without the technology of today, communication was a much more daunting task. Thus, a large family event such as a wedding would be planned even years in advance. This would allow for all the necessary communications and arrangements to be accomplished.

How does Joseph communicate with Mary's family and his own family about the reason for a suddenly expedited wedding schedule? What will they no doubt assume? After all, what did Joseph himself initially assume? Reverend Moon offers insight:

Do you think that naturally he would ask her whose baby it was, since after all he had saved her life? Could she reply that she conceived through the Holy Spirit and expect Joseph to accept it? If the Pope was in Joseph's position would he believe her? Would Billy Graham believe his wife if she told him that? That kind of conversation between Joseph and Mary could have led only to a great argument, with Joseph accusing that even though he saved Mary's life she still was not being honest with him. Though this is not exactly what took place, do you think there was no tension in that family when Jesus was finally born? At first the community would think he was Joseph's son, but it was impossible to keep secrets. Any conversation between Mary and Joseph must have been overheard, even by the birds or insects, and I'm sure rumors spread quickly that falsely suggested that Jesus was an illegitimate child.

More children were born to Mary and Joseph, and they all knew that somehow Jesus was different. The Bible does not speak directly about this, but the fact is that when Jesus was a boy there was a great deal of

tension, and even Mary was distant with him at times because she was
a victim of the everyday situation. Jesus was lonely as a child and often
left the house to be alone. Once his parents even left him behind in
Jerusalem, traveling for a whole day before realizing he was missing.
How could parents leave a young boy behind that way? There were not
many happy days in that family.

"Day of Victory of Heaven," October 4, 1979

Do you think Joseph could convince his extended family by reporting his dream? Can Mary explain that it was the work of the Holy Spirit? As far as we know, Gabriel only appeared to Zechariah and to Mary. There is no other record.

That is why we find Joseph and Mary apparently in total estrangement from their families and in a stable ready to give birth to this "questionable" child. Most important, however, will be the continued relationship of the house of Joseph with the house of Zechariah. Will there be any signs of an uneasy family circumstance spilling over and souring the relationship between Jesus and John?

Establishing the Foundation of Faith

John Thirty Years Later

John the Baptist, like Moses, was called on the foundation of a 400-year period for the separation from Satan. Moses had learned to love his brethren and the traditions of his fathers while living in the Pharaoh's palace. Likewise, John the Baptist learned the way of faith and obedience to Heaven and made preparations for the messiah while living on locusts and wild honey in the wilderness.

John's ascetic life was so exemplary that many people, including the priests and Levites, wondered whether he might be the messiah. **John 1:20, Luke 3:15** In this way, John the Baptist successfully established the dispensation of forty for the separation from Satan and was able to lay the Foundation of Faith for the first worldwide course to receive the Messiah.

The Foundation of Substance

Just as the Israelites were to follow Moses all the way to the promised land, John the Baptist was "to make ready a people prepared for the Lord." This was the Foundation of Substance centering on John. This was to be accomplished through the condition of baptism.

There is no question that John amassed a large following. According to some historical records, John baptized hundreds of thousands of people.

Matthew 3:5

People went out to him from Jerusalem and all Judea and the whole region of the Jordan.

This is why Jesus waited until the age of 30 to reveal himself as messiah. Jesus was waiting for the providential foundation for the messiah to be accomplished by John. John's baptizing Jesus is reminiscent of Jacob's course at the ford of Jabbok, where he received the angel's blessing.

Observing the sign of the dove, the spirit coming down and remaining on Jesus, John gives his most resounding endorsement of Jesus with the words, "Behold the Lamb of God!" This was a key moment in God's dispensation to bring the messiah. This was the moment for John and all his foundation to move with Jesus just as the Israelites had moved with the Tabernacle whenever the cloud appeared overhead.

Yet, strangely, we see that Jesus and John separate. Jesus heads into the wilderness to be tempted by Satan and John continues to baptize.

Even before this moment, inconsistencies with the initial preparation that took place in John's family were beginning to manifest. They begin to reveal themselves as John begins his mission "to make ready a people prepared for the Lord." Remember, for all intents and purposes, John should know that he is Elijah and that Jesus is the messiah. That is, if his parents and kinsmen had been preparing him properly.

John 1:19–23

*Now this was John's testimony when the Jews of Jerusalem sent priests and Levites to ask him who he was. He did not fail to confess, but confessed freely, "I am not the Christ." They asked him, "Then who are you? Are you Elijah?" He said, "**I am not.**" "Are you the Prophet?" He answered,*

"No." Finally they said, "Who are you? Give us an answer to take back to those who sent us. What do you say about yourself?" John replied in the words of Isaiah the prophet, "I am the voice of one calling in the desert, 'Make straight the way for the Lord.' "

This is a very disturbing response because there will be no other Elijah that is going to arrive except the one who "was born in the spirit and power of Elijah."

Why did John answer incorrectly? We will never know for sure, but the direct result of his failure to clearly explain that he was the expected Elijah was that the people would continue to wait for Elijah's arrival and, therefore, would be faced with an apparent contradiction whenever Jesus was proclaimed as messiah. If the orthodox teaching was that the messiah would only come *after* Elijah appears, then how could Jesus be recognized as the messiah as long as John denied he was the Elijah who was to appear?

Matthew 17:10–11
*The disciples asked him, "Why then do the teachers of the law say that **Elijah must come first**?" Jesus replied, "To be sure, Elijah comes and will restore all things."*

You can detect a bit of frustration in their question to Jesus. Obviously they had been trying their best to represent Jesus, the messiah. No doubt, day in and day out, they had to field the question, "If your Jesus is the messiah, then where is Elijah? Did we miss something?"

Jesus continued to explain to them and provided the answer to their question in **Matthew 17:12-13**:

*"But I tell you, Elijah has already come, and they did not recognize him, but have done to him everything they wished. In the same way the Son of Man is going to suffer at their hands." Then the disciples understood that he was talking to them about **John the Baptist**.*

Remember Malachi's warning that God would "strike the land with a curse" if Elijah were not heeded. Jesus indicated that the people did not recognize that John was Elijah and as a result Jesus himself was going to suffer at their hands. Would not John, in denying he was the Elijah, bear the brunt of the responsibility for that circumstance?

This was the bigger problem created when John denied that he was the Elijah. We must consider that if John, in fact, was unaware that *he* was the Elijah, then John too may have begun to struggle with Jesus as messiah for the very same reasons all of Israel struggled: How could Jesus be the messiah if Elijah had not come?

Another curious inconsistency took place when John met Jesus in the Jordan and saw the spirit descend "as a dove" and remain on Jesus.

John 1:29-34

The next day John saw Jesus coming toward him and said, "Look, the Lamb of God, who takes away the sin of the world! This is the one I meant when I said, 'A man who comes after me has surpassed me because he was before me.' ***"I myself did not know him,*** *but the reason I came baptizing with water was that he might be revealed to Israel."*

Then John gave this testimony: "I saw the Spirit come down from heaven as a dove and remain on him. ***I would not have known him,*** *except that the one who sent me to baptize with water told me, 'The man on whom you see the Spirit come down and remain is he who will baptize with the Holy Spirit.' I have seen and I testify that this is the Son of God."*

It was the clearest and most emphatic testimony John gave about Jesus. However, we must examine all of John's words concerning Jesus.

The curious element is expressed by the words, *"I myself did not know him."* And, *"I would not have known him except that the one who sent me to baptize with water told me, 'The man on whom you see the Spirit come down and remain is he who will baptize with the Holy Spirit.' I have seen and I testify that this is the Son of God."*

John is saying that had it not been for the sign from heaven (the dove appearing) he would not have known that Jesus was the messiah because, "I did not know him."

He did not know him? But they were second cousins. John's father Zechariah and his mother Elizabeth both received direct testimony from heaven concerning all these matters. Gabriel had appeared and testified that John was the Elijah. He explained that he was to make a people ready for the Lord. Zechariah called Jesus "the horn of salvation," and clearly stated, "and you, my child will go on before the Lord." Elizabeth referred to Mary as "Mother of my Lord," and exalted Jesus, "blessed is the child you will bear." She also said, "and blessed is she who believes all that the Lord told her will come true."

Why did John need an additional sign of confirmation if Zechariah and Elizabeth had done their job properly? Something *had* gone awry in the house of Zechariah. It would continue to affect John as he sought to accomplish his mission.

Are there similar signs indicating an erosion of support for Jesus in his own house of Joseph?

House of Joseph

Let's start from the most obvious. Consider the resounding affirmations offered to Jesus by angels, shepherds, Magi, Anna the prophetess, Simeon, the teachers at the temple. Keep in mind: Joseph and Mary witnessed all of this. Yet, at age 30, Jesus is a carpenter.

Mark 6:3–4
"Isn't this the carpenter? Isn't this Mary's son and the brother of James, Joseph, Judas and Simon? Aren't his sisters here with us?" And they took offense at him. Jesus said to them, "Only in his hometown, among his relatives and in his own house is a prophet without honor."

This scripture reveals evidence of the same kind of discord in Jesus' family as we saw in the house of Zechariah. Another curious moment took place at age 12. Jesus slipped away from Joseph and Mary and remained in Jerusalem while they returned to Galilee. They "assumed" Jesus is with other relatives. Does this seem like a close-knit family? After a whole day of travel, they were still "assuming."

Mary and Joseph were disharmonious, fighting and quarreling all the time. They quarreled so much that young Jesus' mother even forsook him and left him. Three days later she came and found him with the priests. Jesus was very angry saying, "Where else would I be but in my Father's house?", which was the temple. Today both Christians and Catholics say that Jesus is such a great person so he stayed in his father's house. He was there because he was forsaken by his mother and father! The fact that Jesus could not get married was directly due to this circumstance.
Rev. Sun Myung Moon, "Restoration From the Origin and Rebirth Are for Myself"

Read the story of Hannah, the mother of Samuel. Mary should have patterned herself after Hannah. The story of Rebecca and Jacob is another model for the relationship of Mary and Jesus. It should have been Mary who made sure that Jesus was properly prepared to assume his rightful destiny in the palace, not just become a shop boy sweeping up sawdust at Joseph's worksite.

Hannah pledged that she would give her son, Samuel, to the Lord after he was weaned. She was true to her word and gave her only son to Eli, the temple priest, so that Samuel could be raised in the most opportune circumstances. Because of this, Samuel could fulfill his mission as one of Israel's great prophets.

Rebecca, like Mary, also received a vision of her son's destiny. Even while the twins were in her womb, God told her, "The elder shall serve the younger." Rebekah not only "kept that word in her heart," *she also brought it to pass* a full 40 years later! Did Mary do that? Did Mary bring to pass the things she was "pondering" in her heart?

Certainly the teachers of the temple courts were sufficiently impressed with Jesus' intellectual prowess. Mary should have seized that opportunity right then and there so that Jesus could have remained in Jerusalem and received the finest education in the temple. In fact, there is evidence that Mary, in her youth, had received a temple education in Jerusalem of her own.

In the non-canonical *Gospel of the Birth of Mary*, supposedly written by Matthew, chapter one states, "The blessed and ever glorious Virgin Mary, sprung from the royal race and family of David, was born in the city of Nazareth, and *educated at Jerusalem, in the temple of the Lord.*"

Jesus, effectively, was telling his parents he wanted the same when he said to them, *"wist ye not that I must be about my Father's business?"* But, alas, it was back to the sweatshop in Galilee. How tragically sad! Jesus had to study on his own as best he could. Can you imagine the limited resources available to a country boy from Galilee, a carpenter's apprentice?

Luke 4:22

The Jews were amazed and asked, "How did this man get such learning without having studied?"

An interesting possible indication of Jesus' lack of formal

training is inadvertently revealed in **Matthew 23:35**. Jesus is chastising the Pharisees and teachers of the law for their unresponsiveness. He reviews the woeful history of Israel's prophets. It is a history of rejection, filled with the blood of the prophets.

And so upon you will come all the righteous blood that has been shed on earth, from the blood of righteous Abel to the blood of Zechariah son of Berekiah, whom you murdered between the temple and the altar.

There is one problem with Jesus' narration of this history. It is incorrect. Zechariah of Berekiah was not the Zechariah who was rejected and killed between the temple and the altar. Zechariah of Berekiah is the written prophet Zechariah who came after the Babylonian captivity (with Ezra, Nehemiah, Malachi). This was a time when Israel was heeding her prophets. Zechariah of Berekiah was not killed.

The Zechariah who was killed is Zechariah of *Jehoiada* and is referenced in **2 Chronicles 24:20–21**:

Then the Spirit of God came upon Zechariah son of Jehoiada the priest. He stood before the people and said, "This is what God says: 'Why do you disobey the LORD's commands? You will not prosper. Because you have forsaken the LORD, he has forsaken you.'" But they plotted against him, and by order of the king they stoned him to death in the courtyard of the LORD's temple.

This Zechariah was the last prophet killed. Thus, the list to which Jesus was referring was rightly, from "beginning to end," that is, "from Abel to Zechariah." However, the wrong Zechariah was cited.

The intent here is not to be critical of the Lord. We are seeking to point out that the providential people who were called to assist Jesus were falling away and that such failures bore real consequences. These failures required Jesus to carry additional burdens.

Remember, Joseph's faith relied on a single experience in one dream, in one night. Was it enough to sustain him year after year? Was it enough to salve the wounds of years of ridicule and scorn? Was it enough to comfort him each time he looked into Jesus' face and saw no reflection of his own? Was it enough to stem the tide of sorrow and hurt, the inner doubt caused by the touch of someone else upon his virgin bride? Was it enough to quell the fear that her heart still harbored a secret love? When she seemed pensive and quiet, distant and cold, was she still thinking of him?

No, it was not enough. Joseph instead drew a tight circle around himself and all that he knew was his. He tried to build another life, as normal as possible, within a circle that did not include Jesus. He wanted a life with other sons, his own sons, a life with his own plans and objectives, a life in a real world and not a world of angels, seers and kings. No more dreams. Does the fact that Joseph gave his own name to a later son express subtly a growing need to assert what was his own?

Mary, too, had to choose which world would be her own, in which side of the circle would she be placed. The scripture testifies that she "kept all these sayings in her heart." Yes, she kept them, ever so tightly, and in a place where no one could hear or see, in a place of muted light and distant memory. Were they treasured or merely locked away? Were they placed in an area of deep contemplation or in the realm where dreams slowly fade and die?

John 2:1-4
And the third day there was a marriage in Cana of Galilee; and the mother of Jesus was there: And both Jesus was called, and his disciples, to the marriage. And when they wanted wine, the mother of Jesus saith unto him, "They have no wine." Jesus saith unto her, "Woman, what have I to do with thee? Mine hour is not yet come."

"Woman"? "What have I to do with thee?"

Luke 11:27–28
As Jesus was saying these things, a woman in the crowd called out, "Blessed is the mother who gave you birth and nursed you."

*He replied, "Blessed **rather** are those who hear the word of God and obey it."*

"Blessed *rather* are those?" Not "Blessed *also* are those"?

Some may ask the question, did Mary fulfill her due responsibility? If you ask that question many will jump up high and say, "Don't even talk about that! That is blasphemous!"

In the Bible there is an episode when there was a wedding ceremony in Galilee. Mary went there to serve people and Jesus went there, too.

Jesus' mother said something like, "We don't have wine" and Jesus became very indignant, saying, "Woman, what do you have to do with me?" She was not worried about Jesus' wedding, which was her responsibility to arrange. She was more worried about a wedding that didn't have any meaning.

Jesus knew this and he felt so indignant, saying, "Your son, the center of God's whole dispensation, should go this path, getting married to restore all mankind, and you don't even think about that. You are worried about another person's wedding. What are you anyway?" That is what Jesus said to his own mother.

Now we know that clearly. What is your guess? Do you think that was Jesus' heart at that time? (Yes.) Jesus was thirty-three years old, and the relative who happened to be getting married that day was not even twenty at that time. And Mary had to get Jesus involved, only worrying that there was no wine?

Rev. Sun Myung Moon

In the third chapter of Mark we see Mary and Joseph's other sons in action against Jesus.

Mark 3:20–21

Then Jesus entered a house, and again a crowd gathered, so that he and his disciples were not even able to eat. When HIS FAMILY *heard about this, they went to take charge of him, for they said, "*HE IS OUT OF HIS MIND.*"*

And who shows up, leading the pack, intent on "taking charge" of Jesus, her mentally imbalanced son, in her view?

Mark 3:31–35

Then Jesus' **mother** *and brothers arrived. Standing outside, they sent someone in to call him. A crowd was sitting around him, and they told him, "Your mother and brothers are outside looking for you." "Who are my mother and my brothers?" he asked. Then he looked at those seated in a circle around him and said, "Here are my mother and my brothers! Whoever does God's will is my brother and sister and mother."*

Jesus' mother and brothers arrive "to take charge" of Jesus because they thought that "he was out of his mind." They were there to spirit him away by force. And what was the state of mind of Jesus' brothers?

John 7:1–5

*After this, Jesus went around in Galilee, purposely staying away from Judea because the Jews there were waiting to take his life. But when the Jewish Feast of Tabernacles was near, Jesus' brothers said to him, "You ought to leave here and go to Judea, so that your disciples may see the miracles you do. No one who wants to become a public figure acts in secret. Since you are doing these things, show yourself to the world." **For even his own brothers did not believe in him.***

Jesus is purposely staying away from Judea because the Jews are waiting to take his life. Jesus' brothers, however, are purposely trying to trick him into going there, for that very reason! "For even his own brothers did not believe in him." Not only did they not believe in him, they were trying to have him killed in the same way Jacob's son Joseph was thrown in a well by his brothers.

This was the state of mind of Joseph's family toward Jesus. It became a fortress of disappointment and sorrow. No doubt this lonely family life opened Jesus to a deeper heart in pursuit of "his Father's business."

I'm sure many of you have grown up with a stepparent, and even in an open society like America's today there is tension between a stepparent and stepchildren, so imagine how much more difficult it was 2,000 years ago. In this sense Americans are in a position to be sympathetic with Jesus' position; many young people are experiencing the same kind of suffering Jesus went through.

Rev. Sun Myung Moon

The breakdown within and between the two families was like an open, festering wound in the mission of Jesus. Understanding this dynamic will shed new light on the indecisiveness of John as his message vacillates from, "Behold the Lamb of God" to "Are you the one to come or shall we look for another." It will ultimately reveal why the Lord, for whom the people were to be prepared, must beseech God, belatedly, for assistance to remedy his plight of "few laborers."

And looming on the horizon, the ominous pledge, *"or else I will come and strike the land with a curse."*

The First Attempt to Establish the Foundation for the Messiah Ends

Jesus and John

As mentioned, John's initial testimony to Jesus was direct, assertive and unequivocal. It stands out not only for its eloquence but also because of its contrast to all subsequent testimony from John about Jesus.

For ministers and most Christians, John is a hero and a model for their ministry, "Of those born of women none rose greater than John," Jesus asserted.

The various doctrines about John have exalted him to highest sainthood. These doctrines begat other doctrines, until ministers are unable to see the proverbial forest for the trees. Open eyes and ears are essential, especially when examining a circumstance that is as fluid and shifting as John's relationship with Jesus.

Over time, the Christian perspective often overlooks the real trials and tribulations in God's effort to form effective partnerships with His providential people. Thus, they look at scripture as the record of what God, alone, has done, without any consideration of man's role in a particular providential action or that it is even possible that someone may fall short of God's expectation.

John proclaimed one time, "behold," and that was enough to start a doctrinal legend. By this day, there is no thought whatsoever that John should be judged by what he did or did not do. There is little motive for examining John to see whether he maintained his initial faith in Jesus *over time*. Jesus himself said in **Matthew 24:13,** *"but he who stands firm to the end will be saved."* We must assess John by that standard.

The Results of John's Ministry

James 2:24
You see that a person is justified by what he does . . .

What were the real results of John's ministry? That is, how many people came to Christ as a result of John's testimony? How many of Jesus' disciples started out as John's disciples? Was John a follower of Christ?

As mentioned, there is no question that John amassed a large following. According to some historical records, John baptized hundreds of thousands of people. *"People went out to him from Jerusalem and all Judea and the whole region of the Jordan."* **Matthew 3:5**

Even though he flatly denied that he was Elijah, we can see in his choice of clothing that he, in fact, had at least a modicum of awareness that he and the prophet of old shared some sort of common destiny.

Matthew 3:4 (about John)
*John's clothes were made of **camel's hair**, and he had a **leather belt around his waist**. His food was locusts and wild honey.*

2 Kings 1:8 (about Elijah)
*They replied, "He was a man with a **garment of hair** and with a **leather belt around his waist**." The king said, "That was Elijah the Tishbite."*

John dresses like Elijah, but denies he is the Elijah. There will be other, even more dramatic expressions of conflict within John.

John's Impact on His Own Disciples

John gives his next notable testimony the next day:

John 1:35–37
*The next day John was there again with **two of his disciples**. When he saw Jesus passing by, he said, "Look, the Lamb of God!" When the two disciples heard him say this, they followed Jesus.*

This is the only known account of anyone following Jesus as a direct result of John's testimony. Two disciples.

Even this result is debatable, however. One of the two is Andrew. Matthew's Gospel records that Jesus witnessed directly to Andrew and his brother Peter, with no mention whatsoever of John playing a role. The other disciple spent the day with Jesus, but we never find out if he remained beyond that one day.

We see that John's disciples, even after his initial testimony to Jesus, maintain their separate identity as "John's disciples." Weren't they supposed to be "a people prepared for *the Lord*"? Were they not to follow Jesus as the Israelites followed the Tabernacle?

Matthew 9:14

Then John's disciples came and asked him, "How is it that we and the Pharisees fast, but your disciples do not fast?"

Does this sound like John's disciples have been influenced by John's initial testimony? Notice that they identify more closely with the Pharisees than with Jesus. Why does John still have disciples at this late date?

We conclude that though John's initial testimony was powerful, for some reason it exerted little moral authority over his disciples to drop their nets and follow Jesus. Of course, the fact that John, himself, was not dropping *his* net and following may have contributed to that climate of hesitation.

John's Impact on the Nation

What was the real influence of John's testimony on the nation? There are two scriptures that give us an insight on this.

Matthew 16:13–14

When Jesus came to the region of Caesarea Philippi, he asked his disciples, "Who do people say the Son of Man is?" They replied, "Some say John the Baptist; others say Elijah; and still others, Jeremiah or one of the prophets."

What does this reveal? What is conspicuously missing from this polling data? Was anyone saying, "Jesus is the Lamb of God"? Can you conclude that they never heard of John the Baptist in Caesarea Philippi? Clearly they are familiar with the name and work of John the Baptist. Obviously, they never heard John proclaiming that Jesus of Nazareth was the Lamb of God.

If tape recorders had existed in those days, John's initial testimony could have been recorded, mass-produced, and distributed. Given that was not an option, John should have personally reproduced his initial affirmation by testifying throughout the nation. For some reason, he apparently did not do that.

In Judea, Jesus takes another poll.

Mark 6:14–15

Jesus' name had become well known. Some were saying "John the Baptist has been raised from the dead, and that is why miraculous powers are at work in him." Others said, "He is Elijah." And still others claimed, "He is a prophet, like one of the prophets of long ago."

No one was saying, "Jesus? Isn't that the man John said was the Lamb of God?"

Again, given the scope of John's mission as expressed by Gabriel, "to make a people prepared for the Lord," this appears to fall well short of that measure.

Another telling event is John's experience with Herod.

Mark 6:19–20

So Herodias nursed a grudge against John and wanted to kill him. But she was not able to, because Herod feared John and protected him, knowing him to be a righteous and holy man. When Herod heard John, he was greatly puzzled; yet he liked to listen to him.

John had the king's ear. Herod "feared John," "protected John" and "liked to listen to him." What single most important bit of information for Herod would John possess? Perhaps, John needs to inform Herod that he should be preparing for a career change. Is not Herod sitting on Jesus' throne? Is not Herod residing in Jesus' palace while the true king "has no place to rest his head?" **Matthew 8:20** *Jesus replied, "Foxes have holes and birds of the air have nests, but the Son of Man has no place to lay his head."*)

Herod was an Edomite, a descendant of Esau. Can we not find in Jacob's course the model for King Herod in terms of what he must do and not do? Herod's unrighteousness is of a far greater degree than that of merely marrying his brother's wife, Herodias.

And yet, after John is beheaded, we see Herod strangely puzzled by the presence of this new rising figure: Jesus of Nazareth.

Mark 6:14, 16

For Jesus' name had become well known. But, when Herod heard this, he said, "John, the man I beheaded, has been raised from the dead!"

"John, the man I beheaded has been raised from the dead"? How could Herod be so confused about Jesus if John had done his job effectively?

Obviously, John never witnessed to the king. Not a word? Not, "behold the Lamb of God"? Not, "Herod, come down and worship your new king"?

John had no lasting impact on his own disciples, no impact in Caesarea Philippi, no impact in Judea and no influence with King Herod.

Given these circumstances, how could anyone conclude that John accomplished his mission?

John Begins to Doubt

John's third testimony to Jesus is thought to be a resounding endorsement. But once again, it fails to compel anyone "to pick up their cross and follow." The reason lies between the lines. John expresses ideas that say more about his own unresolved reservations about Jesus than anything else.

This testimony is far less emphatic than the initial "Behold, the Lamb of God." It reveals a growing contradiction within John's mind. This contradiction begins to produce an array of contrary signals, not the least of which is his "You follow him and I'll be over here with my disciples" approach to evangelism.

John 3:22–30

After this, Jesus and his disciples went out into the Judean countryside, where he spent some time with them, and baptized. Now John also was baptizing at Aenon near Salim, because there was plenty of water, and people were constantly coming to be baptized. . . An argument developed between some of John's disciples and a certain Jew over the matter of ceremonial washing. They came to John and said to him, "Rabbi, that man who was with you on the other side of the Jordan, the one you testified about, well, he is baptizing, and everyone is going to him."

To this John replied, "A man can receive only what is given him from heaven. You yourselves can testify that I said, 'I am not the Christ but am sent ahead of him.' The bride belongs to the bridegroom. The friend who attends the bridegroom waits and listens for him, and is full of joy when he hears the bridegroom's voice. That joy is mine, and it is now complete. He must become greater; I must become less."

It sounds good. Many cite it as another example of John's deep exaltation of Jesus. But it is a fatally flawed testimony. It shows that John is stepping away from his initial emphatic endorsement and is, instead, moving toward more of a "wait and see" posture.

It is, again, odd that Jesus is in Judea with "his" disciples and is baptizing while John is in Salim with "his" disciples and they are continuing to baptize. That this is a rather odd situation, given the initial testimony, is displayed in the question, *"Rabbi, that man who was with you on the other side of the Jordan, the one you testified about, well, he is baptizing, and everyone is going to him."* In other words, why aren't you and your disciples over there with "the one you testified about"?

John's answer is an attempt to explain away the issue brought to the surface by that question. The real issue is that John's actions are increasingly inconsistent with the initial expression of conviction in Jesus. On the one hand, John had a personal spiritual experience. He saw "the dove" descend and remain on Jesus. God told him that such a sign would indicate the messiah.

On the other hand, John is publicly denying that he, John, is Elijah even though heaven has declared it and Jesus later affirms it. Also, he should have known Jesus, his second cousin, and he should also have known Jesus was the messiah. Instead, John publicly denies knowing him.

What is John actually saying in this testimony about Jesus? What do these words really mean: *"The bride belongs to the bridegroom. The friend who attends the bridegroom waits and listens for him, and is full of joy when he hears the bridegroom's voice. That joy is mine, and it is now complete. He must become greater; I must become less."*

He is saying that the one to whom the people go is the messiah. The "bride" belongs to the "bridegroom." The "bride" symbolizes the people. The "bridegroom" is the messiah and the "friend of the bridegroom" is John.

What motivates John's words is a desire to remove himself from the position of having to validate, as he did unabashedly at the Jordan River, the figure who is the messiah. He is saying that the validation of the messiah is, instead, determined by the flow of the people to that figure. The one who has the *"bride"* is the bridegroom. Therefore, he is saying, essentially, "I'm done and don't come to me requesting any more personal validations." That is why he insists,

"That joy is mine, and it is now complete. He must increase, I must decrease."

No wonder no one heard in Caesarea Philippi that Jesus was the Lamb of God. No wonder in Judea, no wonder in Herod's palace. John had decided that they were to decide for themselves!

What is wrong with John's "bride and bridegroom" analogy? First of all, the sign for which the people are waiting is the appearance of *Elijah*! John *is* Elijah. On some level, he is aware of this and is *rejecting it*.

Second, if it is true that the bridegroom is the one with the bride, then Jesus is, unequivocally, *not the messiah*! Not in Caesarea Philippi. Not in Judea. Not in Herod's palace where he would be condemned to die. The bride passed him by. He was the deserted Tabernacle and Temple. Jesus ends up in a desperate effort for "laborers unto his harvest." He was deserted by everyone and died nearly alone at Calvary.

The Truth about John

The truth comes out about John in the **Matthew 11:2-6**:

*Now when John had heard in the prison the works of Christ, he sent two of his disciples, And said unto him, **Art thou he that should come, or do we look for another**?*

The truth is that John could never decide.

*Jesus answered and said unto them, Go and shew John **again** those things which ye do hear and see: The blind receive their sight, and the lame walk, the lepers are cleansed, and the deaf hear, the dead are raised up, and the poor have the gospel preached to them. And blessed is he, whosoever shall not be offended in me.*

Notice Jesus says, "Go and show John *again*." John's question was extremely offensive in view of all the signs he had received and all the preparation in his family. What were these mysterious barriers in John's faith toward Jesus? What was this secretive counterweight to the descending dove and the forthright declaration, "Behold"? What were the issues that were holding him back and preventing him from doing his mission to hand over to Jesus a prepared foundation of people? We can only speculate, but certainly the disintegration of the faith and support of the house of Joseph and the house of Zechariah must have been key elements.

Jesus' comment leaves no doubt.

Matthew 11:11

*I tell you the truth: Among those born of women there has not risen anyone greater than John the Baptist; yet he who is **least in the kingdom of heaven is greater than he**.*

Of course, many who cling tenaciously to John's saintly status point only to the first part: "Among those born of women there has not risen anyone greater than John the Baptist." Indeed, John was the greatest of all central figures, for he was the one who was to make the foundation for the messiah on the world level. He was the one who would directly hand over to the messiah the entire historical foundation laid in Israel. However, they conveniently overlook the remainder, and most important, part of the statement: "yet he who is least in the kingdom of heaven is greater than he."

Some will insist that Jesus is merely indicating that John is humble. Others will suggest it is because John was beheaded before the day of Pentecost and so he did not enjoy the full merits of salvation through Jesus and the Holy Spirit.

What does the term, "least in the kingdom of heaven" mean? How does one qualify for such a position? See **Matthew 5:19:**

*Anyone who breaks one of the least of these commandments and teaches others to do the same will be called **least in the kingdom of heaven**.*

What commandment did John break?

Matthew 5:11–12

*Blessed are you when people insult you, persecute you and falsely say all kinds of evil against you **because of me**. Rejoice and be glad, because great is your reward in heaven, for in the same way they persecuted the prophets who were before you.*

Notice, too, that John is conspicuously missing from the list of faithful saints of **Hebrews 11**.

The Second Course on the Worldwide Level

Jesus Continues John's Mission

Why did so many think that Jesus was John the Baptist raised from the dead? It has a lot to do with the fact that Jesus was working in a similar way as John. He was baptizing disciples. He was in the wilderness and fasted for 40 days. He was proclaiming the coming Kingdom. He was casting out demons and healing the sick. He was generating a lot of excitement and renown. It was as if Jesus had taken his cue from John.

In a real sense, because John fell short in his mission "to make a people prepared for the Lord," Jesus had to step into John's role and make his own foundation. **Matthew 4:12–17:**

> *When Jesus heard that John had been put in prison, he returned to Galilee. Leaving Nazareth, he went and lived in Capernaum, which was by the lake in the area of Zebulun and Naphtali. . . **From that time on Jesus began** to preach, "Repent, for the kingdom of heaven is near."*

Most of the Gospel is the record of Jesus attempting to make his own Foundation for the Messiah. In other words, because John had failed in the first course, Jesus had to step into that providential role and accomplish the mission to restore the Foundations of Faith and Substance. This is why so many people thought of Jesus as a resurrection of John the Baptist. In a sense, he was; but how tragic and sad that the Lord, himself, would have to struggle on this level.

Until those conditions were established, Jesus would not reveal his true mission. This is why we see, in **Matthew 16:20**: *Then he warned his disciples not to tell anyone that he was the Christ.*

The Second Course to Establish the Worldwide Level Foundation of Faith

When John the Baptist gradually came to doubt Jesus and finally even undermined his work, the chosen people, who had the highest esteem for John, were compelled to disbelieve in Jesus. As a result, Satan invaded the Foundation of Faith that John had laid for the first worldwide course. Therefore, Jesus himself now had to take on John's mission and restore through indemnity the Foundation of

Faith. When Jesus fasted for 40 days in the wilderness, it was to separate Satan for the very purpose of restoring the Foundation of Faith. For this, he lowered himself to assume the position of John the Baptist.

Jesus' Forty-Day Fast and the Three Temptations

In the national course at Kadesh-Barnea, Moses stood before the rock, disobeyed God, and struck the rock twice. As a result, the rock, symbolizing Jesus (**I Corinthians 10:4**), was under a condition for Satan to invade. This act affirmed the possibility, centuries later, when Jesus came to walk in the footsteps of Moses' course, that John the Baptist might likewise stumble, opening the way for Satan to attack Jesus, the substantial rock.

This was the immediate cause of Jesus undertaking a dispensation of 40 for the separation from Satan by fasting for 40 days and overcoming the three temptations. By doing this from the position of John the Baptist, Jesus restored through indemnity the Foundation of Faith.

At the conclusion of Jesus' fast, Satan tested Jesus three times. First, he showed Jesus stones and tempted him to turn them into loaves of bread. Next, he took Jesus to the pinnacle of the Temple and challenged him to throw himself down. Finally, Satan took Jesus to a very high mountain and offered to give Jesus all the kingdoms of the world if he would fall down and worship him. **Matthew 4:1–10**

The three temptations are directly related to the fundamental mission of the messiah. In the beginning, God told Adam and Eve to "be fruitful, multiply and have dominion." Satan claimed these three great blessings through the fall. Jesus came into the world to accomplish the purpose of creation by restoring these blessings. Therefore, Satan tempted Jesus three times in an attempt to prevent him from restoring the three blessings and accomplishing the purpose of creation.

The first blessing was individual perfection. Satan tempting Jesus to turn the stone into bread is the same course by which Jacob restored the birthright back to God's side. Esau was also hungry, and he gladly traded his birthright to Jacob for bread and stew. Satan is seeking to retrieve the birthright from Jesus. The Lord was having none of it.

The second blessing was for Adam and Eve to multiply God's lineage as True Parents. **Malachi 2:15** In the second temptation,

Satan tempts Jesus to cast himself down from the pinnacle of the Temple. Jesus standing at the pinnacle of the Temple is Jesus standing in the position of True Father and first Son born of God's lineage. The temple upon which Jesus was standing represents God's lineage, restored mankind. The descendants of Jesus and his bride form a "macro temple" of God's spirit.

Revelation 21:3

Now the dwelling of God is with men, and he will live with them. They will be his people, and God himself will be with them and be their God.

Satan was tempting Jesus to lose his position as first ancestor in the same way Adam lost his. Keep in mind that Jesus "was tempted in every way, just as we are, yet was without sin." **Hebrews 4:15**

The third blessing was for Adam to have dominion over all things upon the earth and all angels in heaven. In the third temptation, Satan was challenging this proper order.

1 Corinthians 15:27

*For he "has put everything under **his** feet."[Psalm 8:6] Now when it says that "everything" has been put under him, it is clear that this does not include God himself, who put everything under Christ.*

Jesus was totally victorious, and on the foundation of his offering of a 40-day fast and subjugating Satan three times, Jesus successfully established the worldwide Foundation of Faith in this second course.

The Second Course to Establish the Foundation of Substance

In gathering followers, Jesus was trying to complete the mission of John so that he could then accomplish the mission of the messiah. His own mission was to establish the Kingdom of Heaven on earth and in spirit through establishing True Parents and fulfilling the three blessings.

Jesus begins to gather his own apostles and disciples. We see Jesus' motivation for his mission:

Matthew 9:36–38

When he saw the crowds, he had compassion on them, because they were harassed and helpless, like sheep without a shepherd. Then he said to his disciples, "The harvest is plentiful but the workers are few. Ask the Lord of the harvest, therefore, to send out workers into his harvest field."

The "harvest" was great because "now was the time." However, Jesus was left without laborers for the harvest. Where were those laborers? Why would Jesus be in need of laborers if John had been doing his mission?

In trying to make a Foundation for the Messiah, Jesus employed a very practical methodology.

Mark 6:7

Calling the Twelve to him, he sent them out two by two and gave them authority over evil spirits.

Before he sent them out, he gave them a through training session. After that training, he assigned them to various towns and villages, after which:

Matthew 9:35

Jesus went through all the towns and villages, teaching in their synagogues, preaching the good news of the kingdom and healing every disease and sickness.

After this initial campaign, Jesus expanded the training to include the next tier of the 72 disciples:

Luke 10:1–3

*After this the Lord appointed seventy-two others and sent them two by two ahead of him to every town and place where he was about to go. He told them, "The harvest is plentiful, **but the workers are few**. Ask the Lord of the harvest, therefore, to send out workers into his harvest field. Go! I am sending you out like lambs among wolves.*

We can see that sometimes not everything went smoothly with the campaign:

John 6:58–61

"This is the bread that came down from heaven. Your forefathers ate manna and died, but he who feeds on this bread will live forever." He said this while teaching in the synagogue in Capernaum. On hearing it, many of his disciples said, "This is a hard teaching. Who can accept it?" Aware that his disciples were grumbling about this, Jesus said to them, "Does this offend you?"

Finally, after two years of public ministry, Jesus' disciples could not be successful enough to stem the tide that was building against Jesus:

John 7:1

After this, Jesus went around in Galilee, purposely staying away from Judea because the Jews there were waiting to take his life.

There was no faith in Israel. **Matthew 8:10:**

Verily I say unto you, I have not found so great faith, no, not in Israel.

Because there was no faith in Israel, the providence, as in the time of Jeremiah, turns toward the secondary path of the cross:

Matthew 16:21

From that time on Jesus began to explain to his disciples that he must go to Jerusalem and suffer many things at the hands of the elders, chief priests and teachers of the law, and that he must be killed and on the third day be raised to life.

As we explained in the previous chapter, Jesus was faced with the most painful dilemma. On the one hand, if Israel remained a faithless nation, he had to prepare his disciples and the coming generations until the Second Coming to be able to understand the nature of this prolongation course. His disciples, so enamored with the hope of the immediate establishment of the Kingdom, would turn morose and pessimistic with the prospect of a 2,000-year delay. Jesus had to try with all his heart to convince them of this "happy" outcome, when in reality, in all of his heart, he too wanted to realize the Kingdom that was "at hand," while he was still fighting to establish his Foundation of Substance.

In the last year we see the collapse of his ministry to accomplish the Foundation for the Messiah. With each passing day, the cross loomed larger on the horizon.

From this time many of his disciples turned back and no longer followed him. "You do not want to leave too, do you?" Jesus asked the Twelve. **John 6:66–67**

But even the faith of the 12 apostles begins to show signs of cracking. We see evidence of the condition of their faith at the Last Supper. When Jesus mentions that "one of you here will betray me," each one of them responds tepidly:

Matthew 26:22

And they were exceeding sorrowful, and began every one of them to say unto him, Lord, is it I?

That each one has to ask "Lord, is it I?" indicates that every one of them had been contemplating betrayal, not just Judas.

Gethsemane

Jesus takes his followers and retired to the Garden of Gethsemane. It was here that Jesus shared his soul's true feelings about the impending offering of his life. **Matthew 26: 37-42**:

And he took with him Peter and the two sons of Zebedee, and began to be sorrowful and very heavy. Then saith he unto them, "My soul is exceeding sorrowful, even unto death: tarry ye here, and watch with me." And he went a little farther, and fell on his face, and prayed, saying, "O my Father, if it be possible, let this cup pass from me: nevertheless not as I will, but as thou wilt."

And he cometh unto the disciples, and findeth them asleep, and saith unto Peter, "What, could ye not watch with me one hour? Watch and pray, that ye enter not into temptation: the spirit indeed is willing, but the flesh is weak." He went away again the second time, and prayed, saying, "O my Father, if this cup may not pass away from me, except I drink it, thy will be done."

If, indeed, Jesus' sole destiny was to die on the cross, how could he face this moment so reluctantly? Jesus attempted to convey to

Peter, James and John the content of his sorrow. He explained that his soul was "exceedingly sorrowful, even unto death."

It is so tragic that not one of them could console Jesus in that moment and, perhaps, be able to provide us with a clearer insight into the nature of his overwhelming grief.

Instead, when he returned to them after his tearful prayer, he found them fast asleep. What greater expression could there be of the divide between Jesus and even his closest apostles? How much more alone and deserted could he have been?

For all intents and purposes, this was the close of the second course on the worldwide level to establish the Foundation for the Messiah. Jesus took three apostles and tried to offer a minimum Foundation of Substance, but alas, they broke faith with Jesus and slept.

This lonely domain of incomprehensible sorrow has been his dwelling until today. No subsequent theological ponderings could adequately unlock the secret substance of his pain. In fact, this grieving Lord offends our theologies and the narrow definitions of his purpose.

And in what must be the pinnacle of human arrogance, we presume to apologize for the Lord by explaining away his tears as a momentary lapse of messianic dignity. How relieved Jesus must be to know that he can be forgiven for violating our doctrinal blindness.

Jesus was sorrowful in Gethsemane because it was there that he lay down his foremost aspiration and, instead, burned to ashes all his hopes and dreams for the Kingdom in his lifetime. The gate was shut and then sealed. Jesus was saying farewell to the hope that God had placed in him for the accomplishment of that ideal.

Farewell, to his disciples and his people, faced now with a most arduous course of exile and destruction. Farewell, to the peoples of the next two millennia, peoples of all lands and all languages who had now lost their chance to live in a world controlled by a covenant of peace. A world where knowledge of the Lord covered the earth as waters covered the sea, where swords were beaten into plowshares and spears into pruning hooks. Where weeping and wailing would cease and be no more.

Farewell holy bride who would never be, who would never embrace or excite the warm glowing passions of her perfect husband and provide for him the place of rest. This unknown beloved princess, this royal bride; the king was readied to be enthralled by your beauty. Yet, no mother embroidered your wedding garments interwoven with gold. No house rose up to lead you to your king. No brethren of joy and gladness gathered along hometown streets welcoming the royal procession.

Farewell, to these loves for which only he was worthy. Farewell to the royal seed; the sons, the daughters, princes and princesses that this love would have borne to perpetuate their memory. Farewell, to those hoped for moments of infinite solace and serenity abiding within the sleeping child pressed to Papa's chest. All those moments of love, those treasures, he left behind. Farewell, forever and ever.

Jesus sacrificed more than just himself when he mounted Calvary's cross. He not only laid down his one life but also all of its potential to everlastingly increase as numerous as the stars in the sky and as countless as the sand on the seashore.

The Godly Seed

All these were laid down and left behind in the Garden of Gethsemane. He waits for us there, waiting for us to awaken from our long, deep sleep.

Our nation, despite its Christian heritage, leads the industrialized world in an ever-increasing spectrum of problems that find their root in the breakdown of the family.

The family is declining not just because of the chaos born of the sexual revolution or the problem of homosexuality. Not even because of the vile porno industry. The most essential cause of the decline of the family is our refusal to understand the deeper meaning of Jesus' sacrifice in relation to the family. We have been blind to that deepest measure of family value.

When Jesus put his family on the cross, he grieved. He grieved because he knew the value of the perfect family that he had to sacrifice. His grief, then, was the perfect expression of the value of that family. In his grief, therefore, we have the perfect expression of true family value. If we know not the substance of that grief, we will, likewise, be ignorant of the essence of true family value. That is why the family declines today.

He gave up his family for us. He was compelled to sacrifice only because we defied God's Will for a lineage as certainly as did Onan, whom God killed. We deserved Onan's fate, yet Jesus interceded, beseeching God, saying, "Father, forgive them, they know not what they are doing." We never expressed an appropriate level of gratitude for the full measure of that sacrifice because, to this very day, "we know not."

Thus, until this day, Jesus grieves alone. We stand on the perimeter of Gethsemane and ponder his unhappiness from afar. We stubbornly cling to our man-made doctrines that disqualified him from true marriage and make obscure the very substance of his grief. In this way, like the dozing apostles who exalted sleep over consoling the Lord, we embrace our doctrinal slumber rather than awakening to a grieving Lord. Today, our crumbling family institution bears final witness against us. The blood-stained voices cry out to convince us that as a nation, we must repent.

Today, the family must revive. Only when we find the ultimate meaning of the family will that revival commence. That deeper meaning is implicit in the shed blood of Christ, yet it has been unknown until today. When men and women realize that greatest meaning, then there will be a newborn motive to uplift and cherish marriage. That will is given birth when all believers can feel at one with Jesus' "sorrow unto death." That is the heart with which he placed his family on the altar for us. Jesus called Rev. Moon to awaken us, yet sleeping, for lo these many years:

> *Thus, the prayer at the Garden of Gethsemane will never end. Throughout endless ages and centuries, this heartbreaking and blood-stained voice of the final plea should always stay alive in the human heart. God is working hard, hoping for a day when your heart will resonate with the heart of Jesus, who cried out, "My God."*
>
> *The believers in the last days should inherit the historical and grave heart of Jesus as he prayed on Mount Calvary and in the Garden of Gethsemane. They should awaken the Christians who are in the position of the three disciples sleeping in the Garden of Gethsemane. You should know that such an age is approaching. With the same heart as Jesus, who prayed in the Garden of Gethsemane, "My Father, if it is possible, let this cup pass from me" (Matthew 26:39), you should also pray, "Father, if possible, do not let our messiah be taken to the cross."*
> **Rev. Sun Myung Moon, "The Sorrowful Heart of Jesus as He Went to the Mountain," January 25, 1959**

Jesus gave up his family so that we could have a family. In view of this, can we, then, simply throw it away? Are we not obligated to take up the family mission he left behind? Should not we, the heirs of salvation, be compelled to comfort Jesus by offering to him a family in the spirit of the one he laid down at the cross?

The Third Worldwide Course to Establish the Foundation for the Messiah

The second worldwide course ended in failure due to the failure of the people to recognize and unite with Jesus. That second course required Jesus to take the position of John and to attempt to fulfill "Elijah's" mission. Satan was able to claim the foundation of faith that Jesus had accomplished in the wilderness during his forty-day fast because the people did not unite with Jesus.

The Meaning of the Cross

God had personally been guiding His beloved chosen people until the time Jesus appeared as the messiah. Yet from the moment they turned against His only begotten Son, God tearfully had to turn His back and allow Satan to lay claim to them, as promised in **Deuteronomy 29:25**. As there was a blessing in the law there was, likewise a curse. **Galatians 3:13, Malachi 4:5–6** Israel would determine the outcome by its faith or lack thereof.

In spite of their rejection, God's purpose in sending the messiah was to save the chosen people and all humanity. God was determined to save humankind, even though it meant delivering Jesus, His only Son, as a ransom, into the hands of Satan.

Satan, on the other hand, was totally focused on killing one man, Jesus Christ. Even if it meant that he would have to hand back all of humanity to God, he felt it was worth it. Unless we understand fully what God sacrificed to recover us, will our repentance and gratitude for salvation be anywhere near reflective of its value?

Satan was willing to take Jesus' flesh body as a ransom for all mankind. Jesus' body, therefore, must have contained an immeasurable value, a value even greater than the value of all mankind. What was the basis of that value? "God so loved the world that He gave His only begotten Son." What did God give?

Was Jesus' body inconsequential and simply destined to turn to dust? What about the first Adam's body; it turned to dust, but was it inconsequential to Adam's descendants? Was it inconsequential to Satan's dominion from generation to generation? Adam's body multiplied a legacy of sin. In that sense, Adam's body is still alive in us and, thus, we are all born in Adam's sin.

If Jesus had multiplied a lineage, would those descendants be of the "dead" Adam? No, they would be descendants of Jesus, the living Adam. "A little bit of yeast within the dough" is a parable describing Jesus' expanding lineage. This would be the lineage of God, his "godly seed," "a mustard seed" growing to be a great tree with many branches. This is the lineage that God had promised to Abraham. God was so touched by Abraham's offering of Isaac because "it is through Isaac that your offspring will be reckoned." Abraham not only offered his son but his lineage as well.

When Onan spilled God's seed on the ground he faced immediate retribution. God killed Onan. This is the value of God's lineage. Those who crucified Jesus committed an offense to God far greater than Onan's and deserved a swifter and more severe fate. Jesus implored God, as Moses had done, to forgive them for "they know not what they are doing."

God not only laid His Son on the cross, God laid down His lineage as well. Of all that Satan feared about Jesus, his greatest fear was Jesus' potential to multiply a Godly lineage. Satan knew he would not be able to claim that lineage. Jesus' expanding body would establish God's dominion as completely as Adam's expanded the dominion of Satan. That is why Satan was willing to exchange all mankind in order to block that one potential of Jesus' body. God gave up his chance for the birth of His own lineage. He offered it so that His fallen children could be brought back to His side. This means that God's moment to be fulfilled and loved by His very own had to be thrown aside. Instead, God had to take up the lonely, bitter and tearful course while hoping for the restoration of all things as a faint and distant dream.

Satan knew that the primary goal of God's 4,000-year providence of restoration was to send the messiah for that purpose. He thought that by killing the messiah he could destroy the entire providence of God. In the end, God handed over Jesus to Satan as the condition of indemnity to save all humankind, which had turned against Jesus and fell into Satan's realm.

Satan exercised his maximum power to crucify Jesus, thereby

attaining the goal he had sought throughout the 4,000-year course of history. On the other hand, by delivering Jesus to Satan, God set up as compensation the condition to save sinful humanity. Jesus, therefore, died for you and me. Not only that, his children died for me, his grandchildren, and his great-grandchildren. For every generation of Adam's fallen descendants there is a comparable generation of Jesus' offspring, never born, never welcomed, never loved, all sacrificed on Calvary's cross. How tragic. How sad. Can we begin to understand the blood-stained voice of Christ and his final lonely plea in the Garden of Gethsemane?

How did God achieve this? Because Satan had already exercised his maximum power in killing Jesus, according to the principle of restoration through indemnity, God was entitled to exercise His maximum power. While Satan uses his power to kill, God uses His power to bring the dead to life. As compensation for Satan's exercise of his maximum power in killing Jesus, God exercised His maximum power and resurrected Jesus. God thus opened the way for all humanity to be engrafted to the resurrected Jesus and thereby receive salvation and rebirth.

The Third Course for the Foundation of Faith

After Jesus gave up his body on the cross, he resumed, spiritually, John the Baptist's mission. That is, to spiritually establish the Foundation for the Messiah. During the 40-day period from his resurrection to his ascension, Jesus triumphed over Satan and broke all his chains. By doing so, Jesus restored the Foundation of Faith for the spiritual course in the third worldwide course. This is the reason his period of ascension was a 40-day period.

The Third Course for the Foundation of Substance

The resurrected Jesus stood spiritually in the position of John the Baptist and the position of Abel. The faithful believers stood in the position of Cain. Jesus used the 40-day period after his resurrection to unite his lost foundation.

Peter had denied Jesus three times. In **John 21:17** Peter had to affirm three times that he loved Jesus. This was to restore his position. Likewise, Judas' position had to be restored. In **Acts 1:23–26**, the apostles chose Matthias. Extending from the foundation of the 12 apostles were the 120 who gathered together in the upper rooms and pledged their faith in Jesus. By believing in Jesus and following him devotedly, they fulfilled the indemnity condition to remove the fallen nature and restored the spiritual Foundation of Substance.

The Foundation for the Messiah on the Spiritual Level

Jesus could now stand in his anointed role as messiah. This mission of the messiah is to become the True Parents of physical and spiritual rebirth.

Jesus and the Holy Spirit as spiritual True Parents opened up the channel of regeneration on the Day of Pentecost. Through the spiritual foundation of True Parents we are born anew and stand, on the spiritual level, as the living descendant of God, freed from sin and worthy of eternal life.

Also, with our salvation comes a hope of future glory. Christ will return to build his original Kingdom on the earth.

Just as Moses could only enter Canaan in spirit, Joshua walked the national course substantially and actually conquered the promised land. Likewise, while Jesus has been restoring a worldwide spiritual realm, Christ at the Second Advent is to complete this third worldwide course as a substantial course and build the actual Kingdom of Heaven on earth. Christ at the Second Advent must realize, on earth, God's ideal that was left unfulfilled at the First Coming.

Hebrews 9:28

He will appear a second time, not to bear sin, but to bring salvation to those who are waiting for him.

Chapter Eleven

Resurrection

The resurrection of Jesus Christ is the citadel of Christian faith. It is the belief that Jesus conquered death for us. By believing in him, we gain the gift of eternal life.

Over the course of time, the meaning of "death" and "life" has been greatly influenced by the profound human mystery of our own physical mortality. The seeming totality of one's physical demise coupled with the inability to assess spiritual reality left one with a considerable sense of fear at the prospect of "death."

Christian teaching on the resurrection offered a vision of life transcendent of earthly bounds, and in so doing, offered comfort to troubled souls confronted with the limits of mortality.

How important is it to Christian faith? Consider Paul's words in **1 Corinthians 15:14**:

And if Christ has not been raised, our preaching is useless and so is your faith.

The Meaning of Resurrection

Resurrection means to come back to life. To come back to life implies that we have been dead. To understand the meaning of resurrection, we must clarify the biblical concepts of life and death.

Luke 9:60
Jesus said to him, "Let the dead bury their own dead, but you go and proclaim the kingdom of God."

This verse is significant because it illustrates the fact that there are two definitions of the word "death" and, by implication, two definitions of the word "life." It is important to sort out the definitions in order to conclude which death is subject to resurrection.

Jesus is witnessing to a prospective disciple. He is encouraging him to make his decision today. People involved in any type of sales know that the greatest obstacle to the sale is a tendency for the customer to procrastinate rather than make the decision to buy. A good salesman, therefore, attempts to "close the deal" on the first meeting and is ready to help the customer who insists he wants "to think it over," or "to talk to my wife and get back to you."

Jesus, in this respect, is a "power closer" when it comes to "selling" eternal life. His prospect shows an interest and wants to go forward, but he has an objection. He has to attend his father's funeral. It seems like a condition not to buy, but Jesus skillfully handles the objection and turns the objection into the reason for buying. Jesus is one great salesman!

"Let the dead bury the dead, you go and proclaim the Kingdom of God!" Jesus' response indicates that there are two types of "death." Let the *spiritually dead* bury the *physically dead*.

Other verses in scripture indicate this twofold meaning:

Revelation 3:1
I know your deeds; you have a reputation of being alive, but you are dead.

John 11:25–26
Jesus said to her, "I am the resurrection and the life. He who believes in me will live, even though he dies; and whoever lives and believes in me will never die. Do you believe this?"

The Death Caused by the Fall

To know which death is subject to resurrection, we need to know which death is caused by the fall of man.

In the first chapter, we saw that the original structure and function of a human entails both a spiritual and physical dimension. This is reflected in scripture:

Ecclesiastes 12:7
And the dust returns to the ground it came from, and the spirit returns to God who gave it.

Genesis 2:22–24

*Then the LORD God made a woman from the rib he had taken out of the man, and he brought her to the man. The man said, "This is now **bone of my bones and flesh of my flesh**; she shall be called 'woman,' for she was taken out of man." For this reason a man will leave his father and mother and be united to his wife, and **they will become one flesh.***

Some believe that the physical body was created as a result of the fall. They point to **Genesis 3:21:** "The LORD God made garments of skin for Adam and his wife and clothed them." This was after Adam and Eve fell. Many maintain a vague notion that the temporal nature of the physical body is attributable to sin.

However, **Genesis 2:22–24** clearly indicates that God created flesh bodies for Adam and Eve prior to the event of sin. This would tend to support the idea that the flesh body, too, had an original Godly purpose and function prior to man's sin. Thus, the existence of the flesh body is not an inherent attribute of sin.

In **Genesis 2:17**, we see that if Adam and Eve eat the fruit, they will die on the very day they eat it.

. . . for in the day that thou eatest thereof thou shalt surely die.

In relation to the temporal nature of the physical body, Adam and Eve ate the fruit and died on that very same day. Therefore, this death that they experienced was not physical death. It was a "death" that reflected the initial category of "death" mentioned by Jesus in **Luke 9:60**, that is, spiritual death. There is no scripture that links the event of physical death as a consequence of sin. That is, the temporal nature of the flesh body "returning to dust" is not a condition caused by the fall of man.

What Is Spiritual Death?

1 John 3:14

We know that we have passed from death to life, because we love our brothers. Anyone who does not love remains in death.

Romans 6:23
For the wages of sin is death, but the gift of God is eternal life in Christ Jesus our Lord.

Romans 8:6
The mind of sinful man is death, but the mind controlled by the Spirit is life and peace.

Ephesians 4:18
They are darkened in their understanding and separated from the life of God because of the ignorance that is in them due to the hardening of their hearts.

Spiritual death is the state resulting from sin. It is the state of being separated from God's love. It is where "our hearts are hardened," and thus, we can no longer "love our brothers." John says anyone who "does not love remains in death."

The Meaning of Resurrection

If physical death is not the "death" caused by the fall, then "passing from death into life" (resurrection) is something much more than the mere revival of the decomposed physical body. **Ecclesiastes 12:7**

Therefore, resurrection is the process of man being restored from Satan's dominion back to God's dominion through the dispensation for restoration.

John 5:24
*I tell you the truth, whoever **hears my word** and believes him who sent me **has eternal life** and will not be condemned; he has crossed over from **death to life**.*

1 Corinthians 15:21–22
For since death came through a man, the resurrection of the dead comes also through a man. For as in Adam all die, so in Christ all will be made alive.

Christ is the central figure for the dispensation of resurrection.

The Distinction between Resurrection of the Spirit and Resurrection of the Corporal Body

Scripture gives examples of both. They are not the same in significance and meaning, however.

Matthew 27:52–53
*The tombs broke open and the bodies of many holy people who had died were **raised to life**. They came out of the tombs, and after Jesus' resurrection they went into the holy city and **appeared to many people**.*

John 11:40–44
Then Jesus said, "Did I not tell you that if you believed, you would see the glory of God?" So they took away the stone. Then Jesus looked up and said, "Father, I thank you that you have heard me. I knew that you always hear me, but I said this for the benefit of the people standing here, that they may believe that you sent me." When he had said this, Jesus called in a loud voice, "Lazarus, come out!" The dead man came out, his hands and feet wrapped with strips of linen, and a cloth around his face.

Luke 24:36–39
*While they were still talking about this, Jesus himself stood among them and said to them, "Peace be with you." They were startled and frightened, thinking they saw a **ghost**. He said to them, "Why are you troubled, and why do doubts rise in your minds? Look at my hands and my feet. It is I myself! Touch me and see; a ghost does not have flesh and bones, as you see I have."*

Let's examine these important Bible verses more closely. We will make a distinction between spiritual resurrection and the miracle of corporal resurrection.

Matthew 27:52-53
The many bodies of the saints who had fallen asleep were raised from the dead. They went into the holy city (Jerusalem) and appeared to many.

The key word is "appeared." They "appeared" to many, but not to "all." We will see in other verses how the term "appeared" is used to describe the arrival of spiritualized forms.

If this event were a corporal resurrection, then the saints would have "appeared" to all. If they had appeared to all, then certainly this great event would have received more documentation other than one verse in the book of Matthew (written about 20 to 40 years after the event). For example, Josephus, the great Jewish historian from the first century, makes no mention of this event in any of his records.

Keep in mind, we are not arguing against the *miracle* of corporal resurrection as exemplified by Lazarus (Elijah also raised the dead). We are maintaining that, in this case, the saints were raised in their spiritualized or glorified forms and the expression of spiritual resurrection can be easily confused with the miracle of corporal resurrection as exemplified by Elijah's work and Lazarus.

Jesus "raising Lazarus from the dead" **(John 11:40–44)** is an example of a corporal resurrection. It *is a miracle* and not the same as the providence of resurrection to "eternal life." The purpose for which Jesus performed miracles is explained in **John 10:38:**

Even though you do not believe me, believe the miracles, that you may know and understand that the Father is in me, and I in the Father.

When Jesus raised Lazarus, he explained that the reason he was doing this was *for the benefit of the people standing here, that they may believe that you sent me.*

Even as a miracle, though quite impressive indeed, the ability to corporally resurrect someone, unlike the resurrection of the spirit, is not *exclusive to Christ*. See **1 Kings 17:21–22**

Then Elijah stretched himself out on the boy three times and cried to the LORD, "O LORD my God, let this boy's life return to him!" The LORD heard Elijah's cry, and the boy's life returned to him. . . and he lived.

Jesus was performing miracles in order to help direct the people toward the actual exclusive provision of Christ: eternal life. This was something that Elijah could never have provided. Christ, *alone*, is the providential agent of resurrection.

The conclusion, is, yes, corporal resurrection is a reality *as a miracle*, but it only provided for an extension of Lazarus' physical life. After all, didn't Lazarus later "die" again? Therefore, corporal resurrection is not the manifestation of resurrection to eternal life.

Luke 24:36–39

*While they were still talking about this, Jesus himself stood among them and said to them, "Peace be with you." They were startled and frightened, thinking they saw a **ghost**. He said to them, "Why are you troubled, and why do doubts rise in your minds? Look at my hands and my feet. It is I myself! Touch me and see; a ghost does not have flesh and bones, as you see I have."*

This "appearance" of Christ after his resurrection is the strongest and seemingly most emphatic statement of Christ's post-tomb corporality. We must examine this carefully.

First of all, notice that Jesus suddenly appears in their midst in such a way as to "startle and frighten" them. **John 20:19** mentions that he appeared in their midst, even though the doors were locked.

We see in an earlier appearance in **Mark 16:12:** *Afterward Jesus appeared in a different form to two of them while they were walking in the country.*

Different form? What kind of different form? It is his spiritualized form. We see in **Luke 24:16** this "different form" prevented the disciples from initially recognizing that it was Jesus with whom they were speaking.

When Jesus "appears" to the disciples inside the room in **Luke 24:36–39**, he must, likewise, assure them that it is, indeed, Jesus. They were frightened thinking that this appearance was a "ghost." This fear toward the presence of a "ghost" is very interesting and significant to properly understand what is happening.

The word "ghost" is used in the New International Version. It is meant to imply some sort of "bodiless demon or apparition." When the presence of a spiritualized form does not entail a negative entity, the term used is "spirit."

However, in the King James Version, it is the opposite. The term "ghost" is used to imply a positive spiritual form, the term "spirit" is used to indicate a negative apparition that instills fear when encountered.

The point is that Jesus is seeking to allay their fears so that they can recognize that it is indeed Jesus himself and not some demonic entity.

What about Jesus' assertion that, "A ghost does not have flesh and bones as you see that I have"? Again, Jesus is emphasizing that it is really he. The fact that they can touch him or that he then proceeds to eat a broiled fish does not mean he isn't in his spiritualized form. It means he isn't a "ghost." A "ghost" can't do these things, but a "spirit" can:

Jacob wrestled an *angel* and wrenched his hip.

Eve *fornicated* with Lucifer.

The daughters of men *married* the "bene Elohim," that is, angels. **Genesis 6:2**

Angels *ate a meal* at Lot's table.

Many have entertained angels *unaware*. **Hebrews 13:1**

How Does Jesus "Appear"?

In the following scripture, Saint Paul documents the series of appearances of Jesus after his resurrection. He concludes the sequence with the "appearance" of Jesus to him (on the road to Damascus).

1 Corinthians 15:4–8

That he was buried, that he was raised on the third day according to the Scriptures, and that he appeared to Peter, and then to the Twelve. After that, he appeared to more than five hundred of the brothers at the same time, most of whom are still living, though some have fallen asleep. Then he appeared to James, then to all the apostles, **and last of all he appeared to me also.**

The manner in which Jesus appeared to Paul is explained in **Acts 9:3–7:**

As he neared Damascus on his journey, suddenly a light from heaven flashed around him. He fell to the ground and heard a voice say to him, "Saul, Saul, why do you persecute me?" "Who are you, Lord?" Saul asked. "I am Jesus, whom you are persecuting," he replied. "Now get up and go into the city, and you will be told what you must do." The men traveling with Saul stood there speechless; **they heard the sound but did not see anyone.**

"They heard the sound, but they **did not see anyone**." This is how Jesus "appeared" to Paul. Paul could see, but others could not. Likewise, when the many bodies of the saints "appeared," they appeared to some but not all. This was the spiritualized form in the resurrection of the spirit.

Paul teaches clearly in **1 Corinthians 15:35–52:**

But someone may ask, "How are the dead raised? With what kind of body will they come?"

How foolish! What you sow does not come to life unless it dies. When you sow, you do not plant the body that will be, but just a seed, perhaps of wheat or of something else. But God gives it a body as he has determined, and to each kind of seed he gives its own body. All flesh is not the same: Men have one kind of flesh, animals have another, birds another and fish another. There are also heavenly bodies and there are earthly bodies; but the splendor of the heavenly bodies is one kind, and the splendor of the earthly bodies is another. The sun has one kind of splendor, the moon another and the stars another; and star differs from star in splendor.

So will it be with the resurrection of the dead. The body that is sown is perishable, it is raised imperishable; it is sown in dishonor, it is raised in glory; it is sown in weakness, it is raised in power; it is sown a natural body, it is raised a spiritual body.

If there is a natural body, there is also a spiritual body. . .

I declare to you, brothers, that flesh and blood cannot inherit the kingdom of God, nor does the perishable inherit the imperishable. Listen, I tell you a mystery: We will not all sleep, but we will all be changed, in a flash, in the twinkling of an eye, at the last trumpet. For the trumpet will sound, the dead will be raised imperishable, and we will be changed.

Some key statements in these verses: Paul states that when you sow you do not plant the body that is to be; instead, you are planting just a seed. Likewise, the body that is sown is the natural body, the body that is raised is the spiritual body. The body that is sown, the natural body, is perishable. It cannot inherit imperishability or the kingdom of God (meaning: it can't go to the spiritual world). It is the spiritual body that is raised. It is imperishable and it can inherit (that is, go to) the Kingdom of God (spirit world).

Mark 16:12 testifies that Jesus "appeared in a different form" after he was raised from the dead. This is because, as Paul affirms, "the dead will be raised imperishable, **and will be changed**."

Jesus Gazes into the Spirit World

This is one of the most interesting parables that Jesus ever gave. It provides keen insight into some of the realities of the spiritual world. Most important, Jesus provides a clear definition of "raising from the dead." It involves two men who die. One was a rich man, the other, a beggar. The beggar went to heaven to be with Abraham. The rich man went to hell. (The beggar's name was Lazarus and is not to be confused with the Lazarus whom Jesus raised from the dead.)

Luke 16:19–31

There was a rich man who was dressed in purple and fine linen and lived in luxury every day. At his gate was laid a beggar named Lazarus, covered with sores and longing to eat what fell from the rich man's table. Even the dogs came and licked his sores.

The time came when the beggar died and the angels carried him to Abraham's side. The rich man also died and was buried. In hell, where he was in torment, he looked up and saw Abraham far away, with Lazarus by his side. So he called to him, "Father Abraham, have pity on me and send Lazarus to dip the tip of his finger in water and cool my tongue, because I am in agony in this fire."

But Abraham replied, "Son, remember that in your lifetime you received your good things, while Lazarus received bad things, but now he is comforted here and you are in agony. And besides all this, between us and you a great chasm has been fixed, so that those who want to go from here to you cannot, nor can anyone cross over from there to us."

He answered, "Then I beg you, father, send Lazarus to my father's house, for I have five brothers. Let him warn them, so that they will not also come to this place of torment."

Abraham replied, "They have Moses and the Prophets; let them listen to them." "No, father Abraham," he said, "but if someone from the dead goes to them, they will repent." He said to him, "If they do not listen to Moses and the Prophets, they will not be convinced even if someone rises from the dead."

What is Jesus' definition of "raising from the dead" in this parable?" It is the phenomenon of a spirit in the spirit world "appearing" on the earth plane to perform a providential task centering on people on earth. The rich man wanted Lazarus to "raise from the dead" to warn his brothers to repent so that they would avoid coming to hell.

The Providence of Resurrection

Resurrection means the process through which God restores a fallen person to the original state. The providence of resurrection, therefore, has been a process manifested over many ages. It is the providence by which God has been restoring man.

That process entails principles. In chapters three and four, we discussed the principles by which God has sought to recover His children. The Principle of Restoration through Indemnity is, in fact, the Principle of God's creation as applied to the work of restoring man. Since the providence of restoration is God's work of re-creation, resurrection is, likewise, a work of re-creation. Thus, the providence of resurrection is carried out in accordance with the Principle of Creation.

The first principle of resurrection is time specific. In the history of the providence of resurrection, God called central figures and people to make the Foundation for the Messiah. At the fall, man fell into total depravity. In such a state, God would not send His Word directly. Instead, He called the central figure to offer sacrifices as "conditional objects" representing the lost Word of God. Over time, a foundation of people were resurrected that could receive God's Word and begin a new providential age. Those who could be born in the Old Testament era were, therefore, more fortunate than their counterparts born in the dark first centuries after Adam's fall.

Based on their devotion, they broadened the foundation upon which subsequent generations could form a relationship of heart with God. We call this foundation the *merit of the age* in the providence of restoration. The merit of the age has increased in proportion to the foundation of heart laid by the prophets, sages and righteous people who came before us. Therefore, the age in which one lives will determine the amount of resurrection available. Had you been born 1,000 years after Adam's fall you would have been born in an age that was less meritorious than if you had been born in Israel at the time of Christ. In the same way, those fortunate enough to be alive in Christ when he returns will take part in the most meritorious age of them all.

The second principle reflects the centrality of the Word in man's relationship with God. God gave man the Word and the responsibility to apply it as the tool of co-creatorship. Through faith in the Word, man gains the potential to inherit the very nature of God.

Thus, "man does not live by bread alone." Similarly, in conducting the providence of resurrection, God's responsibility is to give us His Word and guidance, and our responsibility is to believe and practice it in order to fulfill the providence. *And he said unto him, "If they hear not Moses and the prophets, neither will they be persuaded, though one rose from the dead." Luke 16:31*

The third principle of resurrection reflects the fundamental role of our body of flesh. According to God's plan of creation, spiritual growth would be accomplished through the interaction between the spirit and body, our personal "pair system." The body is the soil for the spirit to grow, like fruit on a tree. Once growth of the spirit is fulfilled, the body drops away and the spirit, perfected, would "return to God who gave it." Likewise, in the providence of resurrection, the foundation of the resurrection of the spirit is accomplished on the earth in cooperative relationship with a body of flesh.

The fourth principle is based on the fact that according to God's plan of creation, people are meant to reach perfection through three ordered stages of the growing period. Therefore, the providence of resurrection for fallen people is also to be completed through three ordered stages, manifested as three ages in the providence of restoration.

The Providence of Resurrection for People on Earth

The Providence to Lay the Foundation for Resurrection

God began His providence to resurrect fallen humankind in Adam's family. However, the providence ended in Adam's family when Cain killed Abel. After 2,000 biblical years, Abraham's family accomplished the original foundation separated from Satan. Through Abraham, Isaac and Jacob, God's Will began to be accomplished. Consequently, the 2,000 years from Adam's family to Abraham's family resulted in the establishment of the foundation upon which God could begin His providence of resurrection in the following age. For this reason, we may call this period the foundation for resurrection or the "pre-Old Testament era."

We can see evidence provided by Jesus in his parable in **Luke 16:19–31**. "Abraham's side" is a sanctified realm separated from Satan by a great chasm. Abraham and Lazarus were not born-again Christians, yet they were able to benefit from the degree of resurrection available as a result of Abraham's foundation.

But Abraham replied, "Son, remember that in your lifetime you received your good things, while Lazarus received bad things, but now he is comforted here and you are in agony. And besides all this, between us and you a great chasm has been fixed, so that those who want to go from here to you cannot, nor can anyone cross over from there to us."

The Providence of Formation-Stage Resurrection

During the 2,000 years from Abraham to Jesus, God worked to raise people to the next stage of resurrection, the formation stage. This era may be called the formation-stage resurrection.

All people who lived on earth during this age could receive the merit of the age based on God's work of formation-stage resurrection. By following the laws, decrees and commandments of God the people could receive a conditional justification before God. Therefore, this era has been called the age of justification by works. The people of this era who practiced the law in their daily life were resurrected in spirit to the formation stage and became form spirits. It is not equivalent to salvation, but is rather the next stage of resurrection and the foundation upon which Christ appears. Upon their death, those who achieved the level of form spirits while on earth entered and abided in the form-spirit level of the spirit world.

In **Matthew 17:3**, Moses and Elijah appeared standing with Jesus at the Mount of Transfiguration. Though Moses and Elijah were not born-again Christians when they left this earth, we can see that their faith and deeds on earth resurrected them to the form level in spirit.

The Providence of Growth-Stage Resurrection

After his crucifixion, Jesus rose from the dead on the third day. He spent the next 40 days making the spiritual foundation for our resurrection. On the day of Pentecost, through Jesus and the Holy Spirit, believers could be "born again" and stand as adopted children of God able to inherit salvation and life. The course of resurrection will be completed when Christ returns at his second coming.

The 2,000 years since then have been a time of prolongation of God's Kingdom "on earth as it is in heaven." God has worked the providence to resurrect people to the growth stage via spiritual salvation through Jesus and the Holy Spirit, the True Parents of rebirth. Hence, this era may be called the age of the providence of growth-stage resurrection. All who have lived in this age can receive the merit of the age based on God's work of growth-stage resurrection. In this era, people are to believe, in faith, upon the Word made flesh, be born again, and stand justified before God. Rather than a justification by works, God opens the way to the next level, a justification by faith. Therefore, this era has been called the age of justification by faith.

Those who lived in this era could be resurrected in spirit through a personal relationship with Jesus Christ and believing in the Gospel during their earthly life. By being resurrected to the growth stage, they could become life spirits. Upon their death, those who became life spirits while on earth enter and abide in Paradise, the life-spirit level of the spirit world.

The Providence of Completion-Stage Resurrection

The era when people are to be resurrected both spiritually and physically through the returning Christ and complete the providence of resurrection is called the age of the providence of completion-stage resurrection.

All those who live during this era are to receive the merit of the age based on God's work of completion-stage resurrection. Christ at the Second Advent brings the "salvation that is ready to be revealed in the last time" (**1 Peter 1:5**) and thereby fulfill the promises of the Old and New Testaments; it may be called the Completed Testament. Christ comes, "not to bear sin, but to bring salvation to those waiting for him." **Hebrews 9:28** Believing in this truth, people are to serve and attend the Lord on the earth, that they may fulfill their responsibility for the providence and be justified before God.

Revelation 21: 1–5

Then I saw a new heaven and a new earth, for the first heaven and the first earth had passed away, and there was no longer any sea. I saw the Holy City, the new Jerusalem, coming down out of heaven from God, prepared as a bride beautifully dressed for her husband. And I heard a loud voice from the throne saying, "Now the dwelling of God is with men, and he will live with them. They will be his people, and God himself will be with them and be their God. He will wipe every tear from their eyes. There will be no more death or mourning or crying or pain, for the old order of things has passed away." He who was seated on the throne said, "I am making everything new!"

This is why Jesus asked, "When the Son of Man comes again, will he find faith on earth?" **Luke 18:8** Therefore, this era is called the age of justification by attendance. By believing in and serving the Lord and devoting themselves to his work, people of this era are to be fully resurrected both spiritually and physically, become divine spirits, and live in the Kingdom of Heaven on earth and in spirit. God himself will dwell with mankind and they with God on the earth and in heaven. When they shed their physical bodies, as spirits they will enter and abide in the Kingdom of Heaven in heaven, which is the divine-spirit level of the spirit world.

The Kingdom of Heaven and Paradise

In **Luke 23:43**, Jesus declares to the thief on the right, "Today, you will be with me in paradise."

Certainly many Christians are of the mind that when Jesus said, "It is finished," he meant everything was complete. However, the idea that Christ is returning to complete the work of salvation is an idea solidly grounded in scripture.

The idea that Christ is returning to set up his Kingdom, likewise, is mainstream. It stands to reason, given the idea that "what is sown on earth is reaped in heaven," that the Kingdom must first be established on earth so that it may then be transported to the world of spirit.

Thus, we see the testimony of **Hebrews 9:28,** and **1 Peter 1:5**.

Hebrews 9:28
So Christ was sacrificed once to take away the sins of many people; and he will appear a second time, not to bear sin, but to bring salvation to those who are waiting for him.

1 Peter 1:5
. . . Who, through faith are shielded by God's power until the coming of the salvation that is ready to be revealed in the last time.

That "salvation" won't be revealed until "the Last Days." The clear implication is that even the Bible, as we know it, has not articulated the nature of that salvation. The Bible declares that it will not be revealed until that time.

Acts 3:21

He must remain in heaven until the time comes for God to restore every-
thing, as he promised long ago through his holy prophets.

"Restore everything as he promised long ago through his holy
prophets." This means the Kingdom and all prophecy of glory such
as **Isaiah 65:17**. Do you remember the disciples' question to the resurrected Jesus? **Acts 1:6**: *So when they met together, they asked him,*
"Lord, are you at this time going to restore the kingdom to Israel?"
This is the meaning of "to restore everything" in **Acts 3:21**.

Paul certainly seems to be expecting more in the following scripture.

1 Corinthians 13:9–12

*For we know in part and we prophesy in part, but **when** perfection comes,*
the imperfect disappears. When I was a child, I talked like a child, I
thought like a child, I reasoned like a child. When I became a man, I put
childish ways behind me. Now we see but a poor reflection as in a mir-
ror; then we shall see face to face. Now I know in part; then I shall know
fully, even as I am fully known.

Hebrews 11:39–40 indicates that the saints in heaven are still
waiting for "what had been promised."

These were all commended for their faith, yet none of them received what
had been promised. God had planned something better for us so that
only together with us would they be made perfect.

Those saints in paradise will be made perfect with us. "Us" refers
to the people on earth at the time of Christ's return to "complete salvation." In **Revelation 2:7**, Jesus affirms: "to him who overcomes
I will give the right to eat from the tree of life." Eating from the "tree
of life" signifies the opening of the way to perfection.

The Tree of Life

The tree of life is the symbol of perfect Adam. God told Adam
and Eve that they must first be "fruitful." This was the prerequisite
for their marriage. On that foundation they could receive God's per-

mission to multiply. Man fell and God blocked the way to the tree of life. **Genesis 3:24** Thus, man "died," was cut off from the life of God, and needed resurrection to life.

"To eat from the tree of life" is the key to opening the Kingdom. Without perfection, to be "fruitful," we cannot fulfill the second blessing "to multiply." Thus, we see in the Old Testament the hope to achieve the tree of life.

Proverbs 11:30
The fruit of the righteous is a tree of life.

Proverbs 13:12
Hope deferred makes the heart sick, but a longing fulfilled is a tree of life.

The fruit of righteousness in the Old Testament is the "blessing" brought by Christ when he comes to Israel to establish his everlasting Kingdom. That is the "hope" and "longing fulfilled" of the Old Testament Age. Therefore Jesus is the "tree of life."

Hebrews 5:8–9
*Although he was a son, he learned obedience from what he suffered and, once **made perfect**, he became the source of eternal salvation for all who obey him.*

By achieving "perfection" Jesus became the "perfected Adam," that is, "the tree of life." He is the "vine," we are "the branches."

John 15:4–6
*Remain in me, and I will remain in you. No branch can bear fruit by itself; it must remain in the vine. Neither can you bear fruit unless you remain in me. **I am the vine; you are the branches.** If a man remains in me and I in him, he will bear much fruit; apart from me you can do nothing. If anyone does not remain in me, he is like a branch that is thrown away and withers; such branches are picked up, thrown into the fire and burned.*

However, he said, "My Kingdom is not of this world." The gates were shut because there was "no faith, no, not in Israel."

Jesus comes again to open the gates and open the way to the tree of life.

Revelation 2:7

To him who overcomes, I will give the right to eat from the tree of life, which is in the paradise of God.

Revelation 22:14

Blessed are those who wash their robes, that they may have the right to the tree of life and may go through the gates into the city.

Until we regain the right to eat from the tree of life, we cannot "enter the gate" into the city. The holy city is the Kingdom of Heaven, i.e., "the new Jerusalem."

Thus, until that time, we are in paradise and must "resurrect" to the level of the Kingdom of Heaven.

Why, then, did Jesus indicate that whoever believed in him would enter the Kingdom of Heaven? The original purpose for which he came on earth was to establish the Kingdom of Heaven. However, due to the people's disbelief in him, Jesus had to go the way of the cross and come again to establish the Kingdom.

Jesus promised the thief who was crucified at his right side that he would enter paradise together with him. **Luke 23:43** The thief was the only person who believed in Jesus at the end, when everyone else had abandoned him.

In the first two years of his ministry, however, if Israel had responded in faith to Jesus' message, he could have established his Kingdom on earth and in heaven at that time. It was during those first two years that Jesus' message focused on the primacy of the Kingdom. When Jesus saw that there was "no faith, no, not in Israel" his focus turned toward his suffering to come. Coinciding with that suffering was the closing of the gates to the Kingdom and the declaration that "my Kingdom is not now of this world." This is why Jesus was grieving in the Garden of Gethsemane.

The Kingdom of Heaven on earth was not realized. The earth never saw the appearance of people who had reached the level of divine spirits. No one has ever become a citizen of the Kingdom of Heaven in the spirit world, which was created as the home of divine spirits. Therefore, the Kingdom of Heaven in heaven remains to be realized at Christ's return.

Thus, from the cross, Jesus revealed to the thief that he would enter paradise. Paradise refers to the realm in the spirit world for those spirits who have attained the level of life spirits by believing in Jesus during their earthly life. There they remain in waiting until the day Christ returns and opens the gate to the Kingdom of Heaven on the earth so that it will then be reaped in heaven.

Spiritual Phenomena in the Last Days

Adam and Eve fell during the period of their growth toward perfection. The historical process of restoration through the Old Testament Age and the New Testament Age has resurrected humans to the point from which Adam and Eve originally fell. The "Last Days" is the time period when people return to that spiritual level obtained by the first human ancestors just prior to their fall.

Today, being the Last Days, is the time when people throughout the world are reaching this level. Just as Adam and Eve prior to their fall were able to converse directly with God, today many people on earth can communicate with the spirit world. The prophecy recorded in **Acts 2:17** declares that in the Last Days, *I will pour out my Spirit upon all flesh, and your sons and daughters shall prophesy, and your young men shall see visions, and your old men shall dream dreams.* This phenomenon is occurring today.

In the Last Days, many people will receive the revelation, "You are the Lord." Often these people will be misled into believing that they are the coming Christ. Why do they stray from the right path? This is why Jesus warns us in **Matthew 24:5** that many false Christs will appear in the Last Days. Today there are numerous movements in the world that claim their leader is the awaited Christ.

At the time of Jesus it was the same. There were several existing groups that were proclaiming their leader to be the awaited messiah.

Upon creating human beings, God gave them the three blessings. The third blessing was "to have dominion." It was the stated mandate that God's children were to rule over the universe. **Genesis 1:28**

Yet due to the fall, they have been unable to fulfill this blessing. When fallen people are spiritually restored to the position from which Adam and Eve fell, they will reach the level of heart comparable to that of Adam and Eve just before their fall.

God gives certain people who are at this stage the revelation that they are "the Lord" in recognition that they have reached the level of maturity at which He had once blessed human beings with dominion over the universe. It is reflective of the declaration of **Psalm 8:6**, "You made him ruler over the works of your hands; you put everything under his feet."

In the beginning, all God's children were to inherit the authority of the Father. In this sense, we are "the lord." However, this does not mean, we are "the Christ." In a similar way, Jesus indicated that we are "gods." **John 10:34, Psalm 82:6** This does not mean that we are the almighty God. We do, however, display attributes that reflect God.

This revelation proclaiming lordship could also indicate that the recipient of that revelation may have a John the Baptist-type mission to a certain group of prepared people. John the Baptist came with the mission to "make straight the way" of Jesus. **John 1:23** In the same way, these people of faith are given the mission to prepare, in their particular areas of responsibility, the way for Christ at the Second Advent. Since they are to act as the Lord's representatives in their respective fields, God gives them the revelation that they are the Lord.

Many people speculated about whether or not John was the Christ. His role to prepare the foundation for Jesus put him in a position to reflect the role of the Lord. For this reason, many people who are in a similar position have a tendency to begin to mistake themselves for the Lord.

In addition, when people of devout faith become spiritually open and reach the level of heart comparable to the pre-fallen Adam and Eve, they will face a test similar to that which Adam and Eve failed to overcome. **Hebrews 4:15** reveals that Jesus was tempted "in every way just as we are, yet without sin."

Likewise, we must go beyond the realm of the fall in the process of resurrection. If people of devout faith are not careful, they may commit the mistake of the fall. It is extremely difficult to overcome this temptation without understanding the deep meaning of God's Word. Regrettably, many religious people have failed to overcome this test, nullifying in an instant accomplishments gained through years of devotion and exertion.

Adultery is a problem sweeping not just the secular world, but the world of the church as well. It is a problem not just for church members but also for the clergy. This is because our position as believers waiting for the Second Coming is exactly the same position of

Adam and Eve before the fall. Just as Adam and Eve lost their prize through the illicit relationships of the fall, great champions of faith must guard against following the same woeful course.

The First Resurrection

The "first resurrection" spoken of in chapter seven of the Book of Revelation describes the fulfillment of restoration in providential history. The number 144,000 represents the 12 tribes of Israel, each tribe having 12,000 members. These are the "first fruits" and the Foundation to Receive the Messiah that was to be erected in Israel at the first advent of Christ. Jesus promised that the Kingdom would be "given to another nation who can produce the fruits in their seasons." That new nation is the "New Jerusalem," the new Israel, the new foundation upon which Christ will come. He will cleanse people of the original sin and restore them to their true, original selves, enabling each to fulfill the purpose of creation.

Revelation 7:9 then reveals that on the foundation of 144,000 prepared for the Lord would come "a great multitude that no one could count, from every nation, tribe, people and language, standing before the throne and in front of the Lamb."

This indicates that upon this foundation of 144,000, the whole world will be able to experience the "restoration of all things." All mankind will return to God both spiritually and physically.

The hope of all Christians is to participate in the first resurrection. But who, in fact, shall participate? It will be those who are the first to believe in, serve, and follow Christ at the Second Advent. They will assist him in fulfilling all the indemnity conditions worldwide and in accomplishing the providence of restoration. In the process, they will be the first to have their original sin removed, become divine spirits and fulfill the purpose of creation.

The Providence of Resurrection for Spirits

The Purpose and the Way of Returning Resurrection

According to the Principle of Creation, the growth of the human spirit requires two kinds of nourishment: life elements received from God and vitality elements received through give-and-take action with the physical self. Spirits can neither grow nor be resurrected apart from a physical self. Consequently, the spirits of people who died before they could reach perfection during their earthly life can only be resurrected by returning to earth.

There they will be able to complete their unaccomplished responsibility through cooperating spiritually with earthly people. By assisting people of faith living on the earth to fulfill their missions, the spirits may complete their own undone missions at the same time. "Spiritual cooperation" does not mean that the spirit reincarnates into another body. Instead, centering on God's Word and Will, spirits partnership with people on earth. Herein lies the meaning of **Jude 1:14** that proclaims in the Last Days the Lord will come "with his holy myriads." We call this process *returning resurrection*.

Returning resurrection is alluded to in **Luke 16:19–31**. In Jesus' parable, Abraham admonishes the rich man, "If they won't listen to Moses and the prophets neither will they listen if someone 'raises from the dead.' " Abraham was not speaking against the phenomenon of returning resurrection per se; he was, instead, emphasizing a key principle: without the condition of faith in God's spoken Word, there is no condition for someone on earth to benefit from the phenomenon of returning resurrection.

We see, conversely, in **Matthew 27:52**, that the "many bodies of the saints" were raised and did "appear" to many believers. This is a clear example of the phenomenon of returning resurrection.

It should be stressed that Scripture warns against an indiscriminate communication with the world of spirit. **1 John 4:1** warns us to "test the spirits" to ensure that the spirit is of God. However, once tested and approved, how do spirits help people on earth fulfill the Will of God? When people become receptive to spirits through prayer or other spiritual activities, the spirits descend to them to form a common base with their spirit selves and work with them. This is especially true for one's own ancestors. Our ancestors in spirit have a special connection to us, their descendants on earth, via family traits, common beliefs and values.

Spirits perform various works. For example, they pour spiritual fire on earthly people and give them the power to heal diseases. They help people enter states of grace and perceive the realities of the spirit world. They give people revelations and the gift of prophecy. They can also give deep inspiration to the soul. In these various works, spirits act on behalf of the Holy Spirit, guiding people on the earth to accomplish the Will of God.

The Returning Resurrection of the Spirits of Israelites and Christians

Growth-Stage Returning Resurrection

Spirits who during their earthly life kept the Mosaic law and worshiped God sincerely during the Old Testament Age came to dwell in the form-spirit level of the spirit world. After the advent of Jesus, these spirits all returned to earth and assisted faithful people on earth to accomplish the Will of God. By helping people to attain the level of life spirit, they too received the same benefit: namely, they became life spirits and entered paradise. We call this dispensation growth-stage returning resurrection.

Since Elijah appeared as a spirit before Jesus and his disciples (**Matthew 17:3**), it is clear that Elijah was dwelling in the world of spirit. However, Jesus refers to John the Baptist, who dwelled on earth, as "Elijah." **Matthew 17:12–13** Jesus called him Elijah because John's mission is the continuation of the mission of Elijah. John was effectively taking up Elijah's undone work. In a manner of speaking, John was the "second coming" of Elijah. In the sense of common mission, John's body concurrently served as Elijah's body. The spirit of Elijah cooperated with John the Baptist to help John fulfill the mission Elijah had left unfinished during his earthly life. This was Elijah's returning resurrection.

An interesting parallel expresses the spiritual resonance that existed between the two providential figures.

Matthew 3:4 (about John)
*John's clothes were made of **camel's hair**, and he had a **leather belt around his waist**. His food was locusts and wild honey.*

2 Kings 1:8 (about Elijah)
*They replied, "He was a man with a **garment of hair** and with a **leather belt around his waist**." The king said, "That was Elijah the Tishbite."*

As mentioned, when Jesus died on the cross, many bodies of the saints rose from their tombs. **Matthew 27:52** This event is not a miracle of corporal resurrection. Rather, it describes the spiritual phenomenon of returning resurrection. Remember the definition of "rising from the dead," provided us by **Luke 16:31**. The spirits of the faithful descended to the earth from the form-spirit level of the spirit world where they had been living. They returned to help the believers on earth, who had the opportunity to benefit from the redemption by the cross, to believe in Jesus and become life spirits. In doing so, the returning spirits also became life spirits.

Completion-Stage Returning Resurrection

The spirits of people who believed in Jesus while they lived on earth during the New Testament Age became life spirits and entered paradise after death. After the second advent of Christ, these spirits will all return to the earth to help faithful people believe in and attend the returning Christ. By helping people on earth to attain the level of divine spirit, they too will receive the same benefit and become divine spirits. When the earthly saints pass over to the next world and enter the Kingdom of Heaven in heaven, the returning spirits will also enter the Kingdom. This dispensation is called completion-stage returning resurrection. In this dispensation, the spirits not only help earthly people; earthly people also assist in the resurrection of the spirits.

This is precisely what **Hebrews 11:39–40** explains:

> *All these* [saints of the Old Testament Age], *though well attested by their faith, did not receive what was promised* [permission to enter the Kingdom of Heaven], *since God had foreseen something better* [the Kingdom of Heaven] *for us* [earthly people], *that apart from us they* [spirits] *should not be made perfect* [citizens of the Kingdom of Heaven].

With this explanation, we can understand that these verses accurately depict returning resurrection. It illustrates that spirits living in the spirit world cannot attain perfection apart from the cooperation of earthly people. Furthermore, Jesus said, "Whatever you bind on earth shall be bound in heaven, and whatever you loose on earth shall be loosed in heaven." **Matthew 18:18** Jesus explains that unless the believers on earth first loose what is bound, the spirits also cannot loose what is bound in them. Since spirits can be resurrected only by cooperating with believers on earth to whom they descend, Jesus gave the keys of the Kingdom of Heaven to Peter, representing earthly believers, in order that he might unlock the gates to the Kingdom of Heaven here on earth. **Matthew 16:19**

The Theory of Reincarnation Examined in Light of the Principle of Returning Resurrection

Many people believe in the theory of reincarnation. They report of the experience, for example, of "déjà vu." Have you ever been overwhelmed with the strong sensation that what just happened has happened before?

Some people report vivid memories of days gone by, from before they were born. They can give a clear account of where they were and what they did. Many who sought to verify those accounts have been startled by their accuracy.

Is reincarnation real? Let's consider the example of John and Elijah. It is easy to understand how someone could conclude that John was the reincarnation of Elijah. Jesus said that John is Elijah and they certainly reflected each other in mode of dress.

However, when a spirit engages in returning resurrection, sometimes elements are traded between the two parties. That is, because of the close connection, sometimes an element from the spirit person may slip into the consciousness of the host on earth. The host's "memory" of a past that predates his earthly birth is not his own memory but rather that of the spirit cooperating with him.

In seeking to fulfill the providence of restoration, God has called upon many individuals and has assigned to each a suitable mission. These individuals have passed down their particular missions to other individuals of similar character and circumstances, gradually fulfilling each area of mission over the long flow of history.

Spirits who could not complete their missions during their earthly life must return to people on earth who share the same type of mission as they had during their lifetime. When a spirit assists an earthly person to fulfill God's Will, the person will fulfill not only his own mission, but also the mission of the spirit who has helped him.

From the standpoint of mission, the earthly host person serves, in a manner of speaking, as the earthly body of the spirit. In a sense, he is the second coming of that spirit; hence he may sometimes be called by the spirit's name and appear to be the reincarnation of that spirit.

Whereas the theory of reincarnation does observe actual phenomena and seeks to define them, as a theory it veers wide of the mark. That is, doctrines of reincarnation interpret these outward phenomena without the benefit of knowing the principle of returning resurrection.

The Unification of Religions through Returning Resurrection

The Unification of Christianity through Returning Resurrection

Jesus prayed for all believers "to be one, as God and Christ are one." Yet after 2,000 years of providence, Christians remain divided. The unity of the Body of Christ will not be accomplished by man's effort alone. At the time of the Second Advent, all life spirits who dwell in paradise descend to the people on earth who, by believing in and attending the Lord, can attain the level of divine spirit.

By cooperating with these people to fulfill God's Will for the providence of restoration, the spirits can share the same benefit and enter the Kingdom of Heaven. Accordingly, all spirits will descend from paradise in that day and assist believers on the earth. This is why **Revelations 19:14** testifies that when Christ returns, "The armies of heaven were following him, riding on white horses and dressed in fine linen, white and clean."

At the appointed hour, each believer will be guided by the spirits from paradise to go before Christ at the Second Advent and devote their lives for the sake of God's Will. For this reason, Christianity's destiny is to finally fulfill the prayer of Jesus! We shall be one as are God and Christ. **John 17:21-23**

The Unification of All Other Religions through Returning Resurrection

The relationship of Christianity to the world's other religions is that of central to peripheral. God works through other religions to make a foundation for the message of salvation brought by Christ. Judaism was the foundation for Christ. Judaism could not accomplish salvation; however, God worked through Judaism to prepare the world for the saving message of Christ.

God uses religions that are in a peripheral position to Christianity in a similar way He used Judaism. The true mission of all religions is to form a foundation for Christ. Christianity should not exist for its own sake but should recognize its final mission is the fulfillment of the purposes of all the religions in human history. Christ at the Second Advent, who is to come on the foundation of Christianity, comes to fulfill all religious expectations and prophecy.

For example, Buddhism teaches of the expected return of the person of the Maitreya Buddha. Chinese traditional religions teach of a coming appearance of "The True Man." The return of the religion's founder or a coming of a figure that perfectly embodies the ideals of the religion is a common theme throughout the religions of the world.

These predictions are all reflections of the similar imagery of the Hebrew expectation of a great king who would restore the kingdom to Israel. Certainly Jesus was more than that; however, those expectations served as the basis to point the chosen people toward Jesus and his new message of salvation.

Consequently, at the Second Coming of Christ, all spirits that believed in religions other than Christianity during their lifetime will, like the spirits in paradise, also return to earth to be resurrected, even though the timing of their return will vary depending upon their spiritual position.

These spirits must guide the earthly believers of their respective religions to Christ at the Second Advent and assist them to believe in him and attend him in his work to fulfill God's Will. We can find a parallel example of this at the First Advent: the wise men from the East, who were, probably, Zoroastrians, came in search of Jesus and worshiped him at his birth. **Matthew 2:1–12** Accordingly, all religions will eventually be united around a revived Christianity.

Typically, when we teach the unification of religions, some misunderstand and conclude that we are asserting that "all roads lead to God." However, the Judeo-Christian providence is unique. No one comes to the Father but by Christ. However, there is a relationship of central and peripheral. Simply put, the Judeo-Christian providence is central because it brings the Christ, the central figure of resurrection and salvation. Other religions are used by God to make a foundation for Christ.

God can use other religions; however, God will only use Christianity for the providence of salvation. Not everything claiming to be a religion is automatically subject to God's use (Baal worship, for example).

God could use the traditions of the wise men to lead them to the baby Jesus. Their belief system was neither Jewish nor Christian and yet it was used by God to bring them to the feet of Christ. It didn't save them, but it brought them to the location of salvation.

We see God's heart for all people expressed in **John 3:16**. God "so loved the world." In **2 Peter 3:9** God reveals who are the candidates for salvation. *He is patient with you, not wanting anyone to perish, but everyone to come to repentance.*

No Marriage in Heaven

Many Christians believe that marriage is exclusively an earthly arrangement. It is temporal only. Traditional wedding vows have reflected this belief: "until death do us part."

Ironically, this misconception of thousands of years is one element that stands at the root of the present demise of the family. It is also a substantial barrier preventing Christians from understanding the purpose of creation, the primary mission of Jesus and the purpose of his return. However, Jesus does appear to indicate that there is no marriage in Heaven and that we will be single and unattached "like the angels."

It is rather paradoxical because most Christians, naturally, in their heart long to be with a departed spouse. Most have a deep hope to "meet again." Most would feel deprived if they could not relish again, in heaven, the precious love they had shared with their spouse on earth.

Matthew 22:30

At the resurrection people will neither marry nor be given in marriage; they will be like the angels in heaven.

This is the verse that many Christians cite. Jesus is speaking to a group of Sadducees. The Sadducees, unlike the Pharisees, did not believe in the resurrection. They were inquiring of Jesus to determine with whom a woman would be married in heaven if she had been married seven times on earth. Of course, their only motive was to try to confound Jesus.

Notice that Jesus never says that there is no marriage "in heaven." He says that there is no marriage "at the resurrection"! This is a significant difference.

If you will examine **Luke 20:27–38**, you will find the same story. However, Luke is a bit clearer. He writes, "We will be like the angels, for we will never die." In other words, our similarity to the angels "in heaven" is not that we will be unmarried as the angels, but rather that we will never die. Matthew's expression, however, seems to suggest that our similarity to angels "in heaven" is that we will be single as the angels. This is incorrect.

What, then, does Jesus mean when he says that we will not marry "at the resurrection"? The course of resurrection, as with the course of restoration, is the course of "re-creation." The course of "re-creation" follows the same Principle as the course of "creation." Adam and Eve were to grow to perfection in the position of brother and sister.

To "eat from the tree of life" is the ideal of perfection and the prerequisite for fulfillment of the second blessing. In the beginning, there would be no marriage until the conclusion of the creation process to the tree of life, that is, the first blessing.

Likewise, in the course of resurrection, there is no marriage until the conclusion of the process of resurrection: restoration to eat from the tree of life. Since God "blocked the way to the tree of life." **Genesis 3:24** there has been "no marriage." This is why no child could be born without the stain of sin. "All born of Adam" were without life.

Thus, there will be no true marriage until mankind can resurrect and reclaim the right to eat from the tree of life. It is a permission issue as stated in chapter eight in *The Change of Blood Lineage*. This is the hope of the Second Coming, as stated in **Revelation 2:7** and **22:14**.

Because of the fall of the first human ancestors, all parents and all things pertaining to them are as if they did not exist. It is as if they died. They lost their lives. To make them live again, to resurrect them, is much more difficult than starting the creation all over again. Re-creating is that difficult. It is nearly impossible. Those who have been given birth already must go back to their mother's womb and be born again, literally. This is extremely, extremely difficult. The realm of resurrection is not just one entity, but it involves the whole environment as well as the people living there.

It is not just individuals who are dead and who need to go back to their mother's womb to be born again as living beings. The whole family, the country, and all things in the world must do this, too. The realm of resurrection includes all things in the world.

Today, we yearn for the day of the last resurrection, the day of hope. That time of hope is one that all people can enjoy, but that time does not approach easily. Only those who win over death can own that hope. Only those who fought Satan with God will own that hope. Only those who received persecution with God will own that hope.

Rev. Sun Myung Moon

Chapter Twelve

Christology

Who is Jesus? What is Christ? Christians have been debating for centuries about the nature of Christ's mission, his role in our life, and the substance of his personality.

Some declare that Jesus is God, the creator, himself. In their view, God took on flesh, departed His heavenly throne and came down to live among men. Thus, while Jesus was on the earth, God was not present on His throne in heaven.

Yet this doesn't correspond to Jesus' prayer, "Our Father, who art in Heaven." It would seem to confirm that Jesus is not God Himself.

Some declare that Jesus is just a man, certainly a good man, but no more than a man. In their view, Jesus was good and wise. His mission was to teach us about the truth. We observe Jesus displaying traits of his humanity in **Mark 9:21:** *Jesus asked the boy's father, "How long has he been like this?" "From childhood," he answered.* If Jesus were God himself, would he have to ask this question?

But could a mere man raise the dead? Jesus called Lazarus out of the tomb. There have been many good men in history, but could they even begin to imagine how to raise the dead? Jesus did many more things that seem to indicate that he was not a mere man like you or me. What, then, a prophet?

Many see Jesus as one of the prophets. Certainly in Caesarea Philippi and in Judea when Jesus asked, "Who do the people say that I am?" many responded that Jesus was a prophet. Many of the Islamic faith have a deep respect for Jesus as a prophet. Many of the things that Jesus did were similar to the works of the prophets of old. Jesus called for repentance. He warned of dire consequences if repentance were not forthcoming. Like Elijah, he raised the dead and performed other impressive miracles.

But Jesus said and did things that no prophet had ever done before. **Mark 2:5–7:**

When Jesus saw their faith, he said to the paralytic, "Son, your sins are forgiven." *Now some teachers of the law were sitting there, thinking to themselves, "Why does this fellow talk like that? He's blaspheming! Who can forgive sins but God alone?"*

Who can forgive sins except God? Jesus forgave sins. No prophet can forgive sins and certainly no ordinary man. Then Jesus must be God! We are back to square one.

The voice of scripture describes Jesus as all of these. It is our own inability to reconcile the relationship of divinity with humanity that stands at the heart of our confusion about the nature of Christ. This inability is another manifestation of the historical enmity between the spiritual and physical components of each human. Paul describes this plight in **Romans 7:22–25:**

For in my inner being I delight in God's law; but I see another law at work in the members of my body, waging war against the law of my mind and making me a prisoner of the law of sin at work within my members. What a wretched man I am! Who will rescue me from this body of death?

The human experience with the flesh is one in which defiance of God's Will is the norm. Jesus, in the Garden of Gethsemane, asserted, "The spirit is willing, but the flesh is weak." In the Christian view, therefore, for Christ to take on flesh as a human was extraordinary.

For most Christians, Jesus stands as both God and man. He is integrated into the Trinitarian construct of God the Father, God, the Son and God, the Holy Ghost. Inevitably, in pursuit of understanding Jesus' divinity, many have subtly de-emphasized his human side. Thus, the "man" Jesus is a mystery, as is the expression of his divinity, increasingly through time, more detached and otherworldly.

Hollywood's attempts to express this mysterious man rendered in scripture have all fallen short. Those that seek, primarily, to uphold his divinity will, predictably, invent a Jesus such as the breathless, ethereal, parable-speaking Jesus of *King of Kings* (played by Jeffery Hunter). Those that seek to convey Jesus' humanity, inevitably portray a Jesus such as the less than heroic one of *Last Temptation of Christ*. Everyone, thus far, has missed the mark.

The problem is in finding "the magenta." Jesus is in the magenta. It is in understanding the harmony of pairs. In order to see the magenta one must understand the turning relationship between red and blue. Likewise, in order to fully articulate Jesus Christ, we must understand the principle relationship between spirit and body.

The First Person Who Fulfills the Purpose of Creation

We learn by comparison. Confusion about Christ is furthered by the assumption that there exists no point of reference. Christians view Jesus as a "one time only" creation. Although we are instructed to become "Christ-like," the meaning of that imperative is rather obscure.

This chapter seeks to establish an acceptable point of reference for understanding Jesus. With whom can Jesus be compared? The point of reference is "the person who fulfills the purpose of creation." In other words, the idea of Adam had he not fallen and, instead, achieved perfection. How would have that Adam compared with Jesus?

Divine Value

The relationship between God and a perfected Adam may be compared to that between the dual characteristics of a person, that is, between mind and body or between husband and wife.

Ephesians 5:28–30

In this same way, husbands ought to love their wives as their own bodies. He who loves his wife loves himself. After all, no one ever hated his own body, but he feeds and cares for it, just as Christ does the church— for we are members of his body.

Jesus instructed us to be "one" as God and Christ are one. Clearly to be "one" does not mean "one and the same" but rather entails the perfect harmony between two. This perfect degree of harmony establishes a resonance and reflection between two just as the mind is reflected in the body. The body becomes the exact representative of the mind. In the same way, perfected Adam would have been the "exact representation" of God as is expressed about Jesus in **Hebrews 1:3**.

Having a fully mature character centering on the perfection of

God's love (**1 John 4:12**), the body becomes "the temple" of God's spirit. Thus, when one observed the conduct of such a perfected Adam one would "see the Father." Such a perfected Adam would come to possess a divine nature. This means that a person who has fulfilled the original purpose of creation assumes a divine value.

Unique Value

Let us consider the special value of a perfected Adam from another perspective. Each person is God's substantial object partner who manifests a distinctive aspect of God. Each of us is given the original role to "perfect God's love." Yet each is distinct and unique. Even children compared with their parents, though reflective of their parents' character and appearance, are unique and original. In that regard, when Jesus implored us to "love God" with all our heart, soul and strength it meant that each one is the only one in the entire universe who can stimulate that distinctive aspect of God's nature to bring Him joy. It is the basis for intimacy with God. God is not only the God of billions of past, present and future peoples, He is also the God who "knows the number of hairs on our head." Thus, God is infinitely personal.

Another important uniqueness is manifested in generational order. My elder will eternally stand in that position to me. Elders have the added value of having been there before and therefore have the potential to offer wise counsel. My parents will always be my parents. My generation is eternally linked by the common struggles of "our time."

Also, because the expansion dynamic from two parents to children entails multiplication and horizontal expansion, as we look back vertically through the line of human ancestors we observe a narrowing range in the expanse of each generation. That is, in a pyramid-like development, humanity ultimately finds a common ancestor, standing alone, at the pinnacle.

Thus, the first perfected Adam would stand in the position of first true ancestor to all mankind. This position of first ancestor would be the first point of contact between man and God. This would be the foundation of God's eternal blood lineage and would, therefore, possess the entire value of that eternal lineage of humanity in the sense that without this foundation of a perfected first Adam, there can be no lineage of God. This is the unique value of perfected Adam.

Cosmic Value

"What does it profit a man that he gain the whole world but lose his soul?" Indeed, for the value of perfected Adam is the value of the entire cosmos. The universe was made "through him" means that the cosmos was patterned after the pattern of perfected Adam. That is, as extensions of perfected Adam's material body (the physical world) and spiritual body (the spiritual world). A perfected person's spirit self encapsulates all elements of the spirit world while his physical self encapsulates all elements of the physical world. The man who fulfills the purpose of creation thus encapsulates all the essences of everything in the cosmos. For this reason a perfected person has the value of the entire cosmos.

Jesus and Perfect Adam

Divine value, unique value and cosmic value all describe the value of the man who fulfills the purpose of creation. God created Adam for this destiny but Adam could not fulfill. Jesus Christ is the man who took up this unfulfilled role and was victorious. Paul indicates that Christ's position is comparable to Adam's position:

1 Corinthians 15:21–22
For since death came through a man, the resurrection of the dead comes also through a man. For as in Adam all die, so in Christ all will be made alive.

Romans 5:19
*For just as through the disobedience of the **one man** the many were made sinners, so also through the obedience of the **one man** the many will be made righteous.*

Hebrews 4:15 and 5:7 indicate a Son "tempted in every way just as we are," yet unlike the first Adam, Jesus did not succumb to that temptation. Jesus "learned obedience" in stark contrast to the disobedient Adam. In **1 Corinthians 15:45**, Paul, again, indicates a point of reference between Adam and Christ, "The first man Adam became a living being, the *last Adam*, a life-giving spirit."

Thus, we can conclude that Jesus is the "second Adam." However, though he is the second Adam, he is the first Adam to fulfill the purpose of creation. The first Adam fell, the second Adam "was made perfect" through his course of obedience and overcoming temptations in all areas. Therefore, Jesus, the second Adam, stands as first ancestor to all mankind.

Human history is the history of the providence of restoration. Its goal is the total recovery of mankind and the realization of God's Kingdom. **Revelation 21:1-3** proclaims the future arrival of "a new heaven and a new earth" where God will be our God and we shall be his people. Jesus tells us that at that time he will grant us "the right to eat from the tree of life." This is the same tree of life that stood "in the middle of the garden" in **Genesis 2:9**. It represents the ideal of perfected Adam. When Adam sinned, God barred fallen Adam and all his descendants from the ideal of the tree of life. **Genesis 3:24**

In the Old Testament we find expressed a deep longing for the tree of life in **Proverbs 11:30** and **13:12**. This hope was fulfilled in Jesus who came as the tree of life. It is why he referred to himself as "the vine" and indicated that we were the "branches" that were to be engrafted.

Most significant is Jesus' promise:

Revelation 2:7
To him who overcomes, I will give the right to eat from the tree of life which is in the paradise of God.

Thus, the second coming of Christ will open for the first time the ideal of perfection that was lost in the Garden. In this way, we will stand with Jesus as fellow perfected Adams and Eves who have fulfilled the purpose of creation.

Jesus: God or Man?

The comparison of Jesus with perfected Adam brings us to the issue of Jesus' divinity as God and man. Some Christians believe that Jesus is the Creator Himself. Others believe Jesus is both God and man.

In fact, Scripture gives two distinct views. Some Scripture appears to affirm unequivocally that Jesus is God Himself. However, other passages in Scripture express a view of Jesus that appears to be inconsistent with that view.

We will never be able to clarify this issue if we only focus on a few Scriptures that basically satisfy our doctrinal position. Instead, we must get all the scripture on the table and see if we can discover the existing harmony between Jesus' divinity and humanity.

Bible Verses That Seem to Indicate Jesus Is God

These are the verses that appear to affirm Jesus as God Himself.

1. John 1:2–3
He was with God in the beginning. Through him all things were made.

Jesus was with God in the beginning and all things were made through Jesus!

2. 1 Corinthians 8:6
Yet for us there is but one God, the Father, from whom all things came and for whom we live; and there is but one Lord, Jesus Christ, through whom all things came and through whom we live.

Again, all things were made through Jesus.

3. Colossians 1:15–19
He is the image of the invisible God, the firstborn over all creation. For by him all things were created: things in heaven and on earth, visible and invisible, whether thrones or powers or rulers or authorities; all things were created by him and for him. He is before all things, and in him all things hold together. And he is the head of the body, the church; he is the beginning and the firstborn from among the dead, so that in everything he might have the supremacy. For God was pleased to have all his full-ness dwell in him.

Here Jesus is described as the creator. "For by him all things were created by him and for him!"

4. Hebrews 1:1-2
In the past God spoke to our forefathers through the prophets at many times and in various ways, but in these last days he has spoken to us by his Son, whom he appointed heir of all things, and through whom he made the universe.

5. Hebrews 1:8

*But about the Son he says, "Your throne, **O God**, will last for ever and ever, and righteousness will be the scepter of your kingdom."*

About the Son he says, "Your throne, O GOD"!

6. John 20:28

*And Thomas said to Jesus "My Lord and **My God!**"*

7. 1 John 5:20

*. . . and we are in him who is true—even in his son Jesus Christ. **He is true God** and eternal life.*

8. Romans 9:5

*Theirs are the patriarchs, and from them is traced the human ancestry of Christ, **who is God over all**, forever praised!*

9. 2 Peter 1:1

*. . . To those who through the righteousness of **our God** and Savior, Jesus Christ. . ."*

10. Titus 2:13

*. . . the glorious appearing of our **great God** and Savior, Jesus Christ.*

11. Philippians 2:5–6

*Your attitude should be the same as that of Christ Jesus: Who, being **in very nature, God** . . .*

12. John 8:58

Jesus answered, "Before Abraham was born, I am!"

Jesus proclaims that he existed before Abraham.

Again, for many these statements are enough and that settles it. However the bigger picture is that there are equally assertive verses that cannot be explained from the standpoint that Jesus is the creator. That is, we have Bible verses that seem to affirm Jesus is God while at the same time we have Scripture that seems, just as clearly, to be affirming that Jesus is not God Himself. We must explain all of the Scriptures and bring them into harmony.

Bible Verses That Indicate Jesus Is Not God the Creator

1. Matthew 24:36
No one knows about that day or hour, not even the Son, but the Father only.

Here Jesus makes a distinction between what he knows and what the Father knows.

2. Matthew 26:39
My Father, if it is possible, may this cup be taken from me, yet not as I will, but as Thou will.

Jesus' will is likewise autonomous from God's Will. Jesus is seeking acquiescence to God's will.

3. John 5:26
For as the Father has life in Himself, so he has granted the Son to have life in himself.

Jesus received his life from God. God received His life from no one. He is eternally self-existent.

4. John 5:30
By myself, I can do nothing; I judge only as I hear, and my judgment is just, for I seek not to please myself but him who sent me.

Jesus says, "by myself, I can do nothing." This indicates that Jesus is relying upon his own relationship with God. He is not trying to "please myself" but rather is seeking to please the one "who sent me."

5. John 5:19
The Son can do nothing by himself; he can do only what he sees the Father doing, because whatever the Father does, the Son also does.

Jesus declares that he is following a pattern laid down by God. He is expressing obedience to God.

6. Mark 10:18

"Why do you call me good?" "No one is good, except God alone."

Here Jesus emphatically makes a distinction between himself and God.

7. John 14:28

The Father is greater than I.

This is another strong statement that makes a distinction between Jesus and God.

8. Matthew 6:9

Our Father, which art in Heaven.

Jesus prayed to God "in heaven."

9. Matthew 27:46

My God, My God, why hast thou forsaken me?

Inconceivable if he is God the Creator.

10. John 17:21–23

. . . that all of them may be one, Father, just as you are in me and I am in you. May they also be in us so that the world may believe that you have sent me. . . . that they may be one as we are one: I in them and you in me.

In this prayer Jesus defines the term "to be one." It is clearly accomplished through the relationship of two autonomous beings. Christian believers are to model their relationship (to become one) after the relationship of God and Christ (as God and Christ are one). Notice that "to be one" does not mean to be "one and the same."

11. 1 Corinthians 15:27–28

For he "has put everything under his feet." Now when it says that "everything" has been put under him, it is clear that this does not include God himself, who put everything under Christ. When he has done this, then the Son himself will be made subject to Him who put everything under him, so that God may be all in all.

Paul declares that God put everything under Christ, except God Himself. Instead God rules all things through Christ. (Remember: "through him all things were made.")

12. Hebrews 1:3

The Son is the radiance of God's glory and the exact representation of his being.

Jesus is the **exact representation** of his being. I send my representative to Congress. He is not me, myself. He is my representative.

13. Hebrews 4:15 (compared with **James 1:13**)

For we do not have a high priest who is unable to sympathize with our weaknesses, but we have one who has been tempted in every way, just as we are—yet without sin.

Jesus has been tempted in every way, just as we are, yet he never sinned. See **James 1:13** "When tempted, no one should say, God is tempting me. For **God cannot be tempted** by evil, nor does he tempt."

Jesus was tempted in every way, but God cannot be tempted. This is why Jesus said, "Don't call me good, none are good, only God."

14. Hebrews 5:7–9

During the days of Jesus' life on earth, he offered up prayers and petitions with loud cries and tears to the one who could save him from death, and he was heard because of his reverent submission. Although he was a son, he learned obedience from what he suffered and, once made perfect, he became the source of eternal salvation for all who obey him

Jesus had to walk a course of faith and obedience in order to achieve perfection. By achieving perfection, Jesus "became" the source of eternal salvation.

In the Gospels, Jesus used the term "Son of Man" 102 times. The term "Son of God" was used 76 times (65 times by Jesus). Jesus proclaimed that God was his father 54 times. There are 17 recorded instances of Jesus praying to God.

Are we arguing against the divinity of Christ? Absolutely not! Jesus is the divine son who fulfilled the purpose of creation. However, we must reconcile these Scripture with those verses that seem to proclaim Christ as God the Creator.

Explanation of Verses That Seem to Indicate Jesus Is God

All of the Scriptures testifying to Jesus are true. However, only through understanding the principled relation of the spirit and flesh of perfected Adam can we reconcile all of the scripture concerning Jesus.

1. John 1:2–3
He was with God in the beginning. Through him all things were made.

As perfected Adam, Jesus has cosmic value. The cosmos is patterned after him. The universe is patterned after the form of perfected man's spirit and body. This is so that man can exert dominion over all things. The description rendered in **1 Corinthians 15:27–28** is in harmony with the view of the Principle.

2. 1 Corinthians 8:6
*Yet for us there is but one God, the Father, from whom all things came and for whom we live; and there is but one Lord, Jesus Christ, **through whom all things came** and through whom we live.*

Again, this verse affirms the Son as the basic pattern of all things.

3. Colossians 1:15–19
He is the image of the invisible God, the firstborn over all creation. For by him all things were created: things in heaven and on earth, visible and invisible, whether thrones or powers or rulers or authorities; all things were created by him and for him. He is before all things, and in him all things hold together. And he is the head of the body, the church; he is the beginning and the firstborn from among the dead, so that in everything he might have the supremacy. For God was pleased to have all his fullness dwell in him.

There is dispute with regard to whom the word "him" refers. Does it refer to "the invisible God" or does it refer to "Jesus"? This one is the most problematic. However, be aware that this is disputed in many Christian circles.

4. Hebrews 1:1-2
*In the past God spoke to our forefathers through the prophets at many times and in various ways, but in these last days he has spoken to us by his Son, whom he appointed heir of all things, and **through whom he made the universe.***

Again, it is expressing the idea that God created the universe "through" the pattern of perfected Adam, or Jesus.

5. Hebrews 1:8
*But **about the Son** he says, **"Your throne, O God, will last for ever** and ever, and righteousness will be the scepter of your kingdom."*

The writer of Hebrews is reciting **Psalms 45:6–7** "Your throne, O God." This was a common salutation of respect offered to a person of high regard. See also the next verse:

6. John 20:28
*And Thomas said to Jesus, "My Lord and **My God!**"*

This is a common form of greeting a person of respect. It is not a statement on the divinity of Christ by Thomas.

7. 1 John 5:20
*And we are in him who is true, even in his son Jesus Christ. **He is true God** and eternal life.*

This is another disputed scripture. The dispute is over whom the term, "He is true God" is referring. The proper reading would be in this way: "We are in God ("Him" is God) who is true—even in His (God's) son Jesus Christ. He (God) is true God and eternal life."

8. Romans 9:5
*Theirs are the patriarchs, and from them is traced the human ancestry of Christ, **who is God over all**, forever praised!*

Jesus is "God over all" in the sense that God "has put everything under his feet" as per **1 Corinthians 15:27–28**. However, everything is under his feet, "except God Himself."

9. 2 Peter 1:1

*To those who through the righteousness of **our God** and Savior, Jesus Christ...*

Meaning "our God (in heaven) and our Savior, Jesus Christ." It would be the same, let's say, if Rev. Jones gave a stirring Sunday sermon and a parishioner approached minister Jones and said, "I'd like to thank our Heavenly Father and preacher Rev. Jones for a wonderful word this morning." He is not proclaiming Rev. Jones to be his Heavenly Father. In the same way **2 Peter 1:1** is referring to two:

Our God
Our savior, Jesus.

10. Titus 2:13

*. . . the glorious appearing of our **great God** and Savior, Jesus Christ.*

Same thing here.

11. Philippians 2:5–6

*Your attitude should be the same as that of Christ Jesus: Who, being **in very nature, God.***

We agree that Jesus, in nature, is like God. As in "exact representation" or "in His image".

12. John 8:58

Before Abraham was born, I am!

This is saying, "Before Abraham achieved perfection, I achieved it." Because Jesus was the first perfected man, he assumed the position of "first ancestor," that is, Adam's position. See **Hebrews 5:7–9**, "Once made perfect, he *became* the source of eternal salvation." **John 8:58** is a statement indicating quality and position, not chronology.

Jesus and Fallen Man

The most important realization for fallen man is that he cannot save himself. Fallen man did not commit the original sin; instead, he inherited sin via the ancestorial affiliation with the dead Adam. Thus, man must escape the death of Adam.

We are affirming that Jesus is more than just a wise and good teacher showing us how we should live our lives. We are emphasizing the most vertical perspective of Christ's role and our relationship with him. Jesus is in the position of first ancestor and thus, we must find a way to sever our relationship with the dead Adam and come into the lineage of the living Adam, Jesus. This means we need the process of "rebirth."

For those whose mission it is to "win souls for Christ," the message of rebirth, of course, stands at the heart of that mighty commission.

"Rebirth" means we come out of the lineage of the dead Adam and are grafted onto the lineage of the "living" Adam. Let's examine the pertinent scripture with regard to this topic:

John 15:1–5
I am the true vine, and my Father is the gardener. He cuts off every branch in me that bears no fruit, while every branch that does bear fruit he prunes so that it will be even more fruitful. You are already clean because of the word I have spoken to you. Remain in me, and I will remain in you. No branch can bear fruit by itself; it must remain in the vine. Neither can you bear fruit unless you remain in me.

I am the vine; you are the branches. If a man remains in me and I in him, he will bear much fruit; apart from me you can do nothing.

Romans 11:17–18
*If some of the branches have been broken off, and you, though a wild olive shoot, have been **grafted in** among the others and now share in the nourishing sap from the olive root, do not boast over those branches. If you do, consider this: You do not support the root, but the root supports you.*

John 3:3–6

In reply Jesus declared, "I tell you the truth, no one can see the kingdom of God unless he is born again." "How can a man be born when he is old?" Nicodemus asked. "Surely he cannot enter a second time into his mother's womb to be born!" Jesus answered, "I tell you the truth, no one can enter the kingdom of God unless he is born of water and the Spirit. Flesh gives birth to flesh, but the Spirit gives birth to spirit.

In order for man to be "born again" we need parents. This is the foundation to understand the process of rebirth.

Rebirth is the heart of "salvation." In fact, it is important to understand, from the Christian perspective, the separate and distinct functions of each of the events from the cross to the ascension in Jesus' ministry.

Rebirth and Trinity

Rebirth requires the position of God, father and mother. This will set the stage for understanding the meaning of the Trinity.

Jesus is referred to as "everlasting Father" in **Isaiah 9:6:**

*For to us a child is born, to us a son is given, and the government will be on his shoulders. And he will be called Wonderful Counselor, Mighty God, **Everlasting Father**, Prince of Peace.*

Jesus is in the position of son and father in the work of regeneration. The Holy Spirit accomplishes the role of mother in rebirth.

John 3:6
Flesh gives birth to flesh, but the Spirit gives birth to spirit.

The "flesh" that gives birth is a mother. Likewise, the "spirit" that gives birth is a "mother."

Jesus and the Holy Spirit form a partnership, similar to parents in the work of providing rebirth. Thus, we can think of Jesus and the Holy Spirit as "spiritual True Parents" in the operation of rebirth.

Trinity and the Extent of Salvation

The first manifestation of trinity is within God. Man was created in the image of God. God's image manifests in male and female. At the same time, God is "one" as Jesus declared in **Mark 12:29**. In this sense, God is "red, blue and magenta." This is why God is a God of the number three.

This becomes the standard of the first attempt to make the trinity substantial. The first trinity was to be God, Adam and Eve. This trinity would have been the cornerstone of the Kingdom of Heaven. It would have been a spiritual and physical foundation.

However, Adam and Eve established the spiritual and physical foundation centering on Satan. Because of the spiritual and physical foundation, Satan exerts a spiritual and physical claim over mankind. Thus, Satan's claim and the nature of sin, although spiritual, are passed through the physical lineage of man. This is why Paul declares "by the sin of one man is death for all."

Jesus came to establish his Kingdom by erecting a spiritual and physical trinity foundation. The spiritual foundation of God the Father, the Son and the Holy Spirit would be incarnated as Jesus fulfilled the three blessings.

However, because there was no faith in Israel, Jesus had to turn toward the cross and the atoning work requiring the shedding of his blood.

On the day of Pentecost, Jesus established the spiritual trinity of God the Father, the Son and the Holy Spirit. This established the position of "spiritual True Parents" and, for the first time, a channel of regeneration was made available for fallen man. He could "change his lineage" through Jesus and the Holy Spirit. He could escape the lineage of the Satan-centered dead Adam, and enter, through rebirth, the lineage of the God-centered living Adam.

A Future Hope

Paul states in **Romans 8:23**

*Not only so, but we ourselves, who have the first fruits of the Spirit, groan inwardly as we wait eagerly for our adoption as sons, **the redemption of our bodies.***

Our present salvation through Jesus and Holy Spirit comes with a hope of a future "redemption of our bodies." This is the physical side of rebirth (or regeneration). Although we are fully saved in Christ as an individual, we know that our salvation does not extend to our next generation. For that to take place requires the hoped for "redemption of our bodies."

Until Christ comes again, the gates to the Kingdom are open spiritually through Jesus and the Holy Spirit. We receive the gift of eternal life through that gate. However, if my spouse and I are born again and we conceive a child, that child is still a descendant of the "dead Adam." Sadly, that child must be "born again." This indicates that sin still reigns through our flesh.

Christ will come again to establish the spiritual and physical trinity foundation. He will set up the conditions to "redeem our physical bodies" so that sin no longer passes through the blood lineage from parents to children.

What is the nature of the Messiah fallen man needs? Fallen people do not need a Messiah in the fallen parents' position. The Messiah should be as unfallen Adam and Eve, one with God's will, receiving God's love and God's blessing in the position of True Parents, and able to give rebirth to all people. Otherwise, men and women cannot move to a position which has nothing to do with sin.

Rev. Sun Myung Moon, "The Blessing and Ideal Family"

Chapter Thirteen

The Last Days and
Parallels in History

The Meaning Of The Last Days

History begins with God and His purpose for creating. God's motive for creating was a parental motive that caused Him to seek joy and satisfaction through the interaction of love with His children. The consummation of parental satisfaction takes place when the children fully mature to embody the ideals and values by which the parents have lived. This was God's hope in creating man and woman in "His image."

Thus, human history began with the birth of Adam and Eve. The consummation of that history, however, would be when Adam and Eve fulfilled their mission to establish the Three Blessings. By so doing they would launch the eternal expansion of God's uncontested lineage.

Intended history, then, should have been the on-going record of that expansion from the individual to the family, society, nation and world. That record would also include a clear testimony of the real experience with the world of spirit, a world that would not have been subject to obscurity and human ignorance as a result of the fall.

History would be the record of all mankind together as one family and not as a aggregation of separate tribes, clans, nations and blocks of nations each with competing cultural and religious values engaged in struggles for land and sovereignty. Adam and Eve "walked and talked with God," they had no scripture, no dogma, no rituals other then the direct experience of God's love. Thus, there would be no impetus for the world to divide itself into religious cultures. In short, the intended history was to be the record of the natural unfolding of the Kingdom of Heaven on earth and in spirit.

This intended history came to an abrupt halt on the very day they ate "the fruit". They died losing their opportunity to fulfill those goals of the intended history.

Instead, man fell into darkness and death. Human ignorance became a bottomless pit. The seed of our humanity, our divine spark, was shrouded in a sea of confusion, carnage and corruption. This became the external manifestation of actual history. It was expressing the internal reality that a pretender had usurped the sovereignty God had over His children. Now the record of history, rather than the unending celebration of the expansion of a mighty love, would instead become the requiem of suffering and tears.

Within this history of suffering, hidden deep, was its only completely innocent victim. This was the grieving God, Himself. God had no practical experience with grief until that first moment of the fall. Now He stood alone at the pinnacle of suffering. He had committed no crime nor was any iniquity ever found in Him. He had only sought to selflessly share His divine nature so that the joy of love could be realized. His gift of love was returned unopened. The hoped for heart brimming in joyous satisfaction became instead a bottomless sea of sorrow.

Despite this overwhelming sorrow, God maintained His commitment to humanity and to the ideal for which He had created. God did not disassociate with humanity even though maintaining faith and hope drove Him to the lonely place of sorrow and tears. This is what it truly means to be "God." He is almighty, indeed, yet He is a slave to His unchanging nature of love. How we vacillate toward our own interests in comparison.

Out of this deep compassion and commitment emerges the hidden dimension of fallen history. That hidden dimension is the effort of God to recover humanity and fulfill His original dream of love. God would not merely languish in His own sorrow. He would not seek self-centered solutions whose only focus would be the alleviation of His pain alone. God instead, contested Satan's sovereignty and began a providence to resurrect humanity to become, once again, His uncontested sons and daughters.

Thus actual history became the struggle between God and Satan for dominion over humanity. Satan's goal is the total depravity of humanity; God's goal is the total recovery of humanity.

God is relentless. God will get the victory and His ultimate purpose will be accomplished. God expressed this determination to Isaiah when he said, "I have purposed it and I will do it." This is the steadfastness of our God.

Because of this, we see that the hope expressed in the Scripture is of a time when God would completely fulfill His original purpose.

Revelation 21:1-5:

Then I saw a new heaven and a new earth, for the first heaven and the first earth had passed away, and there was no longer any sea. I saw the Holy City, the new Jerusalem, coming down out of heaven from God, prepared as a bride beautifully dressed for her husband. And I heard a loud voice from the throne saying, "Now the dwelling of God is with men, and he will live with them. They will be His people and God himself will be with them and be their God. He will wipe every tear from their eyes. There will be no more death or mourning or crying or pain, for the old order of things has passed away."

He who was seated on the throne said, "I am making everything new!"

What is "the old order of things" that will pass away? This is the actual history that was founded in corruption. That is, the Satan-centered history of the descendants of the dead Adam and Eve.

And the "new?" This is the beginning of the original history whose inception was thwarted by the fall of the first human ancestors.

Christ, as the new Adam, is the central figure and starting point of that original history.

Thus, the transitional period from the old order of things to the new order of things is called "The Last Days." It is the "last days" of Satan's dominion. Also, because the New Adam is the central figure and starting point of the new history, then, it is Christ who comes, in the Last Days, as the new Adam to begin the new, original true history of mankind.

Since human beings fell, God has attempted more than once to consummate His providence to put an end to the sinful world and restore the original, good world. Nevertheless, at each attempt, human beings failed to fulfill their portion of responsibility, thus postponing the ultimate fulfillment of the Will of God.

Isaiah 5:4

What more could have been done for my vineyard than I have done for it? When I looked for good grapes, why did it yield only bad?

Consequently, dispensations of the Last Days have been repeated several times. This can be confirmed by a close study of the Bible.

Noah's Day Was the Last Days

God said to Noah, "I have determined to make an end of all flesh; for the earth is filled with violence through them; behold, I will destroy them with the earth. **Genesis 6:13** Thus, Noah's day was the Last Days. Sin had expanded from a single family to many families and tribes by the time of Noah. God wanted to destroy the corrupt, evil world that had been ruled by Satan since the time of the human fall. God had Noah warn the sinful people for 120 years in order to elicit their repentance and to separate them from Satan. However, they would not repent. The flood that had been predicted came upon them to, once and for all, purge the sinful history of 1,600 years.

God's providence now focused on one righteous family. He intended to raise up Noah's family and resurrect the world of God's sovereignty upon the foundation of their faith. This is why Noah's day can be considered to be the Last Days. It was meant to be the turning point from evil sovereignty to good sovereignty.

As we studied in chapter five, Ham broke faith with Noah and reaffirmed the Fall. Thus, Noah's family could not fulfill its providential mission to make a Foundation for the Messiah to come at that time. Jesus' words indicate that the time of Noah was a potential time for Christ to come, "As it was in the days of Noah so shall it be in the days of the Son of Man." Because Christ did not come during the era of Noah, the purpose of the Last Days could not be fulfilled.

Jesus' Day Was the Last Days

God's primary will is absolute and will be accomplished. However, God does not determine the accomplishment of man's area of responsibility. If a chosen person, family or nation doesn't fulfill their responsibility, God will call a new person, family or nation to accomplish His primary Will. Therefore, the goal of the providence of restoration is unchanging and shall be fulfilled without fail. Although the providence of restoration was not accomplished through Noah, God called upon other prophets to prepare anew the basis of faith. Upon this foundation, God sent Jesus to destroy the satanic sovereignty that had maintained dominion over the world. After that, Jesus would have established the God-centered ideal world of the Kingdom. Thus, Jesus' day was also the Last Days.

This is why Jesus said that he came to bring judgment (**John 5:22,27**) and why Malachi prophesied of Jesus' coming:

Malachi 4:1
Behold, the day comes, burning like an oven, when all the arrogant and all evildoers will be stubble; the day that comes shall burn them up ... so that it will leave them neither root nor branch.

Jesus came to restore the original ideal world. However, when the people of Israel did not believe in him, the human portion of responsibility was left unaccomplished. This meant that the fulfillment of the Will of God had to be prolonged until Christ's Second Advent. Jesus indicates this in **Matthew 21:43** "thus the Kingdom of God will be taken from you and given to a people who can produce the fruits in their season."

The Day of Christ's Second Advent Is the Last Days

When the faithlessness of the people was an irreversible fact, Jesus turned toward the way of the cross. On the day of Pentecost Jesus established the spiritual foundation for humanity's regeneration. It remains for him to return "to restore everything." **Acts 3:21** Christ returns to redeem mankind both spiritually and physically and restore the Kingdom of Heaven on earth. Hence, the day of Christ's Second Advent is also the Last Days. For this reason Jesus said, "As it was in the days of Noah, so will it be in the days of the Son of man." **Luke 17:26**

Bible Verses Concerning the Signs of the Last Days
The Bible conveys an ominous portrait of the Last Days to come.

According to many expectations, natural calamities and radical changes beyond the imagination of modern men will take place.

However, with the perspective that human history is the history of God's effort to restore His original ideal, we may gain new insight about the nature of predicted events that serve as signs of the Last Days. Let us investigate what the prophecies concerning the Last Days could mean.

1. Heaven and Earth Destroyed, and a New Heaven and New Earth Created

In **Genesis 6:13**, God seems to express His determination to destroy the earth at the time of Noah. Noah's time was the Last Days, yet the earth was not destroyed. Other Scripture appears to declare that the earth will remain forever, "A generation goes, and a generation comes, but the earth remains forever. **Ecclesiastes 1:4** "He built His sanctuary like the high heavens, like the earth, which he has founded forever. **Psalm 78:69** Also, see **Psalm 104:5**, "He set the earth on its foundations, it can never be moved."

What earth was destroyed at the time of Noah? Obviously, "earth" means something other than the literal planet. What, then, is the meaning of the prophecies of the earth's destruction in the Last Days? For example:

2 Peter 3:12-13
The heavens will be kindled and dissolved, and the elements will melt with fire! But according to His promise we wait for new heavens and a new earth in which righteousness dwells.

Revelation 21:1
Then I saw a new heaven and a new earth, for the first heaven and the first earth had passed away.

To "destroy the earth" does not mean the destruction of the planet. When a nation is destroyed it means the overthrow of its sovereignty. Conversely, to erect a new nation is to establish a new sovereignty. Likewise, the prophecies that heaven and earth will be destroyed means that the tyranny of Satan's sovereignty will be overthrown. To create a new heaven and new earth means to restore heaven and earth to God's sovereignty founded on Christ.

In **Revelation 21:5** Christ at his second coming declares, "I am making all things new!" He doesn't say that he is making all new things. Thus, Christ comes to make all things new by breaking down Satan's sovereignty and establishing God's sovereignty over all things.

We should also recall that Isaiah had predicted that the "new Heaven and new Earth" would come to Jerusalem at the time of Jesus. **Isaiah 65:17** However, the people did not have faith in Jesus and so the kingdom was taken from them at that time and given to another people that can bear the fruits. It is the Kingdom on earth and in spirit under the exclusive dominion of God.

2. Heaven and Earth Judged by Fire

What is the meaning of Peter's prophecy in **2 Peter 3:12** that "the heavens will be kindled and dissolved and the elements will melt with fire" in the Last Days? It seems very frightening. We also find a similar prediction by the Old Testament prophet Malachi prophesying about events that would take place at the time of Jesus' first coming. He predicted that it would be a day burning with the fire of judgment. **Malachi 4:1** However, a literal fire never ignited. Instead, a "fire" of a different sort fulfilled Malachi's prediction.

Jesus came into the world to cast judgment, as he said, "For judgment I came into this world. **John 9:39; 5:22** Jesus also said, "I came to cast fire upon the earth." **Luke 12:49**

"Fire" represents the means of judgment for which Jesus came into the world. Nevertheless, there is no record that in his time Jesus judged the world with literal fire. In what context, then, is Jesus using the word "fire"? What does Jesus mean? We can find a hint in the Old Testament.

In **Jeremiah 23:29**, God tells Jeremiah "Is not my word like fire?" Therefore, judgment by fire represents judgment by the Word of God.

Jesus' "fire" was the Word of God:

John 12:48
He who rejects me and does not receive my sayings has a judge; the word that I have spoken will be his judge on the last day.

2 Thessalonians 2:8
The lawless one will be revealed, and the Lord Jesus will slay him with the breath of his mouth. , that is, by his word.

Isaiah 11:4

He shall smite the earth with the rod of his mouth, and with the breath of his lips he shall slay the wicked.

John 5:24

He who hears my word and believes him who sent me, has eternal life; he does not come into judgment, but has passed from death to life.

What is the reason that Jesus judges by the Word? Human beings are created through the Word. **John 1:3** God's plan in the beginning was for Adam and Eve to keep faith in God's Word. That role of faith is what gave them the potential to inherit the divine spark from God: His spirit, His love and His lineage. Yet they did not keep the Word of God and fell; thus, they failed to fulfill the purpose of the Word.

Jesus lamented, "I came to cast fire upon the earth; and would that it were already kindled!" As the incarnation of the Word, he was grieved that the people of Israel did not receive the life-giving words that he proclaimed.

3. The Dead Rising from Their Tombs

It is written in the Bible that in the Last Days the dead will rise from their graves:

1 Thessalonians. 4:16

With the archangel's call, and with the sound of the trumpet of God . . . the dead in Christ will rise first.

We can understand the meaning of this prophecy by examining a similar event, when the dead rose from their tombs at the time of Jesus' death:

Matthew 27:52-53

The tombs also were opened, and many bodies of the saints who had fallen asleep were raised, and coming out of the tombs after his resurrection they went into the holy city and appeared to many.

What does the Scripture mean when it says that the bodies of the saints rose from their tombs? As we studied in chapter eleven on Resurrection, there is the miracle of corporal resurrection and there is spiritual resurrection. Spiritual resurrection is described in **Luke 16:19-31**. The bodies that were raised and who appeared to many were the spiritualized or glorified bodies of the saints.

The believers who "had eyes to see" were the ones who recorded this event. This is much like Moses and Elijah who, as spirits, briefly appeared with Jesus on the Mount of Transfiguration.

Thus, in the Last Days when Christ returns, this time the saints of the New Testament Age will resurrect and appear to many (but not all). This is the meaning of **1 Thessalonians 4:16.**

4. People on Earth Caught Up to Meet the Lord in the Air

1 Thessalonians 4:17
Then we who are alive, who are left, shall be caught up together with them in the clouds to meet the Lord in the air; and so we shall always be with the Lord.

The "air" mentioned in this verse does not refer to the sky over our heads. **Ephesians 2:2** states, "In which you used to live when you followed the ways of this world and of the ruler of the kingdom of the air, the spirit who now is at work in those who are disobedient." Is Satan in "the air"? Satan is also called ruler of "this world" in **John 12:31.**

Satan has a spiritual and physical sovereignty. "Air" represents his spiritual sovereignty while "this world" represents his physical sovereignty. It is the "old heaven and old earth" that is destined to pass away. Meeting the Lord "in the air," doesn't mean "in the sky" but rather that we will be lifted spiritually to the Tree of Life. **Revelation 2:7; 22:14** It is the uncontested spiritual relationship that is then inherited through our redeemed bodies.

Some point to Paul's assertion that the "Lord himself will come down from heaven" in **1 Thessalonians 4:16** as indicative of future celestial happenings. However, keep in mind that Jesus said that he "came down from heaven" in his first coming (**John 3:13**) and yet we know that he was born in a manger. No one observed with their physical eye the Lord's journey from heaven to the earth at that time and no one will observe it that manner when he returns.

5. The Sun Darkened, the Moon Gives No Light and the Stars Fall from Heaven

In the Last Days, Jesus said, "The sun will be darkened, and the moon will not give its light, and the stars will fall from heaven." **Matthew 24:29** How are we to understand this in view of Jesus' assertion that "The Kingdom of God does not come with your careful observations"? **Luke 17:30**

Also, if the literal stars, that are millions of light-years away, are to be observed falling, then they must have done so millions of years ago.

Does Scripture give us insight into the actual meaning of Jesus' prediction? First, it is important to recognize that Jesus is repeating a prophecy given by Isaiah and Ezekiel.

Isaiah 13:10
The stars of heaven and their constellations will not show their light. The rising sun will be darkened and the moon will not give its light.

Why does prophecy of the Old Testament repeat in the New Testament? Two other instances are **Daniel 7:13** with **Matthew 24:30** (predicting Christ's coming in the "clouds of heaven") and **Isaiah 65:17** with **Revelation 21:1** (a new heaven and a new earth).

The most common explanation of this reoccurrence is that Old Testament prophecy, in many cases, is focused beyond the first advent of Christ and is addressing circumstances of the second coming.

But in our careful study of Scripture we could construct a more clear explanation. God's word revealed in **Jeremiah 18:7-10** helps us to understand that all Old Testament prophesies are relevant to Jesus in his first advent. The Kingdom was an achievable goal and the preferred course that Jesus desired to fulfill.

Jesus is renewing predictions for the second coming because, "The kingdom will be taken from you and given to a people who will bear the fruits in their seasons." Thus the "new heaven and new earth" of **Isaiah 65:17** meant for "Jerusalem" is renewed. However, that new heaven and new earth described in **Revelation 21:1** is for a "new Jerusalem."

In other words, it is repeated because it was intended for the first coming but the people fell into faithlessness and God, as mentioned in **Jeremiah 18:7-10**, did not carry out that plan.

Therefore, when Jesus said he will come in the clouds at his second advent, he is actually reaffirming that he will come as he did in the first advent. This means that Jesus "came in the clouds" at his first advent. In that we know that Jesus was born on earth in his first advent we can conclude that "coming in the clouds" does not mean literal clouds.

Likewise, the new heaven and new earth, did come down at the first advent. Jesus said now was the time "the Kingdom is at hand." The fruits are in season. The gates are open. Thus the coming of the new Heaven and new Earth is, likewise, not something visible with the physical eye.

Therefore, the darkening of the sun and moon and the falling stars, likewise refers to some phenomenon that took place at the time of Jesus and will happen again at the second coming. What was that phenomenon? Obviously, the sun that darkened, the moon that did not give its light and the stars that fell at the time of Jesus were not the celestial bodies.

Genesis 37:9-10 gives us insight into the meaning of sun, moon and stars. It tells of a certain dream that was given to Joseph, the eleventh of the twelve sons of Jacob:

Genesis 37:9-10

*Then he dreamed another dream, and told it to his brothers, and said, "Behold, I have dreamed another dream; and behold, the sun, the moon, and eleven stars were bowing down to me." But when he told it to his father and to his brothers, his father rebuked him, and said to him, "What is this dream that you have dreamed? **Shall I and your mother and your brothers indeed come to bow ourselves to the ground before you?**"*

The image of the "sun, moon and stars" bowing down to Joseph was fulfilled many years later when Joseph had risen to a position of power and influence in Egypt. The "sun, moon and stars" that bowed were not the literal celestial bodies but rather his father, mother and brothers. In his dream, the sun and moon symbolized his parents, while the stars symbolized their children. This was made evident in Jacob's shocked response to his young son's dream, "Shall I and your mother and your brothers indeed come to bow ourselves to the ground before you?"

Clearly then, sun means "father," moon means "mother" and stars mean "children." Thus when we read Isaiah's prediction in **Isaiah 13:10**, it means that when Jesus comes to Israel, the "father" will be darkened, the "mother" will not give its light and the "children" will fall.

The "father" of the Old Testament Age is Moses, the "mother" is the Law and the "children" are the Chosen People of Israel. Isaiah is giving a warning to the future generation that will meet Christ. The greater light of Jesus will appear to dim the light of Moses and the Law. Therein rests the possibility that the people will misunderstand, thinking Jesus is blaspheming Moses and the Law. Thus, the children will fall.

It is the very phenomenon that takes place when the sunlight enters a movie theater and bleeds out the screen. It appears that the light of the screen has been dimmed but in reality that light is at the same intensity. It is the more intense light of the sun that creates the appearance that the light of the screen is dimmed.

Paul describes this perfectly in **2 Corinthians 3:7-11**,

Now if the ministry that brought death, which was engraved in letters on stone, came with glory, so that the Israelites could not look steadily at the face of Moses because of its glory, fading though it was, will not the ministry of the Spirit be even more glorious? If the ministry that condemns men is glorious, how much more glorious is the ministry that brings righteousness? ***For what was glorious has no glory now in comparison with the surpassing glory.*** *And if what was fading away came with glory, how much greater is the glory of that which lasts!*

"For what was glorious has no glory now in comparison with the surpassing glory." Christ's light dimmed Moses and the Law. This is, sadly, why the children of Moses and the Law "fell from the sky."

It is most significant that Jesus repeats this warning in **Matthew 24:29**. This time, the warning is extended to the people of the "new Jerusalem." These are the future people who are to "bear the fruit in their season." In effect, Jesus is warning that the struggles transitioning from Old to New Testament age could be repeated in the transition from the Christian age to the final age.

Christians of that age could fall for the same reasons that the people of Israel fell. A greater light emerges and appears to dim the light that serves as the very foundation upon which the people stand.

This is why Jesus also warns,

Matthew 7:21-22

*Not everyone who says to me, "Lord, Lord," will enter the kingdom of heaven, but only he who does the will of my Father who is in heaven. Many will say to me on that day, "Lord, Lord, did we not **prophesy** in your name, and in your name **drive out demons** and **perform many miracles**?" Then I will tell them plainly, "I never knew you. Away from me, you evildoers!"*

The Gospel ends with the declaration, "he is coming soon." Therefore, the return of Christ and his work will not be the Gospel, as we have known it. The work of Christ at his return will involve new truths and dispensations being revealed at that time.

Romans 8:23

*Not only so, but we ourselves, who have the first fruits of the Spirit, groan inwardly as we wait eagerly for our adoption as sons, the **redemption of our bodies**.*

Act 3:21

*He must remain in heaven until the time comes for God to **restore everything**, as he promised long ago through his holy prophets.*

Hebrews 9:28

*So Christ was sacrificed once to take away the sins of many people; and he will appear a second time, not to bear sin, **but to bring salvation** to those who are waiting for him.*

1 Peter 1:5

Who through faith are shielded with God's power until the coming of the salvation that is ready to be revealed in the last time.

Salvation that is to be revealed "in the last time." That means, to this point, it has not been revealed. It is not in the Bible and is not a part of anyone's doctrine of Christ's return. Christ himself will reveal it when he comes.

Can we imagine the potential problems that Christians will face? Can we see a similarity between the stars of old and the new stars of the new Jerusalem?

The "sun" of **Matthew 24:29** is Jesus, the "moon" is the Holy Spirit. As spiritual True Parents, Jesus and the Holy Spirit have been the channel of regeneration through which the descendants of the "dead Adam" have been born again as the children, the "stars" of God.

However, when Christ returns he will come with a "salvation that is to be revealed in the last time." He will be in the position to "restore everything" as promised by the holy prophets.

Jesus predicted that Christ at his return would be recognized as overtly as a lightening bolt flashing across the sky, yet before that victorious day, he will suffer many things:

Luke 17:24-25
For the Son of Man in his day will be like the lightning, which flashes and lights up the sky from one end to the other. **But first he must suffer many things and be rejected by this generation.**

Who will bring suffering upon the Lord of second coming? Will we mistake the Lord for a pretender only preaching "another gospel" and conclude he is deserving of scorn? Will the wrath of the Lord to "depart from me" ring in our ears? Therefore we must pray with a humble heart in order to learn from history and not repeat it.

Why Historical Events Reoccur

The time of Noah was "the Last Days." The "Last Days" came again at the time of Jesus and will return at the time of the Second Coming of Christ. Historians have been well aware that there seems to be a cyclical nature to history. As a result, they have been an ardent voice beseeching the powerful to learn the lessons contained in historical precedents.

Numerous theories of history abound. Much debate rages about the length of periods, the accuracy of dates and the valid sequence of circumstances and events. As historical records constantly expand, so do the areas of contention.

History is more than dates and events swirling through time like leaves blown in a tempest. As more history emerges and extends outward, analytical observation begins to identify patterns and parallels in the same manner an impressionist painting becomes more vivid as the observer backs away.

Historians, naturally, postulate various meanings and predict trends as a result of those observations. Generally they agree that history seems to move in an orderly, purposeful manner. It suggests an initial intention and systematic movement toward an ultimate fulfillment.

People of faith, however, recognize that the unfolding of historical events manifest a deeper reality. The movement of time and events bear the signature of God's intentions. As William Gladstone, the renowned nineteenth century British diplomat, rightly observed, "Diplomacy is the art of understanding where God is going in the next fifty years and planning accordingly."

Where God is going is made that much more clear if we can recognize, likewise, where God has been and from where He is coming.

This means in order to properly understand the ebb and flow of historical events, one must understand the Will of God and the principle by which God is fulfilling His Will. As we have studied, human history is the history of restoration. God is seeking to recover His original purpose for which He created. God created Adam and Eve and sought to have them stand as perfect True Parents. He wanted them to inherit all of His life and love so that when they started the lineage of humanity it would, likewise, be the lineage of God. This expansion of God's lineage would be the original object of historical record.

However, because of the fall of man, the goal of history became the goal of restoration. The goal of restoration is to bring a new Adam who can fulfill the original mission of the first Adam. This accomplishment ends the "old order of things" and begins the new history of God's uncontested expansion of lineage from family, to tribe, to nation, to world.

However, as we have studied, God is not solely responsible to exact the results. He has bequeathed to humanity a vital role and, as we also learned, God will not intervene upon that responsibility. Thus if the chosen persons, tribes or nations do not fulfill their responsibility, then the purpose of restoration in that era will not be fulfilled. As a result, God will recreate at a later time, the new era, the circumstances, events and figures that serve as the context for the accomplishment of that responsibility. In the midst of that recreated environment, God selects a new central person to fulfill the predecessor's responsibility.

This is the hidden dimension that manifests via historical events. It is the essential motive that brings one age in parallel with another. Its fundamental example is the return of the Last Days whose central figure is "the Christ," that is, "the new Adam."

The most basic of historical parallels is the return of Adam. All other cycles of history are peripheral (and debatable) to this core phenomenon. Adam will keep returning until he has accomplished his mission. Likewise, for every "Last Days" period there will be the subsequent need to establish a foundation for that messiah, the new Adam.

Thus central figures, such as Abel, Noah, Abraham, Isaac, Jacob, Moses and John the Baptist are called to establish that foundation. The course to accomplish the goal is the same course: establish a Foundation of Faith and a Foundation of Substance. Each central figure is picking up the same responsibility bequeathed forward from the predecessor who was not able to complete the mission.

This is why parallels appear between these central figures as exemplified with Jacob, Moses and Jesus. It is also why when John the Baptist faltered in his role and Jesus had to take it up, many people concluded that Jesus was "John the Baptist raised from the dead." What is the core lesson we can derive from this phenomenon?

Adam's mission is to become a perfect bridegroom, establish the position of True Parents and to begin God's lineage. It is the core mission that sets up the cornerstone of the Kingdom of Heaven on earth and in spirit. This mission, then, is the responsibility of the "next Adam" .

This is the foundation to understand Jesus' primary mission. This is how we can understand, too, the nature of Jesus' grief as he was rejected by the people and turned away from that primary mission toward the way of the cross.

Likewise, this is the basis to understand the nature of the mission for which Christ returns. His mission is to accomplish Adam's mission, the mission that became Jesus' primary mission. Only then will Christ's "sorrow unto death" be consoled.

Finally, we can conclude, within reason, the approximate point in the Christian era that parallels its counterpart in the history of Israel. The "new Jerusalem" is the recreated people who must take on the responsibility of that generation in Jerusalem that was to do "as Abraham would do," that is, to recognize and unite with Jesus the messiah.

The people of Jerusalem who failed to recognize Jesus came on the foundation of a two thousand year providence from Abraham's family to the arrival of the messiah in Israel. On that foundation, we could expect that the era of "the new Jerusalem" will likewise repeat a historical course of two thousand years from the time of Jesus until his return.

In fact, the second coming of Christ is not just the second coming of Christ alone, but rather, the second coming of all the events, circumstances, and figures faced by Jesus two thousand years ago. Thus the history of Christianity is predicated upon the history of Israel. The history of Israel is the model course, or image, for the history of Christianity.

Thus we can observe interesting and significant parallels between the two histories in the same manner we find parallels between Jacob, Moses and Jesus.

Parallels Between the History of Israel (Jerusalem) and Christianity (New Jerusalem)

The Period of Slavery in Egypt Compared with the Period of Persecution in the Roman Empire

After Jacob entered Egypt with his twelve sons and seventy kinsmen, their descendants suffered terrible abuse at the hands of the Egyptians for four hundred years. This was for the restoration of the four-hundred-year period from Noah to Abraham that had been defiled due to Abraham's mistake in his offering of the dove and pigeon.

The corresponding period in Christian history is the period following Jesus' crucifixion. Just as the Israelites suffered at the hands of the Egyptians, the Christian age begins in suffering and persecution by the hands of Rome. The Roman Empire in this sense was "the second coming" of the pagan sovereignty of Egypt. Jesus' twelve apostles and seventy disciples were the first of many generations of Christians who suffered severe persecution in the Roman Empire over a period of four hundred years. By enduring this suffering, they were walking the same model course as the Israelites who suffered for four hundred years at the hands of Egypt.

We can observe the signature of providence during this period in other areas. God not only recreates a similar time period and a similar time length. He also recreates similar events and circumstances within those periods. For instance, in the period of slavery in Egypt, the chosen people of the First Israel kept themselves pure by circumcision (**Joshua 5:2-5**), by making sacrifices (**Exodus 5:3**) and, as they left Egypt, by keeping the Sabbath (**Exodus 16:23**).

In comparison to that, during the period of persecution in the Roman Empire, the Christians, as the "Second Israel," in a similar way, lived a life of purity by performing the sacraments of baptism and Holy Communion, offering themselves as sacrifices, and keeping the Sabbath. In both periods, they had to follow this way of pure faith as a condition to separate from Satan, who was constantly assailing them for the mistakes of the past.

Let's examine another example that displays the link between the two periods. At the end of Israel's slavery in Egypt, Moses was able to defeat the "hardened heart" of Pharaoh by the power of the three signs and ten plagues. He then led the Israelites out of Egypt for the land of Canaan.

Likewise, toward the end of the period of persecution in the Roman Empire, Jesus increased the number of believers by moving their hearts with his power and grace. By stirring the heart of Emperor Constantine, Jesus led him to recognize Christianity in 313 A.D. Jesus inspired Theodosius I in 392 A.D. to establish Christianity as the state religion. We could say in this sense that the emperor of Rome was modeled after the Pharaoh in Egypt and was a "second coming" in the same way John the Baptist was a "second coming" of Elijah.

Christians thus restored Canaan spiritually inside the Roman Empire, the satanic world. In the Old Testament Age, God worked externally through conditions set by the Mosaic Law; likewise, God had Moses defeat the Pharaoh through the external power of miracles. In the New Testament Age, however, God worked through the internal conditions of faith. He manifested His power internally by moving the hearts of people.

Another important example that links the two periods involves the Word. When the period of slavery in Egypt was over, Moses on Mt. Sinai received the Ten Commandments and God's Word revealed in the Law, which formed the core of the Old Testament Scriptures. By setting up and honoring the tablets of stone, the ark of the covenant and the tabernacle, he paved the way for the Israelites to prepare for the coming of the Messiah.

Likewise, at the conclusion of the period of persecution in the Roman Empire, Christians gathered the writings that had been left behind by the apostles and evangelists and began the process to establish the canon of the New Testament. Based on these writings, they sought to realize God's ideals spiritually. These ideals of the "New Covenant" had been foreshadowed in the Ten Commandments, the tabernacle and the voice of the prophet in the Old Testament Age.

Centering on the Word of the Gospel, they built up churches and expanded their foundation to prepare for the Second Coming of Christ. After Jesus' ascension, the resurrected Jesus and the Holy Spirit guided Christians directly as the Israelites had been guided by a pillar of cloud by day and a pillar of fire by night.

For these reasons we can conclude that the initial four hundred years of the Christian era were patterned after the four hundred years the tribe of Israel was in Egypt. Is this just a coincidence? Let's see if the pattern continues in the next historical period of comparison.

The Period of the Judges Compared with the Period of Regional Church Leadership

Upon inheriting the mission of Moses, Joshua led the Israelites into the land of Canaan. For the next four hundred years, fifteen judges governed the Israelite tribes: thirteen judges from Othniel to Samson recorded in the Book of Judges, as well as Eli and Samuel.

The judges served simultaneously in the capacity of prophet, priest and king. Later, in the history of Israel, each of these functions would merit their own separate office. Israel in this period was a tribal society with no central political authority.

In the New Testament Age, the period of regional church leadership was the period that is modeled after the period of Judges in the Old Testament Age. In this period, regional church leaders—patriarchs, bishops and abbots—led Christian society. Like the judges of the Old Testament Age, they had duties similar to those of prophet, priest and king. As in the time of the judges, Christian society in this period was a tribe-like feudal society set under local authorities.

Thus the pattern continued. We could conclude that the regional church leaders of the New Testament Age were modeled after the Judges in the Old Testament Age.

We can find parallels between the two ages not only in duration and in similar figures but in circumstances as well. The period of the judges began after the Israelites were liberated from slavery in Egypt and the younger generation united solidly under the leadership of Joshua and Caleb to enter the land of Canaan. They parceled out the territory among their clans and tribes. Settling in villages united around the judges, the people consolidated into a chosen nation and established a simple tribal society.

Likewise, the period of regional church leadership in the Christian era began after the liberation of Christianity from the persecution of the Roman Empire, the satanic world. Christians spread the Gospel to the Germanic peoples, many of whom had migrated to Western Europe in the fourth century to escape the invading Huns. In their new land of Western Europe, God empowered the Germanic tribes as a new chosen people and established an early form of feudal society, which later matured into the feudalism of the Middle Ages.

As we discussed earlier, when the Israelites set out for Canaan, they first built the tabernacle as the symbol of the Messiah. In the period of the judges, the Israelites should have exalted the tabernacle and remained obedient to the direction of the judges centering on the laws, decrees and commandments. However, instead of purging the seven Canaanite tribes from Canaan, the Israelites lived among them and were influenced by their customs. They even took to worshipping their idols, thus bringing great confusion to their faith.

Likewise, in the period of regional church leadership, the Christians were supposed to exalt the church, which was the image of the Messiah, and follow the directions of its bishops and monastic leaders. However, they became influenced by the religion and culture of the pagan Germanic tribes, which brought great confusion to the Christian faith.

As the pattern continues, we can begin to sense that Christianity, in the role of the Second Israel and New Jerusalem, is moving in orderly fashion to an ultimate fulfillment along the same path that had been laid out for Israel. Let's examine the next parallel period.

The Period of the United Kingdom Compared with the Period of the Christian Empire

These two periods show parallels in many areas. In the Old Testament age, about eight hundred years after Abraham's descendants had entered Egypt, by God's command the prophet Samuel anointed Saul as the first king of Israel. **1 Samuel 8:19-22; 10:1-24** This began a new era in the history of Israel. Now the twelve tribes of Israel would have to recognize the central authority of the king and become a united kingdom.

In a similar way in the New Testament Age, Pope Leo III crowned Charlemagne and blessed him as the first emperor of Christendom in 800 A.D. Charlemagne stood upon the foundation of the four-hundred-year period of regional church leadership, just as Saul stood on the foundation of the four hundred years of Judges. In this respect, Pope Leo crowning Charlemagne king was the providential echo of Samuel crowning Saul king and establishing a united kingdom.

In the Old Testament Age, in the period of the United Kingdom, the functions of the judge were apportioned to the offices of prophet, priest and king. The prophets received instructions directly from God, the priests kept charge over the tabernacle and later the temple, and the king governed the nation. Each carried on their distinct missions in guiding Israel to accomplish the goal of the providence of restoration.

In the New Testament Age, in the period of the new united kingdom, similar division of missions were apportioned to the offices of monastic leaders corresponding to the prophets, the popes corresponding to the high priests, and the emperors, who ruled the people like the kings in the Old Testament. They were responsible to guide the Second Israel to accomplish the goal of the providence of restoration.

In the period of the united kingdom of Israel, the king was the central figure for restoring the Foundation of Faith. The Law Covenant now focused on the faith or lack thereof of the king. Blessing or curse would be decided by the king's personal standard with the laws, decrees and commandments of God.

However, because King Saul disobeyed the commands of God given through the prophet Samuel (**1 Samuel 15:1-23**), he was in no position to build the temple. Upon his failure, King Saul found himself in the same position as Moses after he had failed in the first national course to restore Canaan.

Likewise, in the period of the Christian empire, Charlemagne's empire realized the ideal of the Christian state as set down in *The City of God* by St. Augustine. Accordingly, in this period, the emperor and the pope were to realize the ideal Christian state by uniting wholeheartedly to follow the Will of God. The spiritual kingdom ruled by the pope, which had been founded upon the spiritual foundation for the Messiah, and the temporal kingdom ruled by the emperor should have united based on Christ's teachings. Had they done so, religion, politics and economy would have harmonized, and the foundation for the Second Advent of Christ would have been established at that time.

In the united kingdom of the Old Testament Era, David replaced Saul and then Solomon succeeded his father David. Finally, the kingdom period came to an unfulfilled close with the failure of Solomon and the collapse of the empire. In each generation of kings it was the relationship of the king with the prophet and the laws, decrees and commandments that were the determining measure of success. As a result of their failure, the seeds of division were sown in Israel.

In the united kingdom of the New Testament Era, Charlemagne, then his sons and finally his grandsons, endeavored to maintain the same type of tenuous relationship of emperor and priest. They, like their counterparts in the Old Testament Age, were unsuccessful. Instead, they too sowed the seeds for a coming division.

The Period of the Divided Kingdoms of North and South Compared with the Period of the Divided Kingdoms of East and West

Because King Solomon was led by his wives and concubines to worship idols, the united kingdom of Israel was divided upon his death, having lasted only three generations. **1 Kings 11:5-13** The kingdom of Israel in the north, which was founded by ten of the twelve tribes, was in the position of Cain, while the kingdom of Judah in the south, which was founded by the two remaining tribes, was in the position of Abel. This was how the period of the divided kingdoms of north and south began.

The Christian empire also began to divide in the third generation. Charlemagne's grandsons partitioned it into three kingdoms: the East Franks, the West Franks and Italy. The descendants of Charlemagne were in bitter and constant conflict with each other. The remnants of the Christian empire soon coalesced into two kingdoms, with Italy reverting to the rule of the East Franks. The kingdom of the East Franks flourished greatly under Otto I and came to be called the Holy Roman Empire. Claiming to be the heir of the Roman Empire, it ruled parts of Western Europe and sought to secure dominion over both politics and religion. The Holy Roman Empire stood in the position of Abel in relation to France, as the kingdom of the West Franks came to be called.

The northern kingdom of Israel was founded by Jeroboam, who had lived in exile in the days of King Solomon. It was ruled by nineteen kings over some two hundred ten years. Through repeated assassinations, its short-lived royal families changed nine times; not one king was righteous in the sight of God. Nevertheless, God sent the prophet Elijah, who prevailed in the contest with 850 prophets of Baal and Asherah on Mt. Carmel when God sent down fire upon the altar. **1 Kings 18:19-40** Other prophets, including Elisha, Jonah, Hosea and Amos, spread the Word of God at the risk of their lives. Yet since the northern kingdom continued to worship foreign gods and did not repent, God had the Assyrians destroy them and took away their qualification as the chosen people forever. **2 Kings 17:7-23**

Solomon's son, Rehoboam established the southern kingdom of Judah. Its royal house continued in one dynastic line from David to Zedekiah, producing many righteous kings out of the twenty who ruled the kingdom for nearly four hundred years of its existence. Nevertheless, a succession of evil kings, combined with influence from the northern kingdom, led to much idolatry and corruption. Consequently, the people of the southern kingdom were taken into exile in Babylon.

In the period of the divided kingdoms of north and south, whenever the Israelites violated their covenant with God, straying from the ideal of the Temple, God sent many prophets—such as Elijah, Isaiah and Jeremiah—to admonish them and move them to repentance and internal reform. However, because the kings and the people did not heed the warnings of the prophets and did not repent, God chastised them externally by sending gentile nations such as Syria, Assyria and Babylon to attack them.

During the parallel period in Christian history of the divided kingdoms of east and west, the papacy was corrupt. God sent prominent monks such as St. Thomas Aquinas and St. Francis of Assisi to admonish the papacy and promote internal reform in the Church. Since the papacy and the Church did not repent, but sank further into corruption and immorality, God chastised them externally by letting their people fight the Muslims. This was the providential reason behind the Crusades. While Jerusalem and the Holy Land were under the protection of the Abbasid Caliphate, Christian pilgrims were received with hospitality. After the Caliphate collapsed and the Holy Land was conquered by the Seljuk Turks, cries of alarm went out that Christian pilgrims were being harassed. Outraged, the popes raised the Crusades to recover the Holy Land. There were eight Crusades, beginning in 1096 and continuing sporadically for about two hundred years. Despite some initial success, the Crusaders were defeated repeatedly.

In the history of Israel, the period of the divided kingdoms of north and south came to an end when gentile nations took the people of Israel and Judah into exile. They put an end to the monarchy in Israel. Likewise, at the close of the period of the divided kingdoms of east and west, the papacy had completely lost its prestige and credibility after the repeated defeats of the Crusades. Christianity thus lost its center of spiritual sovereignty. Moreover, since the lords and knights who had maintained feudal society were decimated by the Crusades, feudal society lost its political power and vigor. Since the papacy and the feudal lords had spent enormous funds to pursue these unsuccessful wars, they were left impoverished. Monarchic Christianity began to erode.

The pattern the binds Israel's history with that of Christianity continues to the next paralleled period.

The Period of Israel's Exile and Return and the Period of the Papal Exile and Return

By falling into faithlessness without repentance, the people of Israel failed to realize the ideal of God's nation founded upon the temple. To make another attempt at fulfilling this Will, God had the people suffer hardships as exiles in Babylon. This was similar to when God had the Israelites suffer as slaves in Egypt to restore through indemnity Abraham's mistake in the symbolic offering.

In the period of the Christian empire, God worked through the pope and the emperor to establish a kingdom prepared for Christ at his Second Coming. God's intention was that ultimately they would bequeath the empire and the throne to the Messiah when he would come as the King of Kings and build God's kingdom upon that foundation. Yet the emperors and popes became corrupt and did not repent. The popes did not lay the spiritual foundation upon which the emperors could stand as the central figures for the Foundation of Substance. Therefore, the foundation for the Second Advent of

Christ was not established. To begin a new dispensation to restore this foundation, God allowed the popes to be taken into exile and suffer captivity.

In the earlier parallel period, nearly seventy years elapsed from the time King Nebuchadnezzar of Babylon took into captivity King Jehoiachin and his royal family, as well as prophets including Daniel and Ezekiel, priests, officials, craftsmen and many other Israelites, until the fall of Babylon and their liberation by the royal decree of King Cyrus. **2 Kings 24,25; 2 Chronicles 36; Jeremiah 29:10**

It then took another one hundred forty years for the exiles to return to their homeland in three waves, until they fully reformed themselves as a nation united around the Will of God as proclaimed in the messianic prophecies of Malachi. Henceforth, they began to prepare for the coming of the Messiah. In the period of papal exile and return, which was to restore this period through indemnity in the form of substantial parallels, western Christianity had to walk a similar course.

The popes and priests, sunk in immorality, gradually lost the confidence of the people. The authority of the papacy sank even lower due to the repeated defeats of the Crusades. The end of the Crusades saw the gradual collapse of the feudal system in Europe and the emergence of modern nation-states. As the power of secular monarchies grew, the conflict between the popes and the kings escalated. In one such conflict, King Philip IV, "the Fair," of France imprisoned Pope Boniface VIII for a time. In 1309, Philip forced Pope Clement V to move the papacy from Rome to Avignon in southern France. For seventy years, successive popes lived there subject to the kings of France, until 1377 when Pope Gregory XI returned the papal residence to Rome.

After Gregory's death, the cardinals elected an Italian, the Archbishop of Bari, as Pope Urban VI. However, a group of cardinals, mostly Frenchmen, rejected him, elected another pope, Clement VII, and established a rival papacy in Avignon. The Great Schism continued into the next century. To resolve this impasse, the cardinals from both camps held a council in Pisa, Italy, in 1409, which dismissed both the Roman and Avignon popes and appointed Alexander V as the legitimate pope. The two popes, however, refused to resign, creating for a short time the spectacle of three contending popes. Shortly afterwards, cardinals, bishops, theologians, royalty and their envoys gathered for the General Council of

Constance (1414-1417). It dismissed all three popes and elected Martin V as the new pope, effectively ending the Great Schism.

The Council of Constance insisted that the general councils of the Church had supreme authority, greater than that of the pope and with the power to elect or depose him, and directed that subsequent councils be held at regular intervals. Thus, it sought to reorganize the Roman church as a constitutional monarchy. However, in 1431, when delegates gathered for the next council, held in Basel, Switzerland, the pope tried to adjourn the meeting. The delegates refused to leave and carried on in the pope's absence, but to no effect; in 1449, they finally disbanded. The plan to institutionalize a constitutional monarchy within the Roman church came to naught, and the papacy recovered the authority it had lost in 1309.

The leaders of the conciliar movement in the fifteenth century had tried to reform the corrupt papacy by setting up a representative council composed of bishops and laymen and giving it supreme authority. Nevertheless, the papacy ended up reasserting its full authority, as it had not enjoyed since before its exile. Furthermore, these councils condemned more fundamental reforms as promoted by John Wycliffe (1320-1384) and Jan Hus (1369-1415), who was personally invited to attend the Council of Constance only to be burned at the stake. At that point, the die was cast for the outbreak of the Protestant Reformation.

This period of approximately two hundred ten years ran from 1309, with the papacy's seventy years of exile in Avignon, through the Great Schism, the conciliar movement and the restoration of papal authority in the Roman church, to the eve of the Protestant Reformation spearheaded by Martin Luther in 1517. Its purpose was to restore through indemnity, in the form of substantial parallels, the 210-year period of Israel's exile and return—from Israel's seventy years of exile in Babylon through the stages of the returning to Israel and the rebuilding of the Temple, until the reform of politics and religion under the leadership of Ezra, Nehemiah and the prophet Malachi.

In fact, from the perspective of Jewish history, Ezra, Nehemiah, Zechariah and Malachi are viewed in the same light as Christian history views its reformers. Even more significantly, as the era of Jewish reformation signaled the beginning of a 400-year period culminating with the arrival of Christ, the Protestant Reformation, likewise, could stand as a similar benchmark.

The Period of Preparation for the Advent of the Messiah Compared with the Period of Preparation for the Second Advent of the Messiah

Following the period of Israel's exile and return, another four hundred years elapsed before Jesus came. This was the period of preparation for the advent of the Messiah. Likewise, Christianity is to meet Christ at his Second Advent only after passing through four hundred years of the period of preparation for the Second Advent of the Messiah, which had followed the period of papal exile and return. It should restore through indemnity in the form of substantial parallels the period of preparation for the advent of the Messiah.

Upon returning from the Babylonian exile, the Israelites established the Foundation of Faith by repenting of their past sin of idolatry, rebuilding the temple (**Ezra 3:7-13; 6:1-15**) that had been destroyed by King Nebuchadnezzar, and reforming their faith based on the Mosaic Law under the guidance of Ezra the scribe. **Ezra 7:1-10; Nehemiah 8** They then began to prepare for the coming of the Messiah according to the word of the prophet Malachi. Likewise, after the papacy's return to Rome, medieval Christians established the Foundation of Faith by seeking to reform the Roman church; these efforts culminated in the Protestant Reformation led by Martin Luther. This movement pierced the gloom of medieval Europe with the light of the Gospel and pioneered new paths of faith.

Specifically, in the Age of the Providence of Restoration, people were justified before God by such external conditions as keeping the Mosaic Law and offering sacrifices. Therefore, during the period of preparation for the advent of the Messiah, the First Israel had to suffer external hardships at the hands of the gentile nations of Persia, Greece, Egypt, Syria and Rome. During the Age of the Prolongation of the Providence of Restoration, Christians have been justified before God by internal conditions of prayer and faith according to the teachings of Jesus.

Hence, in the period of preparation for the Second Advent of the Messiah, the Second Israel has had to walk a path of internal tribulations. The ideologies of Renaissance humanism and the Enlightenment, as well as the call for religious freedom that arose from the Reformation, have created a profusion of philosophies and theologies, causing great confusion in the Christian faith and turmoil in people's spiritual lives.

The period of preparation for the Second Advent of the Messiah has also been restoring the internal preparations and external environment for the worldwide reception of the Messiah, which had first been set up during the four hundred years of the period of preparation for the first advent of Jesus.

In preparation for the first coming of Christ, God sent the prophet Malachi to the chosen people four hundred thirty years beforehand to arouse in them a strong messianic expectation. At the same time, God encouraged the Jews to reform their religion and deepen their faith to make the internal preparations necessary to receive the Messiah. Meanwhile, among the world's peoples, God founded religions suited to their regions and cultures by which they could make the necessary internal preparations to receive the Messiah.

However, the scope of Israel's mission had expanded since the time of Solomon's kingdom:

Isaiah 49:5-6

⁵ And now the LORD says:
he who formed me in the womb to be his servant
to bring Jacob back to him
and gather Israel to himself,
for I am honored in the eyes of the LORD
and my God has been my strength-
⁶ he says:
"It is too small a thing for you to be my servant
to restore the tribes of Jacob
and bring back those of Israel I have kept.
I will also make you a light for the Gentiles,
that you may bring my salvation to the ends of the earth."

Israel's mission was to be beyond its borders. God wanted Israel to "be a light for the Gentiles" as well. This shows that Jesus' mission was to take salvation "to the ends of the earth." Thus God prepared a worldwide foundation for Jesus during this period of four hundred years.

In India, God established Buddhism through Gautama Buddha (565-485 B.C.) as a new development out of Hinduism. In Greece, God inspired Socrates (470-399 B.C.) and opened the brilliant age of classical Greek civilization. In the Far East, God raised up Confucius (552-479 B.C.), whose teachings of Confucianism established the standard of human ethics. Jesus was to come upon this worldwide foundation of preparation, and through his teachings he was to bring together Judaism, Hellenism, Buddhism and Confucianism. He was to unify all religions and civilizations into one worldwide civilization founded upon the Christian Gospel.

As True Parents, Jesus and his bride would establish God's uncontested lineage of true sons and daughters. The vision of **Psalm 45** would be substantially realized. A new history and a new culture would emerge centering on the True Parents and their nation. By today, our world would have been entirely transformed into the living culture of Jesus. As we know, sadly, this did not take place.

In the Christian era, God has been recreating the events and circumstances that were used to prepare Israel and the world for the coming of Jesus' first advent. Since the Renaissance, God has been creating the religious, political and economic environment conducive to the work of Christ at his Second Coming. This has been the age to restore through indemnity, in the form of substantial parallels, the earlier period when God had set up the worldwide environment to prepare for the coming of Jesus. Beginning with the Renaissance, progress in virtually every field of human endeavor, including politics, economy, culture and science, has increased at a rapid rate.

Today, these fields have reached their zenith and have created a global environment conducive to the work of Christ at his Second Coming. In Jesus' day, the Roman Empire ruled the vast domains around the Mediterranean Sea, integrated by an advanced and extensive transportation system reaching out in all directions. This was the center of a vast Hellenistic civilization founded on the Greek language. Thus, all the necessary preparations had been made for a swift transmission of the teachings of the Messiah from Israel, where Jesus lived, to Rome and the world.

Similarly, in the present era of the Second Advent, the influence of the Western powers has expanded the democratic political sphere throughout the world. The rapid progress of transportation and communication has greatly bridged the gap between East and West, and the extensive contact among languages and cultures has brought the world much closer together. These factors have fully prepared an environment in which the teachings of the returning Christ can freely and swiftly be conveyed to the hearts of all humankind. This will enable his teachings to bring rapid and profound changes all over the globe.

God's objective in the second coming is as it was in the first coming. That is, to "bring salvation to the ends of the earth."

A 400-year period of preparation from the time of Martin Luther and the Protestant Reformation brings us squarely to the 20th century. The 20th century of the Christian era, then, stands in parallel with the age of Jesus in Israel.

This means that in the 20th century we can begin to see the appearance of events, circumstances and figures that parallel the very age of Jesus. The second coming of Christ is not just the second coming of Christ alone, but rather is the second coming of all the circumstances, attitudes and figures faced by Jesus.

However, at the right time, the crowning glory of all reoccurring history, the personage of Christ, will be revealed. Indeed, when the time is right and the pieces are all put in place, Christ, himself, will return in our era. We are the generation that stands in parallel with the generation of 2,000 years ago. That is, the ones who walked this world with Jesus.

Chapter Fourteen

The Second Coming of Christ

Rev. 7:9–10

I looked, and behold a great multitude, of which no one could number, of all nations, tribes, peoples, and tongues, standing before the throne and before the Lamb, clothed with white robes, with palm branches in their hands, and crying out with a loud voice, saying, "Salvation belongs to our God who sits on the throne, and to the Lamb."

In his letter to the Hebrews, Saint Paul referred to this physical reality as a "copy and shadow" of the heavenly, or spiritual, realm. **Hebrews 8:5** The Bible makes clear that life does not cease with the death of the flesh. Indeed, most major religions hold the concept that a person's soul continues on after his or her physical body passes away. Where in the spirit world a person goes is determined by the quality and character of his or her life on earth, especially the quality of faith and depth of love.

Up to the present, the realms of heaven and hell have been divided, separated by the same barriers of religion, nationality, race and culture that have divided people on earth. This is because people on the other side continue with the same prejudices and limitations they had on earth. However, in the Last Days, when God establishes His Kingdom, there should be unity in Heaven as well as on earth. **Zechariah 14:9:** *"The Lord shall be one and His name be one,"* and **Revelation 11:15:** *The kingdoms of this world become the kingdoms of our Lord and of His Christ, and He shall reign forever and ever.*

Today, many people are thirsty for knowledge about the heavenly world, and they seek out all manner of sources, some of dubious worth. A reliable source would be someone whom God has chosen to convey His message, for genuine prophecy "edifies the church". **1 Corinthians 14:4 Acts 2:17–19** reveals that in the last days, *"I will pour out My Spirit on all flesh, your sons and your daughters shall prophesy . . . and I will show wonders in the heavens and in* *the earth.*" This text indicates that the Spirit will move gifted individuals to have visions of the spirit world, showing people on earth the wonders of heaven. It also indicates that God's activity may encompass both realms. A study of the book of Zechariah, for instance, shows that prophets sometimes worked with heavenly spirits to better grasp the meaning of their revelations.

At a time when religious conflict seems rampant on earth, this vision of the gathering of heaven's forces united as one mind under the one God comes as a welcome message of hope.

Knowing that this information is new and unusual to many readers, I encourage you to digest it with a prayerful yet open mind. Much of its contents may be challenging, particularly as it concerns the Second Coming of Christ. Therefore, by way of orientation, we offer some additional explanation.

The Second Coming of Christ in Our Age

When will Christ come again? Jesus said that we couldn't know. In **Matthew 24:36**, *"Of that day and hour no one knows, not even the angels in Heaven, nor the Son, but the Father only."* However, in **Amos 3:7**, we see that God does nothing without revealing His secrets to "his servants the prophets."

This would seem to suggest that God will give us a "heads-up" before He sends Christ again. In fact, we can see that Jesus goes to great lengths to clearly describe the "signs" of the time to which Christ returns. Evidently, Jesus expects the generation of Christians alive at that time to be able to identify the moment and stand at the ready.

Most preachers' favorite sermon is the one that proclaims the Second Coming of Christ as the culminating hope of our faith. What believer cannot be stirred by the rendering of the "signs of the times" mentioned by Jesus in **Matthew 24** and the report of their fulfillment, one by one, in our time. In fact, one of the signs of the times that Jesus mentioned was, *And this gospel of the kingdom will be preached in the **whole world** as a testimony **to all nations**, and then the end will come.* **Matthew 24:14** Clearly, this didn't happen until the end of the 20th century.

From the standpoint of the "signs," there is good reason to conclude that our generation is the one that will be on the earth when Christ returns. In a modern world whose airwaves are increasingly dominated by news of biological, chemical and nuclear weapons of mass destruction and the likelihood of their use, it is most welcome news.

Consider that Jesus spoke a message in **Matthew 24** that would be relevant to only one generation. It is very clear that Jesus wanted Christians of that single generation to be aware of the special age in which they lived, and to be prepared for the Second Coming. Why else would the Lord be so adamant about describing the signs of that age and urging that generation to be on the alert?

Is it to prepare for the rapture? Yet what special preparation does one need beyond traditional faith in Christ to participate in that sudden event?

Is it because the final judgment will occur? But doesn't accepting or rejecting Christ before one dies just as conclusively judge every generation?

Or could it be that the particular generation on earth at the time of Christ's return will be faced with a unique responsibility, a responsibility never faced by any previous generation of Christians? Could Jesus' urgency reflect the fact that there are possible unprecedented benefits as well as adverse consequences if that generation fulfills or fails to recognize its unique historical role?

This is where learning from history is vital. As it has been said, "Those who refuse to learn from history are doomed to repeat it." Never has that been truer than for this generation of Christians.

Parallels to Jesus' Day

To better understand the challenges facing the generation of Christians that welcomes Christ at his Second Coming, it is instructive to look at the challenge faced by the religious leaders of Jesus' day. If we can learn from those figures of the past, it can bring us into greater recognition of our responsibility in this providential age.

What was the great challenge faced by the religious leaders of Jesus' day? Why was it so hard for them to recognize Jesus as the long-awaited messiah?

The law judged every generation in Israel since the time of Moses to the time just prior to the birth of Jesus. It was their standing in relation to the laws, decrees and commandments of God that would determine their standing in front of God.

However, when Christ was born, the standard of judgment

suddenly changed. From that moment on, the standard of judgment was no longer obedience to the law, but was, rather, judgment based upon the extent they could recognize and unite with Jesus as Israel's messiah.

It was a great challenge, but it was not insurmountable. We see that Simeon and Anna the prophetess were able to accomplish recognition of Christ. **Luke 2:25–37** Initially, John the Baptist was able, as were the 12 apostles and 70 disciples.

Clearly, though, the teachers of the law, the Pharisees and Sadducees and the masses of the people were unable to establish faith in Jesus. That is why Jesus proclaimed, *"Verily I say unto you, That the publicans and the harlots go into the kingdom of God before you."* **Matthew 21:31** He also lamented that they did not know the time of their visitation. **Luke 19:44**

In biblical history, we observe that God re-creates the circumstances of the past, in order for the new central figures to undo the wrongful conditions laid down by their predecessors. For example, Cain, the elder, killed his younger brother Abel, starting a historical trend of violence and debauchery. Generations later God restored this wrongful start when Esau, the elder brother, submitted and united with his younger brother, Jacob, to begin the new history of God's people.

Did the behavior of the Pharisees and Sadducees constitute a sin that needs to be restored? Was their unbelief an acceptable response to the coming of Jesus Christ? Clearly not! It was a failure that should be restored by a later generation of religious leaders. To restore it, they should be placed in the same position as the Pharisees and Sadducees of old. That is, the position to welcome the Christ at the Second Coming.

If it is the case that Christian ministers today are placed in the same position as the religious leaders of Jesus' day, then what obstacles might they expect in their path?

Jesus came to establish his Kingdom, but not according to the doctrines of the Old Testament. Likewise, in this age, in order for Christians to effectively unbind the failures of 2,000 years ago, Christ will come in a way that does not harmonize with every doctrinal expectation.

No one in Israel came to Jesus as a natural conclusion of any doctrine. Those who recognized Jesus did so by drawing on other internal faculties. **Matthew 16:16–17:** Simon Peter answered,

*"You are the Christ, the Son of the living God." Jesus replied, "Blessed are you, Simon son of Jonah, for **this was not revealed to you by man, but by my Father in heaven**."*

Over the course of the last 2,000 years, each Christian generation has been judged by faith in the Gospel. However, the generation alive in the day of Christ's return will no longer be judged only by faith in the Gospel, but by the extent to which they will be able to recognize the dispensation of the return of Christ and the completion of salvation.

1 Peter 1:5 says that Christians will be *"shielded with faith, **until** the coming of the salvation that **is to be revealed in the last days**."* This is a very significant statement. First, it indicates that Christian faith will shield believers "until." This means there will be an expiration date. Why? Will it be because Christian faith will pass away? No, it is because they will have to transfer their faith-center from the Gospel to the revelation of salvation that comes in the last days! The Gospel concludes with the hope that Christ will come soon. Therefore, arrival of Christ and the revealing of the completion of salvation is not the traditional "Gospel" message. Many may mistake it for "another Gospel" that Paul warns against.

Our generation may be the generation that has been given the responsibility to unbind the chosen people's failure of 2,000 years ago. Can we Christians do what Israel was unable to do when faced with having to transfer their center of faith from the law to Jesus? Unless we are able to transform our faith of expectation of Christ's coming into one of recognition of Christ's coming, we are liable to repeat the same failure of the Pharisees 2,000 years ago. A new season requires new duties, yet Christians of our generation can readily give the same reasons as to why they should remain bound to their traditional faith.

How Will Christ Return?

Based on what we have already explained, could Christ come any other way except by being born on earth? Adam was born on earth to accomplish his mission. Jesus was born on earth to accomplish his mission. Jesus was on earth poised at the gate of his primary mission, but that gate was closed. When Christ comes again, he must come to the earth to open that gate.

Matthew 24:30: *They will see the Son of man coming **on the**

clouds of the sky *with power and great glory.* Does "coming on the clouds" mean literal clouds?

The idea that Jesus is coming on the clouds is one of the most cherished and comforting beliefs in the Christian faith. Literally millions of believers have been comforted in the hope of Christ's imminent return. Especially in times of hardship and trouble, all good preachers know that is the time to pull out the "clean-up hitter" of sermons: Jesus is coming soon!

Yet, no other article of faith divides Christians more. For example, some Christians have a pre-millennial view of Christ's return. That is, Christ will return "in the air" to collect the faithful and 1,000 years later establish his Kingdom on the earth. Then there are those with a post-millennial view, who believe Christ will come only after the millennial reign. Still others hold an a-millennial view. They don't accept the idea of a millennial reign at all. There are numerous other Second Coming issues on which Christians fundamentally differ.

The important issue is how Jesus must feel about this circumstance, especially after he prayed so fervently that all believers should be one as God and Christ are one. Surely God and Christ are not debating about the manner of the Second Coming.

Surveying the diverse expectations of Christ's return we see three possible options that would most accurately describe the actual situation:

Option #1: There is one denominational body out there whose expectation is doctrinally correct. They are right and everyone else is wrong. That would mean, of course, that the majority of Christians are wrong and are not prepared for the event of the Second Coming.

Option #2: Everyone is completely wrong! We will all miss it.

Option #3: Most people have something right and something incorrect. We are a mixed bag of various points overemphasized, underemphasized, points hit right on the nose and points completely overlooked.

No doubt, every minister agrees, it is option #1. Unfortunately, every minister, every church and every denomination believes that it alone is prepared for the Second Coming of Christ.

In other words, if any minister stood up and explained to others, outside his denominational affiliation, his particular doctrinal expectation of Christ's return, he would meet with stiff resistance. And that's the problem that we have to solve.

The truth is that one denomination cannot fulfill God's purpose for sending Christ again. That purpose is nothing less than the establishment of God's Kingdom. Yet most Christians only see God's purpose for the second coming in terms of Christ coming for me. But what is the point in that? Aren't we going to die and head his way anyway?

Christianity has been losing influence in the world because it has retreated from an overall sense of God's Will for the nation and world. It has broken into pockets of believers, each making pronouncements of God's Will for me and my church alone. As a result, not enough people feel responsible for the nation or the world. This, in spite of God having "so loved the world that he gave his only begotten Son." Consider the consequences.

Despite its Christian heritage, the United States leads every other nation in the industrialized world in the:

- Percentage of single-parent families (23 percent),
- Abortion rate (22.9 per 1,000 women aged 15–44),
- Sexually transmitted diseases,
- Teenage birth rate,
- Use of illegal drugs by students (44.9 percent using in 1998),
- Size of the prison population (327 per 100,000) [Source: *Lost in America* by Tom Clegg and Warren Bird].

In truth, the reality of today's Christianity is more reflective of what is described in option #3. Everyone, in some respect, has a bead on the truth while at the same time, in other areas, is missing the mark.

That means that no matter how hard Jesus might try, he will not be able to come back in a way that would satisfy more than a small minority. Wouldn't it seem likely that before his coming, he would send into the world a clarification of the important truths germane to his coming? Indeed, that has been one of the missions that needs to be fulfilled. For more than 40 years it has been the teaching of the Divine Principle to help all Christians recognize that their responsibility is comparable to that of our historical counterparts of 2,000 years ago.

On the Clouds

Will Christ come on literal clouds? Well, no he won't, not the fluffy ones. Before we explain the meaning of clouds, let's first establish that it was predicted that Christ would come in the "clouds" at his first advent also. Of course, we know that Jesus was born on the earth and did not float down out of the sky.

Daniel 7:13–14

*In my vision at night I looked, and there before me was one like **a son of man, coming with the clouds of heaven.** He approached the Ancient of Days and was led into his presence. He was given authority, glory and sovereign power; all peoples, nations and men of every language worshiped him. His dominion is an everlasting dominion that will not pass away, and his kingdom is one that will never be destroyed.*

Of course, many conclude that Daniel, who appeared roughly 600 years before Jesus, was already leaping over the first coming and was speaking about the Second Coming. This reasoning falls apart, however, as we consider the salient point made by Jesus in **Matthew 11:13:** *"For **all the Prophets** and the Law **prophesied until John.**"* Jesus indicates that *all* Old Testament prophecy was relevant to his coming in Israel.

We can also demonstrate this in another way. The 7th chapter of Daniel is a dream sequence in which Daniel sees the rising of four beasts. It is during the time of the fourth beast that Christ comes in the clouds and establishes his everlasting Kingdom. In **Daniel 7:17** the meaning of the four beasts in his dream is explained to be "four great kingdoms that will rise from the earth." The four great kingdoms that arose from the time of Daniel to the time of Jesus were: (1) Babylon, (2) Persia, (3) Greece and (4) Rome. The fourth beast is the most formidable and is the beast (nation) that has dominion when Christ comes. The Christ who came during the time of Rome was, of course, Jesus. Jesus did not come on a literal cloud. However, he did "come down from heaven."

Why does Jesus say in **Matthew 24** that in his second coming he will also "come in the clouds?" We have to understand that he is repeating or renewing **Daniel 7:13** in the same way that **Isaiah 65:17** is renewed by **Revelation 21:1**. In essence, Jesus is declaring that the Second Coming will come in like manner as the first coming.

If we take his coming "in the clouds" to be symbolic, then we can understand that Jesus did in fact come in the clouds at his first coming. What is the symbolic meaning of "clouds"?

Hebrews 12:1

*"Therefore since we are surrounded by so great a **cloud of witnesses** let us lay aside every weight."*

The "cloud of witnesses" is the spiritual aggregation of saints that the writer describes in **Hebrews 11:39–40**: *"These were all commended for their faith, yet none of them received what had been promised. God had planned something better for us so that only together with us would they be made perfect."* **Jude 1:14** likewise reports of Enoch's prophecy that Jesus would come with "thousands and thousands of holy saints." This was "the cloud" upon which Jesus came.

At the mount of Transfiguration, Moses and Elijah appeared with Jesus and "while he was still speaking, **a bright cloud** enveloped them, and a voice from the cloud said, *'This is my Son, whom I love; with him I am well pleased. Listen to him!'"* **Matthew 17:5** This could only be seen with their spiritual eyes. It was not a physical event.

When we seek to understand the meaning of clouds we also have to incorporate the meaning of "waters." Clouds come from water and in deciphering symbols you will find waters and clouds are related. Scripture uses the symbol "water" to represent people, but people of a different quality than the "clouds."

Revelation 17:15: *The waters that you saw, where the harlot is seated, **are people, multitudes, nations and tongues**.* Also in **Jude 1:13**, we see that unrighteous men are called "wild waves of the sea." Therefore, "waters" is a symbol of unrighteous, unsanctified people.

A cloud is drawn out of the water and is purified. Thus, water is a symbol of sinful people, and clouds are a symbol of sanctified people.

Then, what does Jesus mean when he proclaims that Christ, in the Second Coming, will be "coming with the clouds of heaven"? He means that, as at the first coming, the Second Coming will also be accompanied by a massive holy entourage of heavenly saints. **Revelation 19:14,** in announcing the Second Coming, describes this clearly: "The armies of heaven were following him, riding on white horses and dressed in fine linen, white and clean."

This phenomenon, like at the first coming, will not be perceived with physical eyes. **Luke 17:20:** *"The kingdom of God cometh not* *with observation.*" Jesus scolded the Pharisees for seeking after a sign:

Matthew 12:38–39
*Then some of the Pharisees and teachers of the law said to him, "Teacher, we want to see a miraculous sign from you." He answered, "**A wicked and adulterous generation asks for a miraculous sign!**"*

The reason people get so enamored with the concept of a readily observable, cataclysmic arrival of Christ is that it takes us out of the realm of responsibility to recognize Christ. We prefer the external, obvious validation rather than having to rely on the internal tools of faith—such as were manifested by Anna, Simeon and Peter.

What about Acts 1:11?
At the time of Jesus' ascension, an angel instructs the disciples,

Acts 1:11
Ye men of Galilee, why stand ye gazing up into heaven? This same Jesus, which is taken up from you into heaven, shall so come in like manner as ye have seen him go into heaven.

On the surface, this seems to be an unequivocal declaration of a celestial return of Christ. Upon closer inspection, however, we find another meaning than what is generally assumed.

The first curiosity is that the angel confronts the men of Galilee who were looking into the sky. He asks, "Why do you stand there looking in the sky?" This seems to indicate that he is being critical of their focus. His next statement seems to be a correction, as if to say, "If you really want to see Jesus come again, you had better be looking in some area other than the sky." He tells them, "This same Jesus which is taken up from you into heaven, shall so come in like manner as ye have seen him go into heaven."

Is this a case of "what goes up, must come down?" No. He will come in the same way you have seen him go. How did Jesus go into heaven? See **John 3:13:** *No one has gone into heaven, except the one* ***who came down from heaven,*** *the Son of Man* ***which is in Heaven.***

Jesus wasn't aloft in the sky when he said this. He said he "came down from heaven." The "heaven" from which the Son of Man came down doesn't mean "sky." The "heaven" in which the Son of Man stayed was not the "sky." Likewise, when the angel chided the disciples for "looking into the sky" he meant that Jesus is not coming from the sky. Rather, he will come down from heaven in the same way as he did before. It will not be observed with physical eyes. When **1 Thessalonians 4:16** asserts that "The Lord himself will come down from heaven," it means as he came down the first time.

In fact, the New International Version makes this very distinction in its rendering of **Acts 1:11**: *"Men of Galilee," they said, "why do you stand here looking into the **sky**? This same Jesus, who has been taken from you into **heaven**, will come back in the same way you have seen him go into **heaven**."* The translators interpret the first "heaven" to be "sky." This is because the angel's point, again, is that Jesus is not coming down from the sky, but rather, is coming down from "heaven" as per **John 3:13.**

History Repeats Itself

There is probably another reason why Jesus said he was coming with clouds. As was said, Jesus in **Matthew 24** repeated or renewed the prophecy about his first coming on the clouds given in **Daniel 7:13**. In order that Christians at the time of the Second Advent might restore the mistake of the people at Jesus' first advent, God is setting up the same circumstances, figures and responsibilities of 2,000 years ago. Included in that mix are the reasons that the chosen people could not have faith in Jesus. One of those circumstances was that they, too, had very mixed expectations with regard to the end times and the coming of their messiah.

Some Jews expected that Christ would come on the clouds of heaven as prophesied by Daniel. Others pointed to **Micah 5:2** that declared Christ would be born in Bethlehem. This scripture was cited for Herod when the Magi came calling. However, in **John 7:27**, it seems that many others were of the mind that no one could know from where Christ would come.

God has re-created those same circumstances today. Some people expect Christ to come from the clouds, some expect he will appear on the Mount of Olives, others think that his Second Coming took place on the day of Pentecost. Again, the question of the Second Coming is among the most divisive issues in all of theology.

Jesus' warning about false Christs also reflects a circumstance that was prevalent at his time. Jesus' group was one of many groups that were following a person they thought was the expected messiah. In **Acts 5**, Gamaliel refers to some of the more prominent messiahs who had fallen by the wayside.

Acts 5:34–37

*But a Pharisee named Gamaliel, a teacher of the law, who was honored by all the people, stood up in the Sanhedrin and ordered that the men be put outside for a little while. Then he addressed them: "Men of Israel, consider carefully what you intend to do to these men. Some time ago **Theudas** appeared, claiming to be somebody, and about four hundred men rallied to him. He was killed, all his followers were dispersed, and it all came to nothing. After him, **Judas the Galilean** appeared in the days of the census and led a band of people in revolt. He too was killed, and all his followers were scattered."*

We see in scripture that, initially, people speculated that perhaps John the Baptist was the Christ. Jesus warns of a similar phenomenon at the time of his return. It is because the circumstances faced by Jesus will be repeated at the Second Coming. Thus, Christ's Second Coming may well emerge out of a similar environment of suspicion and confusion.

The challenge for Christians is to do what the chosen people could not do: translate their faith of expectation of Christ into a faith of recognition of Christ.

Christ Will Be Born on Earth

Revelation 12:5

*She gave birth to a son, **a male child**, who will rule all the nations with an iron scepter. And her child was snatched up to God and to his throne.*

Why must Christ be born on the earth?
- The first Adam was born on earth to establish the Kingdom.
- Jesus, the second Adam, was born on earth to establish the Kingdom.
- What is sown on earth is reaped in Heaven.
- The third Adam will be born on the earth to establish the Kingdom.

As we have mentioned in our study of history, in order for "the New Jerusalem" to unbind the failure of former Jerusalem, the people of the New Jerusalem must walk the same course as the people of the former Jerusalem. In the re-creation of the events, figures and circumstances of 2,000 years ago, the key re-creation will be the appearance of a Christ who comes again in an unanticipated way as Jesus came in an unanticipated way. This will require the New Jerusalem to recognize him in the same manner as Peter, Simeon and Anna. This requires an on-earth presence of the returned Lord.

Of that future appearance, Jesus said in **Luke 17:24–25:**

For the Son of Man in his day will be like the lightning, which flashes and lights up the sky from one end to the other. But first he must suffer many things and be rejected by this generation.

But first he must suffer? Who will make him suffer? It is obvious that this could only happen if his Second Coming begins in an unexpected fashion. Certainly every eye will eventually see him, but only after an initial period of rejection and suffering. Who will cause him to suffer?

Some conclude that the suffering to which Jesus refers is that which takes place at Calvary. In other words, Jesus is predicting his own impending suffering and death at Calvary's cross. This is incorrect, however. Most credible Bible scholarship records three occurrences of Jesus predicting his suffering to come, and **Luke 17:25** is not considered one of those three. The reason is because he is clearly speaking within the context of the future, second coming of Christ. Read from the 20th verse and you will see.

Again, Jesus stressed that his coming would not be accompanied with "signs to be observed." Instead, Jesus asks the more pertinent question in **Luke 18:8:** "When the Son of Man comes, will he find faith on earth?" He doesn't mean the faith of expectation. There is plenty of that. He is referring to the faith of recognition, the rare faith as displayed by Anna, Simeon and Peter.

The prospects for a returning Christ to experience suffering as Jesus did are set up by the same conditions faced by Jesus in his first coming. That is, people today, as then, are looking for a Christ to come in a way that will validate their doctrinal expectation. As we have already seen, because of the wide diversity of doctrines on this issue, no matter in what way Christ actually comes, the majority of Christians will ignore him or stand against him.

Thus Jesus warns, in **Matthew 7:21–23:**

*"Not everyone who says to me, 'Lord, Lord,' will enter the kingdom of heaven, but only he who does the will of my Father who is in heaven. Many will say to me on that day, 'Lord, Lord, did we not **prophesy** in your name, and in your name **drive out demons** and **perform many miracles**?' Then I will tell them plainly, 'I never knew you. Away from me, you evildoers!' "*

To whom is Jesus referring? Some will assert that Jesus is explaining that you can't be a CINO (**C**hristian **I**n **N**ame **O**nly) and enter into Heaven. But notice that Jesus is describing a believer of a very active faith. You certainly cannot be a CINO and drive out demons! You can't be a CINO and prophesy and perform many miracles!

Jesus is warning us that the faith of expectation shaped by doctrinal assertions will not, in and of itself, transform into a faith of recognition of Christ. Christians who are driving out demons, prophesying and doing many miracles are doing so centered on their faith in the Gospel of Christ. However, that "shield of faith" is "until" the coming of the salvation that is to be revealed at the time it is to be granted.

Will Christians be able to put aside "the glass, darkly" in order to take up the clear? Or will they succumb to the historical tendency of the past, reject that completion of salvation and misidentify God's new Word as nothing more than "another Gospel"? Consider this actual minister's reaction:

You speak with a forked tongue! How do you explain Galatians 1:6–9, which says ". . . But even if we or an angel from Heaven should preach a gospel other than the one we preached to you, let him be eternally condemned!" **Rev. B.D., Pentecostal**

What did Paul mean by "Gospel"? He did not mean a particular doctrine of the Bible. There was not even a canonized version at that time. Paul had not even written all his letters, nor had there been the revelation to John. For Paul, the "Gospel" refers to the fundamental kerygmatic message:

Christ was born sinless, conceived by the works of the Holy Ghost, was the fulfillment of the Davidic Covenant and prophecy, his death at Calvary atoned for sin, His resurrection conquered death, he opened the channel for man's regeneration on the Day of Pentecost and he will return at the end of the age to bring judgment and the Kingdom.

We fully affirm the Gospel message, but not every jot and tittle of everyone's doctrine, which in innumerable ways disagree. The problem is that many Christians take **Galatians 1:6–9** as a personal sanction from Paul for their particular denomination's doctrinal perspective.

Why Does Christ Come Again to the Earth?

Christ, the second Adam, returns to the place where Adam's undone responsibility resides. As Adam came to the earth, the second Adam came to the earth. Likewise, at the Second Coming, the third Adam comes to the earth.

What would Jesus have done if he had been received in Israel? He would have established the Kingdom for which we now are waiting. How would he have set up that Kingdom? Jesus would have fulfilled the purpose of creation, God's original word to Adam and Eve, to be fruitful, multiply and have dominion. Consider Reverend Moon's insight:

> *Jesus' desire was indeed to get married. Why did Jesus need a wife? It is because human history began with fallen ancestors; therefore, humankind has not had true ancestors. God's ideal of creation was to make the true ancestors hold their holy marriage ceremony united with God's love. Through this, it was the purpose of creation to make a family lineage formed from a God-centered direct blood lineage. However, the blood lineage became different. Therefore, no matter how much faith people living on this earth had, they could only be adopted children. Adopted children do not have the same lineage . . .*
>
> *Think about it. The fall occurred on earth, so the restoration should be done on earth as well. What is lost on earth should be found on earth. Are you saying that it was lost in the air?*
>
> **Blessing and Ideal Family**

Jesus and his Bride were to establish the true family ideal and become the True Parents of all mankind. They would have become the new Adam and Eve, completely restoring the first family of God that was lost at the fall. As Jesus mentioned, he had the authority to forgive sin on earth. Jesus and his Bride would "bless" marriage and eliminate the consequences of the original sin.

Consider God's purpose for marriage. **Malachi 2:15**: "Has not the Lord made them one? In flesh and spirit they are his. And why one? Because he was seeking godly offspring." Are Christian married couples today able to become one eternally in God's love, uniting flesh and spirit to produce godly offspring? No matter how faithful the parents may be, their children are still born with original sin and need to be born again in the grace of Christ and the Holy Spirit. That means they are not, from birth, "godly offspring." Every Christian, individually, needs to be born again because we all inherit a false lineage. God's desire from the beginning was to have His own uncontested lineage. Had there been no fall, Adam and Eve's children would have been of God's lineage, without any trace of sin. The entire human family would have belonged wholly to God. Because this could not be restored in Jesus' day, Christ will return to complete salvation:

Romans 8:23
*"Not only so, but we ourselves, who have the first fruits of the Spirit, groan inwardly as we wait eagerly for our adoption as sons, the **redemption of our bodies**."*

Act 3:21
*"He must remain in heaven until the time comes for God to **restore everything**, as he promised long ago through his holy prophets."*

Hebrews 9:28
*"So Christ was sacrificed once to take away the sins of many people; and he will appear a second time, not to bear sin, but **to bring salvation** to those who are waiting for him."*

1 Peter 1:5
Who through faith are shielded with God's power until the coming of the salvation that is to be revealed in the last time.

We fully affirm that we are completely saved to eternal life through Jesus and the Holy Spirit. Salvation for the individual is complete. However, when a saved husband and a saved wife join together and conceive a child, that child is born as a descendant of the dead Adam and must be "born again."

The union between husband and wife *has not* been reconciled to God because when Jesus had to go the way of the cross, he not only laid down his flesh and shed his blood, but he also sacrificed God's seed and lineage as well. When on the cross he beseeched God to forgive us for we "know not what we do," he was hinting that the crucifixion had a tragic side, that something was left unfinished. Marriage, conception and birth were not reconciled to God.

Christ must return on earth to establish the position of True Parents and accomplish the reconciliation of husband and wife through the blessing of marriage. Christ comes to give the blessing to marriage so that not only can individuals conquer death, but marriage and family can conquer death as well. The family blessed by God is the foundation of the Kingdom.

Thus the blessing of marriage means:

1. The end of "until death do us part" in marriage. Marriage is eternal.
2. Conception is reconciled to God. Children are conceived in grace, not sin.
3. Children are born without the stain of original sin.
4. They are born as a descendant of the living Adam.
5. No need for rebirth. It is the end of the era of religion.
6. The Kingdom expands on the earth by multiplication of sinless children.

Will It Be Jesus?

"I am coming soon," Jesus said. The angel in **Acts 1:11** even stressed, *"this **same** Jesus."*

If Christ is born on the earth, will it be Jesus himself? Will Jesus reincarnate? Let's examine the pattern displayed in other documented "second comings."

Malachi 4:5 said that Elijah would come again. He didn't say that someone other than Elijah would come to assume the mission of Elijah. He simply said "Elijah" would come again. Thus, the chosen people were anticipating the return of the actual figure of Elijah, the prophet of old. However, Jesus said that John the Baptist "is Elijah who is to come." **Matthew 11:14** Furthermore, the angel

Gabriel had informed Zechariah that his son John was born "in the spirit and power of Elijah." **Luke 1:17**

Therein is revealed the biblical principle of second comings. The mission is entitled with the name of the predecessor. Thus, Elijah's mission is called "Elijah." John takes up Elijah's mission and is the "Elijah." John the Baptist was the fulfillment of **Malachi 4:5**.

Adam's mission was taken up by another "Adam" and so Jesus was called the "last Adam." Esau and Jacob take up Cain and Abel's mission. A "New Jerusalem" takes up Jerusalem's mission. "Jesus" will come again means that Jesus' primary earthly mission will be accomplished not by Jesus reincarnating into another body, but rather by Jesus anointing his representative on earth. That representative on earth will carry out Jesus' primary mission that was laid down in Gethsemane in sorrow and tears. He who takes up that mission, of course, must be able to commune with Christ in the "sorrow unto death."

Jesus explains this in his own words. In the **Book of Revelation**, chapters 2 and 3, the spirit of Jesus speaks to John the revelator.

Revelation 2:7

*"He who has an ear, let him hear what the Spirit says to the churches. To him who overcomes, I will give the **right to eat from the tree of life**, which is in the paradise of God."*

Jesus explains, "to him who overcomes" he will give him the right to eat from the tree of life. Adam's original hope was to "eat from the tree of life," however because of his sin, he was banished. In **Genesis 3:24**, God places a cherubim and a flaming sword to "guard the way to the tree of life." Thus Jesus granting someone "the right to eat from the tree of life" means that Jesus will give a particular person the right to assume the role and unachieved perfection of Adam. Some might say, at this point, that "to him who overcomes" could mean "whosoever overcomes" and not a specific chosen person. We will see, however, that the "him who overcomes," is, in fact, a specific person chosen by Jesus.

Revelation 2:17

*"I will also give him a **white stone** with a **new name** written on it, known only to him who receives it."*

The "white stone" is a symbol of Christ. In **1 Peter 2:4**, Jesus is the "living Stone." In **1 Corinthians 10:4** "That rock was Christ." Thus, Jesus is declaring that he will send "Christ" with a "new name." Just as Elijah had "a new name"—John the Baptist—so Christ at his Second Coming will have a new name. This means that Jesus is anointing and sending his chosen person, "him who overcomes."

Revelation 2:26–28

*"To him who overcomes and does my will to the end, I will give **authority over the nations**, 'He will rule them with an iron scepter; he will dash them to pieces like pottery'—just as I have received authority from my Father. I will also give him **the morning star**."*

Here Jesus proclaims that he will give this chosen person his own authority. What kind of authority is made clear by the statement: "He will rule them with an iron scepter." Iron scepter is from **Psalm 2:9**. It is a symbol of Christ's royal authority. Jesus also affirms that he, Jesus, would be with "him." "I will also give him the morning star." The "morning star" is Jesus. **Revelation 22:16**

Revelation 3:12

*"Him who overcomes I will make a pillar in the temple of my God. Never again will he leave it. I will write on him the name of my God and the name of the city of my God, the new Jerusalem, which is coming down out of heaven from my God; and **I will also write on him my new name**."*

This is a most amazing scripture. Jesus states that he will "write on 'him' my own new name." As we look at **Revelation 19:11–16**, keep in mind that Jesus "will write" and this unknown "him" will be written upon:

*I saw heaven standing open and there before me was a white horse, whose rider is called Faithful and True. With justice he judges and makes war. His eyes are like blazing fire, and on his head are many crowns. **HE HAS A NAME WRITTEN ON HIM THAT NO ONE KNOWS BUT HE HIMSELF.** He is dressed in a robe dipped in blood, and his name is the Word of God. The armies of heaven were following him, riding on white horses and dressed in fine linen, white and clean. Out of his mouth comes a sharp sword with which to strike down the nations. **"HE WILL RULE THEM***

WITH AN IRON SCEPTER." *He treads the winepress of the fury of the wrath of God Almighty. On his robe and on his thigh he has this name written:* **KING OF KINGS AND LORD OF LORDS**.

This scripture is thought to be describing the return of Jesus at his Second Coming. Indeed it is, except for one important difference. The figure that comes, "whose eyes are like blazing fire and on his head are many crowns," has "a name written on him that no one knows but he himself." What did Jesus say in **Revelation 3:12**? "I will write on him." Therefore, the coming figure of **Revelation 19:11–16** is not Jesus, but is, rather, the person that Jesus anoints to fulfill his primary mission. This person will come and the "armies of heaven will be following him." Notice too, "He will rule them with an iron scepter." Where did he receive the iron scepter? From Jesus, **Revelation 12:5**. Which, again, states that "a male child born on earth" will indeed be the recipient.

And what else does Jesus write on him? It is this: "KING OF KINGS AND LORD OF LORDS." This person is given the title of King of Kings by Jesus himself.

Are There Two Messiahs?

Jesus is the Christ, the messiah, and the unique savior of humankind. Through his death on the cross he atoned for our sins, and his resurrection delivers us from death and brings us into the power of new life. There is no other name in heaven or on earth by which we can be saved.

However, once Jesus has appointed another person to fulfill the mission of the Second Coming of Christ, how should we view this new person in relation to Jesus? Since Jesus appointed him, surely they are not rivals! Nevertheless, it is a human failing for churches to be rivals. Christians should guard against projecting their human rivalries into the relationship between Jesus and Christ at the Second Coming.

In **John 9:28–29**, some Jews accused a man born blind who was testifying to Jesus:

Then they hurled insults at him and said, "You are this fellow's disciple!
We are disciples of Moses! We know that God spoke to Moses, but as for
this fellow, we don't even know where he comes from."

Comparing Jesus and Moses from a human point of view, they regarded them as rivals.

Yet Scripture teaches that Jesus and Moses were united with one purpose, to fulfill the will of God. On the Mount of Transfiguration, Jesus could be seen having a conference with Moses and Elijah. They were discussing his path to Jerusalem that would lead to his crucifixion.

Luke 9:30–31
Two men, Moses and Elijah, appeared in glorious splendor, talking with
Jesus. They spoke about his departure, which he was about to bring to
fulfillment at Jerusalem.

Moses brought the law, to which the Jews were so devoted that it became a stumbling block to receiving Jesus. After all, Jesus healed on the Sabbath and violated the Mosaic Law on numerous occasions. Moses brought the Law, but Jesus brought a higher truth— the Gospel. Hence, many Jews could not recognize Jesus as the messiah.

Nevertheless, Moses certainly recognized Jesus as the messiah.

Hebrews 11:24–26
By faith Moses . . . chose to be mistreated along with the people of God
rather than to enjoy the pleasures of sin for a short time. He regarded
disgrace for the sake of Christ as of greater value than the treasures of
Egypt, because he was looking ahead to his reward.

Moses endured a difficult life with the hope of reward in Christ, and on the Mount of Transfiguration he could meet him and support his mission directly.

Moses supported Jesus' mission, even if ordinary Jews did not. Moses and Jesus were of one mind and heart when Jesus set off to Jerusalem to consummate his Passion. In truth, Jesus' victory over death through the cross and resurrection was also Moses' victory.

Likewise, how could there be any gap between Jesus and the man he has appointed to the mission of the Second Coming? In the eyes of God, they are completely united. They work together, Jesus in paradise and the person of the Second Coming on earth, to fulfill the dispensation of the Second Coming that will "restore everything." **Acts 3:21** It is none other than Jesus who gives him the authority. **Revelation 2:26–28**

Jesus' heartfelt desire during his lifetime was to establish the Kingdom of God on earth, and thus he taught his disciples to pray. **Matthew 6:10:** *"Thy kingdom come. Thy will be done in earth, as it is in heaven."* Christ at the Second Coming likewise appears on earth to establish the Kingdom. **Revelation 11:15:** *"there were great voices in heaven, saying, The kingdoms of this world are become the kingdoms of our Lord, and of his Christ; and he shall reign for ever and ever."* For this purpose he comes with the "armies of heaven" to rule the nations. **Revelation 19:14–15**

The heartfelt desire of Jesus to establish God's Kingdom—a hope that he could not see accomplished in his lifetime—is the same desire as that of the person in the role of the Second Coming. They are of one heart and mind to do the Father's will.

John 5:30: *"I do not seek My own will but the will of the Father who sent Me."* Jesus came to do his Father's will, and so does the messiah at the Second Coming. Jesus laid the cornerstone by bringing salvation to individuals, but as we saw above, the will of God also includes the restoration of "everything." In particular, the Will of God requires the sanctification of marriage, conception and birth by restoring the family to the circumstances prior to the fall. This is the key to the establishment of God's true family that embraces all humanity. This greater salvation that is the work of Christ at the Second Coming brings the Will of God to its completion.

Therefore, the victory of the Second Coming is also Jesus' victory. Their struggle is a common struggle; their suffering is a common suffering; their victory is a common victory.

This explains why Jesus said that he would spurn those faithful Christians who reject the Second Coming, for by opposing him they are opposing Jesus and crucifying him yet again: **Matthew 7:22–23:** *"Many will say to me on that day, 'Lord, Lord, did we not prophesy in your name, and in your name drive out demons and perform many miracles?' Then I will tell them plainly, 'I never knew you. Away from me, you evildoers!' "*

Yet if the Second Coming is truly a different person, not Jesus reincarnated or coming on the clouds, how difficult will it be for many faithful Christians to support him! For example, **John 14:6:** *"I am the way, the truth, and the life. No one comes to the Father except through me."* If Christians follow this verse strictly, they are likely to reject Christ at the Second Coming when he appears as a different person than Jesus. This trial can be overcome with deep prayer that leads to the conviction that indeed it is Jesus who stands behind the person who stands in the role of the Second Coming of Christ.

Is there any other way for Christians to overcome this trial? The Bible does not leave us in the dark. Jesus instructs us that the way to overcome the last judgment is by practicing charity to all.

Matthew 25:31–41

"When the Son of Man comes in his glory, and all the holy angels with him, then he will sit on the throne of his glory. All the nations will be gathered before him, and he will separate them one from another, as a shepherd divides his sheep from the goats. And he will set the sheep on his right hand, but the goats on the left. Then the King will say to those on his right hand, 'Come, you blessed of my Father, inherit the kingdom prepared for you from the foundation of the world: for I was hungry and you gave me food; I was thirsty and you gave me drink; I was a stranger and you took me in; I was naked and you clothed me; I was sick and you visited me; I was in prison and you came to me.' Then the righteous will answer him, saying, 'Lord, when did we see you hungry and feed you, or thirsty and give you drink? When did we see you a stranger and take you in, or naked and clothe you? Or when did we see you sick, or in prison, and come to you?' And the King will answer and say to them, 'Assuredly, I say to you, inasmuch as you did it to one of the least of these my brethren, you did it to me.'"

What Shall We Call Him?

If another person is fulfilling the mission of the Second Coming of Christ, what shall we call him? Messiah? Savior? King of Kings? These are some of his biblical titles, and a faithful Christian would call him nothing less. The mission of the Second Coming is the most glorious mission, and that glory should redound on his person.

Nevertheless, while he is walking the earth, his glory is hidden, just as Jesus' glory was invisible to the people of his day. When a blind man praised Jesus as the Son of David, the Pharisees who heard it immediately declared that Jesus was possessed by demons. **Matthew 12:23–24** Likewise, whenever someone proclaims him the Lord at the Second Coming and the messiah, cries of "pretender" and "false Christ" come thick and fast. One might think he would be better off to just keep quiet. Wearing the title of messiah is quite a heavy burden. To proclaim it invites a cross, not glory.

Because the title "messiah" is uniquely applied to Jesus Christ, who is our savior, we may overlook the fact that in the Old Testament, the term "messiah," Hebrew for "anointed one," was a title used of all the kings of Israel and Judah, from Saul to Zedekiah. They were all "anointed ones" and could thus be termed "messiahs." High priests were also "anointed ones." **Zechariah 4:14** So there is biblical precedent for regarding more than one person as a "messiah." That usage of the term "messiah" is only a type and shadow of what was to come, but it may also foreshadow the circumstances at the time of the Second Coming.

Jesus' role as savior and messiah will never change. Still, Jesus predicted that those who believe in him could equal or even surpass him. **John 14:12:** *"He who believes in me, the works that I do he will do also; and greater works than these he will do."* When Jesus was accused of making himself God in **John 10:33–35,** he answered by quoting Psalm 82: *"I said, 'You are "gods"; and all of you are children of the Most High,'"* comparing his divinity to that which all are meant to inherit.

When will this inheritance occur? **1 Corinthians 15:22–23:** *"For as in Adam all die, so also in Christ shall all be made alive. But each in his own order: Christ the first fruits, then at his coming those who belong to Christ."* During the dispensation since the resurrection of Jesus up until the Second Coming, only Jesus was resurrected. He stood alone as the "first fruits." But at the Second Coming all those who belong to Christ will be resurrected to the same life that Jesus enjoys. This suggests that at the Second Coming, the title "messiah" might apply more broadly to all sanctified people who come to resemble Jesus in spirit and who take up his mission.

Consider, in particular, the person commissioned by Jesus to fulfill the mission of the Second Coming of Christ. He and Jesus are separate individuals, yet united in purpose to fulfill the Will of God and establish the Kingdom. Signs of the Kingdom's manifestation are multiplying over the earth, as more and more marriages are blessed and true, God-centered families are established. They are but a prelude to the Kingdom's greater manifestation as the age-old problems of racism, nationalism and religious conflict are solved through the ministry of the Second Coming. For those who, through the eyes of faith, grasp this movement of the Providence in our time, it is proper that they give honor to this person by calling him the messiah and savior, even the King of Kings.

In the year 1936 on Easter Sunday morning, Jesus Christ appeared to a sixteen-year-old Korean boy. His name was Sun Myung Moon. He is the person whom Jesus has chosen to carry out the mission of the Second Coming of Christ.

On April 5, 2001, Jesus appeared again, this time to a Korean woman named Ms. Young Soon Kim. The testimony entitled, *Jesus' Message to Christians and All People on Earth,* is an account of what Jesus revealed to her.

Please prayerfully read these words and consider their meaning for our age.

Jesus' Message to Christians and All People on Earth

Jesus, who was born in Bethlehem, is using this opportunity to send this new message to people on earth, including the Jews who are still waiting for the coming of the messiah. Whether Christian or non-Christian, people know my name, Jesus.

The heart of Jesus who is sending this message to the earth is complex and perplexing. I feel sad that I cannot summarize and convey my message in a few words. In particular, I know that Christians will doubt the message rather than believe it. However, as a person who came to the earth with the mission of saving the world as the messiah in the New Testament Age, since the time to reveal the truth has arrived, I am telling you the truth before heaven and earth.

I came to earth with the mission from God to be the messiah. In the Bible I could not reveal all of the conflicts between the religious believers and non-believers in those days. In fact, there are many providential matters that the Bible does not reveal. With the flow of each providential age, God could not avoid changing His immediate plan. I am revealing clearly a part of this hidden providential content to the numerous clergy who have been waiting for the Lord's return.

God created human beings to need a physical body during their earthly life. Once they lose it, they go to the spirit world and live there for eternity. Dear saints who are waiting for my return, why don't you pay attention to the fact that God gives dual prophecies in the Bible [blessings for those who follow His will, curses for those who disobey His will]? I came to earth as the messiah in the New Testament Age. What do you think is the meaning of the crucifixion? Do you really think that it was God's Will from the beginning, or could it have been the result of human error? Have you thoroughly studied my life? I certainly came with the mission of the messiah, yet I lived eating and sleeping like any other man on earth. Even though I lived as an ordinary human being, my mission as the messiah was unique. To state the conclusion, the way of redemption through my crucifixion was not God's original intention.

Dear Christians and all people on earth, please pray over this matter while fasting. Then I will appear to you and clearly tell you the truth. When you do it, you should be totally focused on praying with a pure heart. Reverend Sun Myung Moon is the one who came to Earth to complete my mission that was not fulfilled through the redemption of the cross. He comes as the True Parent to conclude God's providence in the Completed Testament Age.

I came with the mission of the messiah in the New Testament, but people at that time crucified me. That is why there remained a task for God to fulfill, and the necessity of a Second Coming. The messiah in the New Testament Age brought salvation to people in the spirit. Still, history continued with the homework of physical salvation remaining to be fulfilled. Wandering in the alleys of grievance, suffering, sorrow and pain, God endured endless tension and pressure while He waited to send the messiah again to earth. After separating good and evil in order to prepare His lineage, God could send Reverend Sun Myung Moon.

You know where I was born; it was in a manger. Do you know what the heart of Mary was like at that moment? Dear fellow Christians, could you easily understand it from reading the Bible? Have you not struggled over some incomprehensible events or insoluble questions? How could you understand my heart, when I could not fully reveal all the secrets of heaven? How could you understand the intricacies of the providence, when so much was not recorded in the Bible? Why was the womb of Mary, Joseph's fiancée, growing large? You cannot understand all the secrets that have been veiled during the providence of restoration. Since human beings are children of God, God cannot help but love them. It is also difficult for you to fathom the heart of God.

Reverend Sun Myung Moon is the returning messiah for whom you have been waiting and waiting. He inherited my mission at the age of 16. Dear Christians, are you still looking up and waiting for Christ to return on the clouds? Reverend Moon travels throughout the world on the clouds. He is investing all of his heart and soul for the realization of world peace. Even today, although he is over 80 years old, he is fighting on the frontline.

Are you going to hang him on the cross again, like the Romans who persecuted me 2,000 years ago? Aren't you aware of the destruction of Sodom and Gomorrah? God is love. He is waiting. Please receive the messiah who has descended in the Completed Testament Age. Do not reject his achievements and his dispensation for the salvation of humanity. Pray with sincerity. I, Jesus, will be with you in your earnest prayers.

I sincerely wish that Christians would reflect deeply upon the circumstances when I, the messiah of the New Testament Age, was crucified. I hope they pray about my life and about God's view on human salvation.

Think about the circumstances that I could not be married even though I was 33. Think of how my twelve disciples and I often went hungry. My life was filled with grievances. Christians surmise that everything that happened to me was the will of God. However, think whether there was any responsibility on the part of human beings. I came as the messiah and the Son of Man. As the begotten Son of God, I did my very best to fulfill my messianic mission, but I could not fully accomplish my dreams and desires. Had my will been entirely fulfilled, would it be necessary for me to return?

Dear fellow Christians and religious believers, I am truly the messiah. However, the one who returned to fulfill the messianic mission today is Reverend Sun Myung Moon. He is the Second Advent of the Lord. Think of the question John the Baptist asked me, when I was being hounded as a ringleader of heretics: "Are you the one who is to come?" How do you now see Reverend Moon? Think of the flow of time and examine the incredible achievements he has wrought. Could he do this by human power and ability alone?

Jesus who died physically cannot come back to physical life and appear to you. Human flesh is to return to the earth as dust, once it gives up the spirit. That is the truth and a heavenly law. Read again the Bible verse that states that people will rise from the tombs. God is the Author of science and mathematics as the Being of the Principle. The theory that a dead body that decomposed will be reassembled and float in the air assumes that God can do anything and everything. However, to have God violate His own Being is extremely contradictory! You cannot solve questions that way. Look at the world of nature. Look at the process of human growth and the design of human life. God and human beings are in a relationship of parent and child. You will have to experience the heart of God now, who has been leading the providence of salvation for humankind so patiently. What if you Christians could see me right now, sitting and talking with Buddha, whom you consider to be an idol worshipper? What would you think of me?

Dear fellow Christians, fellow Buddhists, and believers of various religions! The four great religious founders, Jesus, Buddha, Confucius, and Mohammed, and saints such as Socrates, Augustine and others, have already held this seminar a number of times. Its theme is always the same: "God is the Parent of All Humankind." During the seminars, we are always studying the Divine Principle revealed by Reverend Moon. We analyze and discuss it in depth. That is the homework given us by God, who carefully observes all the activities of Reverend Moon on earth. God has also directed that the major religious leaders in the spirit world unite and cooperate with earthly people for the salvation of humankind.

We religious founders have no barriers among us. We are united as one, through the messiah who appears on earth in the Completed Testament Age and gives rebirth to all humankind as the children of God. We are praying about and discussing how to create one world centered on God. The conflicts and confrontations often seen among religious people are resolved here in the spirit world. It took a long time for this to happen, to persuade people to understand one ultimate truth: the Creator of human beings is God alone. Likewise, in order to bring peace on earth, it will be necessary to break down the barriers among all religions on earth.

Earthly leaders of each religion should discuss the commonalities and differences among their different faiths. Together they should choose the strongest points from each, while showing the virtue of humility before others. Would non-believers not be guided in the right direction by following their example? I hope that all religious followers, especially Christians, can unite as one, and that I can meet them all in one place.

The fact that Jesus from Bethlehem in Judea could send a message to earthly people is due to the benefit of the age wrought with the arrival of the Completed Testament Age. Reverend Sun Myung Moon is the master of this era because he is the Messiah of the Second Coming.

What will you do with him? Are you going to put him on the stand for judgment? Are you going to hang him, as I was hung 2,000 years ago? Are you willing to pray and fast about this? I hope that you will make a wise decision as a religious follower. I send this message to earthly people with a desire to teach people about my responsibility as Jesus, the Messiah of the New Testament Age.